SEEING OURSELVES:
Exploring Race, Ethnicity & Culture

CARL E. JAMES
York University

THOMPSON EDUCATIONAL PUBLISHING, INC.
Toronto, Ontario

Requests for permission to make copies of any part of the work should be mailed to:
Thompson Educational Publishing, Inc.
14 Ripley Avenue, Suite 105
Toronto, Ontario, Canada M6S 3Np
Telephone (416) 766–2763 Fax (416) 766–0398
e-mail: thompson@canadabooks.ingenia.com
WWW site: http://canadabooks.ingenia.com

Canadian Cataloguing in Publication Data

James, Carl, 1952-

Seeing Ourselves : exploring race, ethnicity and culture

Rev. ed.
Includes bibliographical references.
ISBN 1-55077-069-1

1. Canada - Race relations. 2. Canada - Ethnic relations.
3. Multiculturalism - Canada. I. Title.

FC104.J35   1995   305.8'00971   C95-930834-2
F1035.AIJ35   1995

Cover design: *Mike McAuliffe*
Photo credits:
Dick Hemingway: x, 3, 8, 12, 18, 27, 31, 34, 41, 45, 56, 63, 68, 75, 82, 86, 88, 90, 93 105, 152, 162, 165, 168, 178, 185, 192, 202, 206, 234
Carl James: 22, 39, 51, 99, 110, 114, 122, 138, 200, 213, 220, 224, 228
Adrienne Shadd: 130

Printed in Canada.
  2 3 4   96 97 98 99

Table of Contents

Preface

Since the publication of the first edition of this book in 1989, I have been fortunate to meet and talk with many of its readers. I have engaged in many discussions with a number of high school, college and university students. I have also used the book in many of my classes and it has generated a number of questions and other very good reflective essays, some of which have been included in the present edition. From all of this I have gained new insights and perspectives which I am again sharing in this edition.

My notion of a "Canadian culture" of which everyone living in this society is a part often generates much discussion. Having had the opportunity to engage in many of these discussions, I hope that in this edition I am able to articulate much more clearly my perspective. I hope that I will have provided readers with a lens through which to view the complexity, dynamism, diversity, tensions and conflict which characterize culture in any society, and a perspective which will illuminate some of the issues that plague individuals' and groups' interactions.

This book provides critical insights into the thinking and analytical processes of "naive" or "non-expert" individuals as they discuss and reflect on issues of ethnicity, race and culture. Most books in this area are written typically from the perspectives of "experts" or "academics," who provide analyses and interpretations. While my voice is indeed present, I also present the voices of the students and the ways in which they articulate their information, ideas and analyses. The concept of culture as a structure that is constructed and acted upon by all members of a society provides a framework with which to contextualize the lives and experiences of the writers.

We believe that effective dialogue necessarily involves the use of a common language, or in the very least a common understanding of a shared terminology. For this reason, we present definitions, not as a way of simplifying the complexity of the concepts involved, but to provide a common reference.

Ultimately, any discourse that deals with anti-racism must be about preparing people to engage in social change. This means that there must be collaborative efforts, and individuals must know themselves and each other in order to engage in social action which will bring about change. Hopefully, the essays will provide further insights into the issues and will contribute to the discussions and dialogues in which we all must engage in order to bring about the necessary changes in our society.

Carl E. James

Acknowledgements

That this book has been written is due to the contributions and efforts of several people to whom I owe a tremendous debt. It is appropriate that I start by acknowledging the many students (who, of course, were at the same time teachers) who participated in my classes and trusted me enough to share with me their experiences, thoughts, ideas and feelings during classes and through their essays. To all of them I am sincerely grateful. Their individual and collective contributions, I am sure, will further the debate and discussion of race and intercultural relations, as well as anti-racism education.

I wish to acknowledge with gratitude the significant contribution of Maxine McKenzie. She gave generously of her time and energy in providing critical insights and editorial suggestions which helped to strengthen the manuscript.

Thanks to the folks at Thompson Educational Publishing, particularly Paul Challen for his superb editing job and Keith Thompson for his support and counsel. I am grateful to Jane Larsson, Elise Malka, Joanne Blake, and Elma Thomas for the computer, word processing and general assistance that they provided me throughout the preparation of this manuscript. I am indebted to Verna Frayne, Lisa Sutcliffe and Alix Yule of Sheridan College whose support was crucial to the publication of the first edition of this book.

Special thanks to my colleagues and friends, particularly Paul Anisef, Carol Geddis, Gottfried Paasche, Adrienne Shadd, Christine Almeida, Denny Hunte and Sabra Desai, who have been constant with their support and advice. Some provided essays, conversations and pictures for inclusion in the book.

To Kai, Milderine and Dorne, I express my sincere thanks for their constant support of which I am always assured. To them I must also dedicate this book since they have been, and will continue to be, my most significant teachers and students.

Introduction

Racial and ethnic diversity have characterized Canada's population from its beginning. But it has been only in recent years, particularly with the increase in the country's racial and ethnic minority population due largely to immigration, that we have begun to pay attention to the ways in which our political, educational, cultural and social systems are meeting the needs of these people, and addressing their issues. This is also due to the fact that as Canadians racial and ethnic minorities expect not only to have access to, and participate in, all of the country's activities and institutions, but also to receive all the services to which they are entitled. Given this reality, educational institutions have been initiating programs and courses to prepare students to work and live in our multiethnic, multiracial, multireligious and multicultural society.

Through their essays, this book shares the experiences, feelings and reactions of students who have participated in both compulsory and elective courses with me as they prepare themselves to live and work in our multicultural society. The essays presented are students' works gathered over a period of eight years. Since the colleges and universities in which I have taught are in southern Ontario, most of the students tend to represent the postsecondary population and program interest of students in this region. Generally, the students were primarily white females.

What was particularly striking—and understandably so—about my classes in race relations or cross-culturalism (or whatever the particular institutional designation) was what each person expected. Some wanted to hear about the Italians, "West Indians," Indians, South Asians, Sikhs. As the educator I was expected to tell about these groups since the students anticipated encountering a multi-ethnic working world upon leaving school. And there were the regular questions: "Why do we have to cater to these people when they come here? After all it was they who decided to come. Why do we have to change our way of life to please them?" And there were the statements: "If I went to their country I would have to adopt their culture. When you are in Rome, you do as the Romans do." "The immigrants are coming and taking all the jobs." "It is the immigrants, they are causing all the crimes." "The minorities are causing the racism; they cry racism for everything, especially when they don't get the jobs." "The government is just trying to please the minorities, that is why they have employment equity." "People are getting hired because of their race, they are not qualified for the jobs." Evidently, each student had a position on the issues and were taking the class for particular reasons. Getting them to articulate their positions and their expectations is fundamental to the pedagogical approach used in the course, for we can only engage that which is articulated, even though it may seem unacceptable (Britzman, 1991; hooks, 1988).

Generally, I begin the class by asking participants to introduce themselves by name only and the program in which they are registered (if they are full-time students) or their occupation (if they work full-time). Then, we have another round of introductions, in which participants introduce themselves by telling us their ethnic background, race, nationality and culture. I usually go first, in order to provide an example. I always make it clear that everyone in the room is Canadian—that is our nationality, citizenship and to varying degrees part of our culture. Therefore, unless the person is an Aboriginal, then she/he must give the place (country or area) of origin of their ancestors. Similarly, Caribbean participants are told that the same applies. Unless, their ancestors are Caribs or Arawaks then they too must name their European, African or Asian origin.

Typically, participants of British origin, particularly those whose parents and grandparents were born here, tended to insist that they were Canadians. When asked to think back to their ancestors, they would refuse. Some contend that it is not important, or it is irrelevant, it means nothing to them because their family has been here for a long time. They do not practise anything of their ancestral culture. Others say that they will have to go home and ask their parents because they have never talked about this at home. Very often some of the participants will say that it is the first time they have had to think about themselves in these terms, and more significantly, to articulate the word "white" to describe themselves. This exercise at times produces tension, because these "Canadian" participants feel uncomfortable because of the challenges they experience. On the other hand, many Black Caribbean participants, particularly the younger (less than 22 years) and older (over 50 years), often insist on identifying their ethnicity as West Indian, Caribbean, Jamaican, Trinidadian etc., and not African. Also, some South Asians from that region would, to a lesser extent, do the same.

Some participants have trouble acknowledging the realities of racial, ethnic and cultural forces in their lives. This reflects the fact that these forces are so much a part of us that they are taken for granted. It is much easier, particularly for ethnic majority group members, to see these characteristics as significant to the lives and behaviours of "other" Canadians—immigrants and "multicultural" Canadians (those with cultures like the Italians, Chinese, Jamaicans and others). For those Caribbean Africans, the negative images that have been presented to them and their miseducation have made them want to disassociate themselves from Africa.

The aim of the introductory exercise is to have participants begin to reflect and examine their worldview, and to try to understand how factors such as ethnicity, race and culture help to structure the way we think of ourselves and others within the context of Canadian society. Further, it is intended to make participants begin to "paint themselves into the picture," to give them the message that, contrary to their commonly-held notions, the course is not intended to study the "other" Canadians—immigrants or "multicultural Canadians"—to learn about their "culture," or to study the victims of racism. The aim is to have participants begin to interrogate their ideas and experiences as minority and majority group Canadians, to reflect on their personal contradictions and challenges, and to begin to critique the varied ways in which inequalities of power and privilege exist in our society (see Dei, 1994).

Some of the greatest challenges I faced as an educator lay in persuading participants (a) that race, ethnicity and culture are not abstract notions, but that they affect all of us personally, from how we see ourselves and others to the way the institutions in our society operate; (b) to see how they themselves and others have internalized the meaning that society has given to these factors; and (c) to understand that culture is a social structure that shapes and informs the lives of all Canadians. Consequently, while reading created the framework for our explorations of the issues, it was the discussions, debates, reflective essays and projects that were particularly useful in the participants' process of discovery and understanding of themselves and others.

Because we were dealing with deeply-felt attitudes and experiences and with the participants' construction of reality, it was incumbent on me to present myself both as a facilitator and a learner. Therefore my presentations were largely in the form of a dialogue in order to facilitate students' input and to encourage them to articulate their perspectives.[1] This was not always easy, since there were some strong oppositional or negative views expressed that needed to be processed. However, these views were valuable, since I believe they represent and reflect the diversity of ideas and opinion in our society. It is necessary for individuals to present them so that they may be discussed in what is hoped will be a safe and non-threatening manner. This view is carried over in the present work.

As the book's editor, my role is not to be the "expert" or to interpret or impose meaning on the participants' experiences and beliefs, but to present for discussion the various ways in which they construct themselves and others in terms of race, ethnicity and culture. These essays are presented so that we may learn from these students of anti-racism education, and move beyond ourselves to learn about each other. Cases with which we identify, or where we see some of our own experiences reflected, present a means of assuring us of shared perspectives and experiences. Such reflections are catalysts for change and growth where necessary.

Some racist or prejudiced information or positions are presented in the essays. This is not intended to legitimize these views, but rather to engage, expose and examine them. All existing perspectives, ideas, histories and beliefs need to be included as part of a dialogue. There is a legitimate risk in doing this, for it is possible that readers will merely add more stereotypes, prejudices and racist information into the existing pool of misinformation, or feel validated in their misinformation. On the other hand, it is possible that the ideas stated in this context will help us to challenge our learned "truths" and "facts."

The Approach

Presenting an approach which facilitates the study and discussion of race, ethnicity, culture and racism is not an easy task, for there are

---

[1] Hooks in her essay "toward a revolutionary feminist pedagogy" (1988) stresses the importance of encouraging students "to come to voice" by providing a space where they can participate without feeling that they have placed themselves at risk.

different schools of thought on how to proceed. There is little possibility of establishing a single, universally-accepted approach to analyzing and presenting the issues. On the other hand, a complete synthesis of all approaches is not feasible. Nonetheless, we have made an attempt to provide a general understanding of the major issues and questions that have held the attention of many students of anti-racism, race relations and multiculturalism.

In Chapters One through Three, we examine sociological and psychological concepts and theories to provide a context for comprehending and analyzing the issues. The terms used in the book are defined so that a shared understanding is acquired for the purpose of the discussion. As Jackson and Meadows point out, "Individuals' definitions or conceptual frameworks. . . may either hinder or facilitate an understanding of the behaviours and experiences that occur in their lives and the lives of others. Often a change in the conceptual framework can open a whole new realm of understanding of these behaviours and experiences" (1991: 72).

In Chapter Four, individuals compare themselves with others. Chapter Five presents people's writings about themselves. In these two chapters, complete essays are presented to show how individuals have struggled and dealt with the issues and questions that relate to their own identity and those of others. Chapter Six is a discussion of three of the major issues that emerged in class discussions (immigration, multiculturalism and employment equity). In Chapter Seven, participants reflect on what has been learned: how their ideas and interpretations have changed or been reinforced as a result of the course.

This book does not pretend to provide a comprehensive theoretical treatment of the subject. In fact, no single book that discusses race, ethnicity and culture can hope to present all the information, variations, etc., that there is to learn and know. If the present work serves to identify the many interpretations and introduces questions, issues and the challenges they present, and if our approach brings awareness, new insights and sensitivity to the issues, then the goal of this project has been achieved.

Not everything that is faced can be changed,
But nothing can be changed until it is faced.
  James Baldwin

It is what we think we know already
that often prevents us from learning.
  Claude Bernard

If I cannot see myself I cannot see others clearly;
and if I cannot see others clearly,
seeing myself becomes more and more difficult.
  Lyn

1

CULTURE: A SOCIAL STRUCTURE

If birds were suddenly endowed with scientific curiosity they might examine many things, but the sky itself would be overlooked as a suitable subject; if fish were to become curious about the world, it would never occur to them to begin by investigating water. For birds and fish would take the sky and water for granted, unaware of their profound influence because they comprise the medium for every act. Human beings in a similar way occupy a symbolic universe governed by codes that are unconsciously acquired and automatically employed. So much so that they rarely notice that the ways they interpret and talk about events are distinctly different from the ways people conduct their affairs in other cultures (Barnlund 1988: 14).

According to Barnlund, "cultural myopia" characterizes the members of every society. This explains how individuals understand, and are able to identify, culture. Jackson and Meadows (1991) point out that "for most people the term is vague because individuals live the culture and seldom explain it or consciously think about or evaluate it" (p. 72). The fact is, no society is without culture—that core set of values and expectations that exerts tremendous influences on our lives, structures our worldview, shapes our behaviours, and patterns our responses to experiences. Adler (1977) asserts that "all human beings share a similar biology, universally limited by the rhythms of life" (p. 27), and we all move through life's phases in a similar sequence of events: birth, infancy, childhood, adolescence, adulthood, middle age, old age and death. Yet he continues:

The ultimate interpretation of human biology is a cultural phenomenon; that is, the meaning of human biological patterns are culturally derived. Though all human beings are born, reproduced, and die, it is culture which dictates the meaning of sexuality, the ceremonials of birth, the transitions of life, and the rituals of death (Adler 1977: 27).

Any group of people who reside in a given geographic area, or in a particular community, will share that set of cultural values and expectations which will govern their lives.

This chapter explores culture as a social construct which influences the life experiences and responses of all who live in Canada. The objective is to explore the question: Is there a Canadian culture—a core set of norms, values and expectations to which Canadian residents must adhere? We do this by assessing (a) the meaning of the term "culture"; (b) social stratification, ethnic and racial diversity and their relation to culture; and (c) the interplay between multiculturalism, assimilation and Canadian culture.

What Is Culture?

Simply defined, culture is the way in which a given society organizes and conducts itself that distinguishes it from other societies.[1] Culture is a dynamic and complex set of values, beliefs, norms, patterns of thinking, styles of communication, linguistic expressions and ways of interpreting and interacting with the world, "which a group of people has developed to assure its survival in a particular physical and human environment" (Hoopes and Pusch, 1981: 3). Therefore, members of any given society will not only be influenced by the culture of that society, but can also help contribute to shaping its culture. The location of the various groups within the social stratification system will determine the extent to which they may be able to influence the overall culture of the society. The term "social stratification" refers to the hierarchical system in which segments of the population are ranked on the basis of their power and access to wealth and prestige. This ranking or social class structure is determined by a complex interplay of property ownership, income, edu-

---

[1] Carroll (1990) defines a "society" as any fairly large group of people who share common cultural values; have inherited a common set of historical traditions; engage in a relatively large amount of mutual interaction; and are associated with a particular geographic area (p. 23).

cation and occupation, as well as identities such as gender, ethnicity, race, time of arrival in country and citizenship status.

Given this stratification, and the resultant hierarchical or social class positioning of the various groups in society, the culture that emerges will largely mirror that of the group with the most economic and political power. Specifically, the cultural elements—i.e. the norms, values and expectations—of the ethnic group with the most power will be those that will be dominant in the society's culture.

Culture is a dynamic and complex set of values, beliefs and norms.

It is important to stress the dynamic nature of culture. Changes within cultures are due to global influences, the movement of people from one country and/or region to another, and the interaction of various racial, ethnic and social groups. Changes also result as structures respond to the tensions and conflicts that occur as groups agitate for space, resources, recognition and survival.

Culture is therefore much more than costume, food, music and dance. As Jackson and Meadows (1991) explain: "Culture must not be treated as a loose amalgamation of customs, as a heap of anthropological curiosities" or seen merely in terms of artifacts such as languages, specific knowledge of customs, and rituals (p. 70). These are the symbols of a culture, and they too, change. Observable aspects of culture are merely tangible reflections of a complex interconnected set of elements that fulfil specific functions in the lives of the members of that society.

Simple actions like boarding a bus, making a dental appointment, dropping by to see a friend, and attending classes are aspects of culture. These behaviours are governed by the shared assumptions and rules of the culture. The existence of these commonly-held values make it possible to predict and control behaviour. Teachers and students with similar social histories know what to expect of each other, on the basis of commonly understood rules about schooling. As teachers and students, we routinely operate on the assumption that all of us know the same rules and will conduct ourselves accordingly. It enables us to depend upon each other to behave in predictable ways. Students and teachers from other cultures may not share these assumptions or unspoken rules.

It is not only that we adhere to particular rules or ways of doing things, and expect others to conform, but also that these are the things on which we place a value. We respond to the ways in which we and others behave with disgust, horror, pleasure or disdain, because not only do we consider some rules useful, but view them as a gauge of rightness and wrongness. And while we continually evaluate these rules, societies' members are still punished and rewarded on the basis of their loyalty to them. The result is that people are powerfully motivated to abide by societies' rules and to attempt to enforce them upon others.

Variations in cultural expressions within a society exist as a result of historic factors which preserve and generate differences. For instance, the region, gender, class, race, ethnicity, religion and sexual orientation with which people identify are factors which contribute to the variances. These social characteristics influence what groups or individuals internalize of the culture—what they value—and determine which *subcultures* are developed to ensure that these individuals survive and participate in the society. For instance, though individuals may share the belief that formal education is related to future career success, their definitions of career success may differ depending on the norms, values and expectations of their subcultural groups. This would then determine the kind and quantity of education that they pursue.

A *subculture* is expressed by "a group of people within a larger socio-political structure who share cultural (and often linguistic or dialectical) characteristics which are distinctive enough to distinguish it from others within the same culture" (Hoopes and Pusch, 1981: 3). The elements of the subcultures which find expression in the society, are those that are not in conflict with the "culture of the society" as a whole; and are therefore accommodated. Individuals can be members of a number of different subcultures (or subcultural groups), and will possess combinations of values, customs and patterns of thinking derived from the culture of the society in which they live, as well as from the many subcultures to which they belong. Adler points out that "the cultural identity of a society is defined by its dominant group, and this group is usually quite distinguishable from the minority sub-group with whom they share the physical environment and the territory they inhabit" (1977: 26).

Social Stratification, Ethnic & Racial Diversity and Culture

To add some clarity to our discussion of the complex relationship between social stratification, ethnicity and race, it is appropriate to first define these terms. *Ethnic group* refers to a group of people who share a common ancestry and history, who may or may not have identifiable physical or cultural characteristics, and who, through the process of interacting with each other and establishing boundaries with each other, identify themselves as being members of that group (Smith, 1991: 181). Ethnic group members often, but not always, speak a common language. They are identified as a distinct group by a common set of values, symbols and histories (Smith, 1991: 182). Sometimes religion or religious affiliation is also part of the ethnic identification. The group's identity is maintained over generations not only because new members enter the society, but also because members develop or maintain interest in their ancestral group and subculture.

According to Jones, *racial group* refers to "a group of people who share biological features that come to signify group membership and the social meaning such membership has in the society at large. Race becomes the basis for expectation regarding social roles, performance levels, values, norms and morals of the group and non-group members alike" (1991: 9). Skin colour is often the basis upon which status-allocation and group membership take place.

Ethnicity and race are significant when groups are identified and acquire status according to social and physical traits. Subcultures based on ethnicity and race are not related to any inherent qualities. Rather, they exist as a reflection of the *social meanings that society has attached to these characteristics,* and the ways in which individuals and groups have internalized these meanings and acted upon them, as well as the meanings that the respective groups give to these characteristics in the context of the society in which they live. It is the behaviour patterns that individuals develop as a consequence of these social meanings that we refer to as ethnic or racial subcultures.

The terms *dominant group* and *minority group* represent the relative relationship of groups to the power structure. The dominant group is the group in society which controls the economic, political and social participation of other members of society. Members of the dominant group usually occupy elite or privileged positions. Power and access to economic and political resources, rather than greater absolute numbers, characterize the dominant group. For example, while women outnumber men in most societies, they lack the power base of men, and are therefore considered a minority group.

Minority groups are usually defined by the dominant group on the basis of perceived physical, subcultural, economic and/or behavioural characteristics. Members of these groups are seen as subordinates in society and often receive different or negative treatment. According to Smith (1991):

We use race and ethnicity to define one's power status within the society. Each multiethnic/multiracial society develops a social distance scale which is usually anchored in the mainstream society's cultural value and feeling about the minority group. Those groups against which majority members have strong sanctions are those that they perceive as being the most unlike them, and therefore, the group from which they feel the greatest amount of social distance (p. 70).

Inevitably, social stratification will influence the subcultures' patterns with respect to the dominant and minority ethnic and racial groups. The dominant group enjoys the privileges of its status in society and gains access to all the social, economic and political institutions without compromising its cultural identity, or having to overcome barriers related to race, ethnicity or language. Minority groups usually experience exploitation and oppression (Smith, 1990: 70). Minority group members are very aware of the dominant group's cultural norms and values. Therefore, they are "inescapably bicultural" having the knowledge of their own subculture and that of the dominant group. They understand that this knowledge is often necessary for survival (Hoopes, 1981: 22).

Given its power and control over institutions, the dominant cultural group often forces minority group members to conform to the existing culture of the society.[1] Driedger (1989) refers to this as "a nationalist attempt" at getting the minorities in society to inculcate the values, norms and habits of the society; in other words, to acculturate or assimilate.

Acculturation is defined as a process which minority groups and immigrants go through in response to overt or systemic pressures from the dominant group to adopt, conform or adjust to dominant values, customs, behaviours and psychological characteristics (Sodowsky, Lai & Plake, 1991: 195). *Assimilation* is an aspect of the acculturation process. During acculturation individuals incorporate cultural elements of the dominant ethnic group, while in assimilation, considerable elements of their ethnic or racial subcultures are relin-

---

[1] It should be noted that many theories have been developed to explain what happens in modern, heterogeneous, technological societies. These are (a) assimilation and amalgamation which "assume that the urban industrial forces of technology and majority power will cause some loss of ethnic identity;" (b) modified assimilation and modified pluralism which "predict that minorities will retain ethnic characteristics partially or in changed forms;" and (c) ethnic pluralism and ethnic conflict which "emphasize that ethnic solidarity and identity can be maintained despite industrialization in both rural and urban settings" (Driedger, 1989: 34). Our argument is that given the power of the dominant ethnic group, acculturation, more than any other factor, characterizes the process of accommodation of the various minority groups in industrial-technological societies.

Acculturation and assimilation occur at different rates for different cultural groups in Canada.

quished in order to "fit in." This theory of assimilation is premised on the idea that the power of the dominant group will be too much for any minority group to resist, and therefore the group will assimilate into the majority (Dreidger, 1989).

As racial and ethnic minority group members interact with dominant group members, particularly in the major institutions[1] where the dominant group's norms and values predominate, assimilation is probable. This is all the more likely as these minority groups recog-

---

[1] Major institutions refer to government (political), education, social, cultural (ballet, opera), recreation (hockey, baseball).

1 / CULTURE: A SOCIAL STRUCTURE

nize that success or upward social mobility depends on being able to operate within the larger society. Often poverty, alienation and harassment are consequences of the sanctions against those whose cultures stray too far from the "norm". It would seem unlikely then, that ethnic and racial minority groups would maintain entirely distinct or different customs.

Many factors affect the rate of acculturation including the relative number of the groups involved in the contact situation; the rate of entrance of the minority group; where they settle; the extent to which they are isolated or segregated; the age and sex composition of the groups; the influence of individuals either in opposing or encouraging assimilation, and the crises which are experienced (Berry, 1958: 240).

Within societies are mechanisms which foster acculturation and seek to ensure stability and survival of the culture and subcultures. Ethnocentrism, prejudice and racism, often sustained by stereotyping and discrimination, are the mechanisms on which we will focus. These concepts will be explored in further detail in Chapter 5. For now, suffice it to say that ethnocentrism, prejudice and racism are attitudes and ideologies which are premised on the *assumed* superiority of one group over others. Stereotyping, the overgeneralization and categorization of individuals based on preconceived notions related to ethnic, racial or religious group affiliation, has a negative effect on minority groups' and individuals' capacity to influence the core set of cultural norms and values of the society. Discrimination is the structural and behavioural expression of the ideologies and attitudes which support cultural values, norms and ways of thinking. It is expressed through laws, regulations and policies as well as through individuals' behaviour. The significance of these mechanisms is evident in the role they play in preserving and perpetuating the structure and the cultural ethos of the society which favour the dominant group.

Is There A Canadian Culture?

Andrea: Call me naive, ignorant, or sheltered from the real world, but I thought in order to have a culture a person had to be of a different racial group. Since I was born in Canada I thought I was just "Canadian." Now I am being told I have a culture ...

Richard: As far as my culture goes, I am at a loss. I am Canadian. Period. There are no special traditions or attitudes that have been passed on to me by my parents or grandparents. My parents have taught me what they think is important for me to know. I have no traditional food or drink, no cultural costume. I am Canadian.

These comments by two students reflect the common notion held by Canadians that those with culture are primarily "ethnics"—in other words, ethnic and racial minorities, non-English-speaking people and immigrants who identify with their country of origin and maintain the language and traditions of that country while living in Canada. The students' failure to recognize that as Canadians they have a culture is in part a reflection of their concept of culture as something made up of observable, distinguishable elements. Indeed, the fact that they conceive of culture as possessed primarily by immigrants and people who are racially different is indicative of what has been communicated to them by the larger society. Further, it illustrates the observation made by Barnlund (1988) that the cultural norms of the society so completely surround them, so permeate their thoughts and actions, that they do not recognize the assumptions and the structures on which their lives and worldview rest (p. 14).

In discussions, students often asserted, "we are multicultural, there isn't *a* Canadian culture." There is no denying that our society is multicultural, but if we acknowledge that we live in a society that is Canadian, then there must be a core set of values, norms, expectations and practices to which all of us within the geographic boundary of Canada must adhere—a culture. So, despite our differences, our diversity as Canadians or our multiculturalism, we all generally live by the same laws, and have some ideas, knowledge, symbols, customs, goals, and aspirations in common. We also share similar views about how people should or should not behave. Furthermore, we relate to the same historical and contemporary issues which are unique to this country, and which help to shape the values, mores and ultimately the behaviour of every Canadian. Social interaction and behaviours are governed by rules, values, etc. which are reinforced through family, school, work, peer and media socialization. As Adler (1977) stated, culture serves "to organize, integrate, and maintain the psychological patterns of the individual, especially in the formative years of childhood," and every culture has patterns "that are unique, coherent and logical to the premises and predispositions that underlie the culture" (p. 28).

Towards An Explanation of Canadian Culture

From its beginnings, the country which is today known as Canada has been settled by peoples of different ethnicities, languages and subcultures. While the Aboriginals might have appeared to the Europeans as a homogeneous group, they were in fact a very diverse population. With the coming of Europeans, Canada became even more diverse, particularly in terms of racial and religious composition. Although many of the early settlers and immigrants were not uniformly English (or French), the institutions (e.g., government, religious, educational) established in the new country tended to be. Institutions are crucial in maintaining a culture; they are carriers of culture.

Historical evidence shows that the British settlers expected that through the legal, political, economic, and cultural institutions that they established, the Aboriginal people, the French and subsequent immigrant populations would assimilate to an Anglo-Saxon way of life. Leaders like Lord Durham had hoped that "somehow even the French would finally amalgamate into the dominant culture although not without conflict and competition. They assumed the desirability of social institutions and expected all others to learn the English language" (Driedger, 1989: 41). It was felt that the core of nationalism must remain English while French institutions, language and history had to take a lesser role.

In Upper Canada the education system established by Egerton Ryerson, a former Methodist minister, influenced educational institutions throughout Canada. It was premised on the principle of "fitting children for their place in the social hierarchy" (cf McNeill, 1974: 134). In the words of Ryerson, the purpose of education was to

... impart to the public mind the greatest amount of useful knowledge based upon and interwoven throughout with sound Christian principles (and that they must) render the system in all its various ramifications and applications the indirect but powerful instrument of British Constitutional government (cf McNeill, 1974: 133).

Over the years, education, like other institutions, has operated to Canadianize immigrants and minorities. Ashworth (1988) writes that "the goal of public schools was to assimilate immigrant children into the Canadian way of life. The 'hidden curriculum' was biased to-

The educational system has a powerful "Canadianizing" effect.

wards white Anglo-Saxons ... Concepts contrary to the religious beliefs of some groups were stressed, and Christian beliefs and values were promulgated" (p. 27-8). Hence, as the English had authority over the government, the courts, religion, the educational system, and all the other important structures of the society, this ensured the survival of the British culture.[1]

---

[1] It should be noted that education was established under provincial jurisdiction as a consequence of the British North America Act. It meant that the education systems of each province developed differently. In Québec for instance, while French education was supported, English control over education and the possibility of assimilation was very much a fear (Jaenen, 1977). Provinces such as Ontario, Manitoba, Alberta and Saskatchewan committed what Jaenen (1977) refers to as "linguistic genocide in the name of efficiency" in which by instructing students in English alone, they would be "Canadianized," i.e., produce "Anglo-conformity" (See also Tomkins, 1977).

One signature aspect of Canadian culture is the institutionalization of two "official languages"—French and English. This has resulted in a duality of institutions, and has fostered a state of mind throughout Canada that has influenced the way in which ethnic minority groups are treated. It has created a precedent for the preservation of cultural differences. (We will return to this point later.)

The size of the respective ethnic groups, their history, their roles in the building of Canada, the degree of difference between their sub-culture and the dominant culture, as well as their level of commit-ment toward maintaining their ancestral culture, all determine the extent to which their values and norms will survive in Canada. Racial and ethnic group members interact in the market-place, the centre of Canadian society where all must meet to make a living (Driedger, 1989: 50), it is reasonable to expect that elements of these groups' subcultures will be evident in the mainstream Canadian culture. And, insofar as some of their subcultural practices are not in conflict with the dominant cultural norms and values of the society, they may persist over time and eventually elements will become absorbed into Canadian cultural norms.[1]

For the most part however, minority groups and non-Anglo and non-French immigrants must adjust aspects of their cultural practices or behaviours in order to take advantage of opportunities and access the institutions in society. Given the social stratification and inequal-ity in our society, these adjustments will vary in degree and intensity from group to group. So too will the degree of assimilation for each group. Those ethnic groups that are closer in appearance and cul-tural practices to the dominant Anglo-Saxon ethnic group will adjust or assimilate much more readily. Northern Europeans, as Driedger (1989) points out, have considerable cultural affinity with Anglo-Saxon culture, and being white they are subject to little racial preju-dice and discrimination. They have some level of influence and control over their situation in the society, and they voluntarily assimi-late to the culture of the society by adopting the language as well as conforming and accommodating themselves. This has enabled them to compete quite well economically.

---

[1] For example, most Canadians have had "Chinese" dinners and pizza, which we tend to assume were brought here by the Chinese and Italians, respectively. Also, signs in languages other than English or French are common in many areas of Canada. Institutions, including governments, communicate to members of communities in languages other than French and English.

Figure 1:
Outside
sources help
to determine
Canadian
culture.

While immigrants and ethnic and racial minority group members in Canada may maintain some aspects of their ancestral culture, by and large their principal cultural practices will be Anglo-Canadian if they are to participate equally and freely in the society. In reality then, they have a mixture of both their subcultures and the Anglo-Canadian culture by which they are expected to live. It is the Anglo-Canadian culture which is expressed in public or in general interactions; and it is this culture into which all Canadians are socialized by educational, political, legal and social institutions.[1]

Outside sources also influence and determine Canadian culture. As shown in Figure 1, Canadians receive information from other countries through T.V., newspapers, magazines, books, etc. In these ways, elements of other cultures (e.g., styles of clothing, cars, accessories, etc.) are transmitted to us. Through this constant interaction, many

---

[1] Of course, the situation is different in Québec. While Anglo-Canadians are the dominant group in Canada, the political power of the French in Québec is used to influence the acculturation and assimilation of the minority groups in that province. Minority group members in Québec are caught between the expectations of the dominant English ethnic group of Canada, and that of the French.

1 / CULTURE: A SOCIAL STRUCTURE

elements of the American, European and other cultures become selectively incorporated into what is Canadian. In essence then, there is a Canadian culture in which all members of the society participate, irrespective of race, ethnicity, religion, etc. The variations which exist in subcultures do not detract from the fact that we all ultimately adhere to, and participate in, the same activities and are able to understand and predict each other's behaviour and expectations. This is what makes us a society.

But I often hear, "We are a multicultural society, therefore, how can you talk of one culture?" There is no question that Canada is a "multicultural society" if by this we mean that the society is made up of a number of racial and ethnic group. Fleras and Elliot (1992) claim that "Canada is also multicultural in the sense that these [ethnic and racial] minorities are not only different, but also wish to retain their identity within the framework of full and equal participation in Canadian society" (p. 52). But this would be evident in most societies. What makes us Canadian is that the meaning given to ethnic groups here relates to their national or ancestral origins (e.g. Italian, African, Asian etc.)[1], and the fact that there exists a federal policy of multiculturalism.

The official federal policy of multiculturalism was inaugurated on October 8, 1971[2] by then-Prime Minister Pierre Elliott Trudeau. At that time he declared that:

[T]here cannot be one cultural policy for Canadians of British and French origin, another for the original peoples, and yet another for all the others. For although there are two official languages there is no official culture, nor does any ethnic group take precedence over any other ... A policy of multiculturalism within a bilingual framework commends itself to the government as the most suitable means of assuring the cultural freedom of Canadians ... First, resources permit-

---

[1] In Canada ethnic origin is also identified in terms of the geographic regions from which groups have come. This is why ethnicity is considered to be socially defined, and is related to the societies in which they are found. This is why Aboriginals present a different case. While we refer to them generally as one group, they are in fact several ethnic groups.

[2] Some writers (e.g. Anderson & Frideres, 1981) claim that, dating back to Confederation, Canada practised a form of cultural pluralism, since the British, French and Aboriginal Peoples were able to maintain their cultural and linguistic differences. However, as we have discussed earlier in this chapter, the government had policies which were aimed toward achieving the Anglo-conformity of all other Canadians. There were indeed specific government initiatives, for example residential schools, that were aimed at assimilating Aboriginal Peoples. It can be argued that placement of Aboriginal Peoples on reserves, because they were considered unable to participate in the society, was definitely not in accordance with *cultural democracy*—the acceptance, support and preservation of the subcultures of all ethnic groups.

ting, the government will seek to assist all Canadian cultural groups that have demonstrated a desire and effort to continue to develop, a capacity to grow and contribute to Canada, and a clear need for assistance, the small and weak groups no less than the strong and highly organized. Second, the government will assist members of all cultural groups to overcome cultural barriers to full participation in Canadian society. Third, the government will promote creative encounters and interchange among all Canadian cultural groups in the interest of national unity. Fourth, the government will continue to assist immigrants to acquire at least one of Canada's official languages in order to become full participants in Canadian society (cf Palmer, 1975).[1]

Fleras and Elliot (1992) point out that the policy of multiculturalism addresses the experiences and expressions of members of society at the "individual, group, institutional, and societal levels" (p. 23). At the individual and group levels, the policy makes the assumption that discriminatory attitudes and cultural jealousies can be overcome if all Canadians share the same amount of cultural freedom.

But can this belief in cultural pluralism as the very essence of Canadian identity be practised in a society in which inequality and racial and ethnic stratification are institutionalized? Probably Jaenen (1977) answered this question best when he observed:

It should not be assumed ... that by defining Canada as bilingual and multicultural the federal government and the various provincial governments are making a definitive sociological analysis of Canadian society. Rather politicians are responding to electoral exigencies, to lobbies, and more optimistically also to the historical context and constitutional dialogue. It was obviously impossible to maintain the initial policy rubric of biculturalism, although bureaucrats as well as social scientists realize that the term multiethnic comes closer to defining Canadian social reality than does the term multicultural (p. 81).

The notion of cultural pluralism therefore can be seen as a way in which Canada sought to accommodate different groups, as well as to avoid or resolve tension and conflict between the various groups in the society. But it remains true that our society is stratified by gender, ethnicity, race and class upon which acculturation and assimilation have operated since "there are limits beyond which cultural freedom cannot go" (Berry, 1958: 339). In a society based on pluralism,

---

[1] Today, the multiculturalism policy is law. It is the Canadian Multiculturalism Act (Bill C-93) passed in July, 1988. In addition to reinforcing the sentiments of the earlier policy, today's Act emphasizes the promotion of positive race relations and cross-cultural understanding in a society where multiculturalism is a "fundamental characteristic of our evolving Canadian heritage and identity."

groups, though speaking their own language and following their own customs with respect to food, dress, rituals, recreation and worship, must carry out their day-to-day living within the boundaries of society's laws and regulations if they are to be acceptable members of the same society. Most of these laws and regulations, in the case of Canada's racial and ethnic minorities, represent the perspective and worldview of the dominant cultural group.

Assimilation at Work: Being Canadian

I was born in Delhi, India ... In 1968, in search of peace of mind and a better life for my family, I came to Canada ... I became a Canadian citizen as soon as I was qualified. After that, every time someone asked me where I came from I felt annoyed and threw back, "I am Canadian." When some people retorted, "You certainly don't look like one," I felt insulted, but forgave them their ignorance. I thought that my funny Indian accent must be the culprit and worked at losing it. I learned to speak Canadian English ... I seriously considered changing my name ... We then took care of our attire and appearance. I forced myself to acquire a taste for Big Macs. I even munched on hot dogs once my Canadian friends convinced me that there was no dog meat in them (Adhopia, 1988).

Above is the experience of an immigrant who wished to identify with, and actively participate in, his adopted society. The writer, Ajit Adhopia, illustrates that immigrants sometimes must make many conscious efforts to become "Canadian." This may involve changing behaviour and adopting attributes of the host society. Consider another example given by a class participant:

As compared to India, I have spent a very short time in Canada (less than two years). Therefore, in many ways I remain unaffected. Still there have been some significant visible changes. First of all, I have started wearing trousers (albeit infrequently). I watch television a whole lot more. After the leisurely lifestyle of India, my life in Toronto seems to be moving at a very fast pace. Instead of living and enjoying every day, I seem to exist here from week to week. My daily diet is still Indian but instead of the three regular meals I now have to make do with only one meal at night. And yes, I do call 967-1111.

We go to the Canadian National Exhibition and Wonderland. We celebrate Christmas but most of the Indian festivals go unobserved ... I was never a devout temple-going Hindu and that has not changed ... My race prevents me from participating freely in the "normal" Canadian humdrum of life. Before coming to Canada race was never an impor-

There are many aspects of North American culture that contribute to the integration and assimilation of immigrants.

tant part of my life ... My stay in Canada has taught me that the colour of my skin differentiates me from majority group Canadians and I feel alienated. I can no longer choose my friends freely; the society plays a large part. There is no daily interaction with the neighbours. If I want to talk to someone I have to call them by phone or drive over to their home.

Writing about the process of integration, another recent immigrant from Asia noted:

In my homeland, students are taught to show reverence for their elders and teachers by agreeing and believing in whatever was taught to them. Now in Canada, I have the liberty to challenge or criticize my elders and teachers, but even if I think I have justifiably and rightfully done so, I still cannot help but feel a twinge of guilt and unease.

Also, I was taught to maintain social harmony by being pleasing and agreeable and to apply tact and delicacy as much as possible. Upon interacting with the frank and honest Westerners, no matter how earnest and well-meaning their convictions, subconsciously I feel I'm being judged and attacked personally. Admiring their truthfulness, and in order to overcome my own sensitivity and insecurity, I am now trying very hard to adopt their open and confrontational behaviours and attitudes. As I venture to become candid, this new behaviour and attitude pose yet another conflict in my conscience. I have to tell myself that I am not out to deliberately hurt others' feelings.

The process of assimilation is not necessarily a self-imposed pressure to change or adjust to a new and dominant culture, but pressure is sometimes directed at minorities and immigrants by members of the society. This pressure sometimes takes the form of racism and prejudice. For example, in telling of her attitudes toward those "who hold unfamiliar values and customs," one class participant wrote:

> ... recently a Chinese lady came to the bank where I am employed, and presented me with documents stating her Chinese name had been changed to a Canadian name. I asked if changing her name would make her life easier. "No," she replied, "it will make things easier for *you*." How true! This brief incident clarified for me how Canadian immigrants struggle with the attitudes of the dominant group, how they are often forced to adapt and assimilate to our Canadian ways.

French Canadians, though one of Canada's so called "founding" ethnic groups, face similar pressures of assimilation. As one group member notes:

> Imagine you grew up in Sudbury in a French neighbourhood. Although you've always spoken French at home and all your friends are French, you can't remember a time when you didn't know English. The movies, the music, most of the T.V. and radio are in English. So, you grow up switching naturally between the two languages: French at home; English at your part-time job; French at church. You use both languages at school, depending where you are and who you're talking to, even what you're talking about.
>
> After high school, you want to get away from small town life and go to university, so you head for southern Ontario. Suddenly, everyone around you speaks English. There are no French newspapers, T.V., or radio. You find a small group of other people from Sudbury and stick together. You don't really notice that even among yourselves you speak French less and less.

After graduation, you get a job teaching in Ontario. The nearest Franco-Ontarian community is too far away to participate in. The other French teachers at the high school where you work are all English so you don't speak French to them. Suddenly it seems that the only time you do speak French is when you are teaching it.

A few years pass. You are engaged to be married. Your fiancé is English, but he knows a little French. Still, when you go home to Sudbury you use English so he won't feel excluded.

You get married in a Catholic church—an English service. The year you turn twenty-five you have your first baby. Your first child understands you when you use French words but your husband doesn't. You have two more children.

When you visit Sudbury now, you feel ashamed. Your French is rusty and you keep using English words. Your first child is nearly ten and the others are seven and five. They know only a few words of your language. They will probably never know more. In the span of one generation, your language has been lost and with it, your culture.

We cannot overlook the cultural debasement and social indoctrination of the Aboriginal peoples as a testament to the importance placed on assimilation in the institutionalization of Anglo-Canadian cultural norms. At the beginning of European settlement, First Nation peoples spoke different languages, and lived in complex self-governed societies. There are today few Aboriginals alive who have not been influenced by the enormous impact of European culture on their traditional way of life (See Adams, 1989; Wotherspoon and Satzewich, 1993).

The 1876 Indian Act was a determined effort to eradicate the cultures of the Indian Inuit and Metis peoples. The act declared that all Indians who married non-Indians, or who received an education in a Christian residential school would be recognized as "civilized ... fit for white society." All of these "enfranchised" Indians and their families would then be required to leave the reserve. Frideres points out that the assumption by many was that the longer "our individual native resides in an urban area, the more likely integration into the dominant society becomes" (Frideres, 1993).

The process of assimilation, of course, has its consequences, as one participant explains:

Canada is a so-called "multicultural society." All ethnic and racial groups have different customs, values, and beliefs, so in Canada they are entitled to preserve them. In order for a cultural group to maintain their heritage, they must practice their specific customs and beliefs. If they weren't permitted to practice these habits then they would soon assimilate. I believe this would lead most of them to having low self-esteem, possibly no pride, and an eventual feeling of loneliness.

The fact that some ethnic and racial groups reside in enclaves in large urban centres, or on rural reserves, does not mean that they do not undergo an acculturation process. While it may be true that many still practice aspects of their ancestral cultures (or subcultures) to varying degrees, it is important to note that all reside in Canada and must conform to popular morality and the laws that support that morality. Furthermore, members of these groups must attend educational institutions through which they are taught the dominant values, norms and behavioural practices. Like other Canadians, minority group members are socialized to elements of culture through the textbooks used, the languages spoken and the daily routines of educational institutions.

SUMMARY

There is a culture in which all members of Canadian society participate. Culture, and by extension subculture, are dynamic, and are influenced by the social and physical contexts in which they exist. The cultural practices and customs of the Italian, African, Scottish, Portuguese, Asian or South Asian groups in Canada differ from those in the countries where they are dominant. Through acculturation and assimilation, ethnic and racial minority group members come to share the dominant Canadian culture. The variations which exist in Canadian culture do not fundamentally dispute the fact that we must all at some point adhere to, and participate in, the same activities. Furthermore, the variations that are found among groups and individuals are a reflection of the socialization process and factors related to characteristics such as ethnicity, race, religion, citizenship, etc. Through agents of socialization such as the family, school, work and peers, we conform to the expectations, rules, and philosophy of living required to function in the society while trying to minimally disrupt or change our core values.

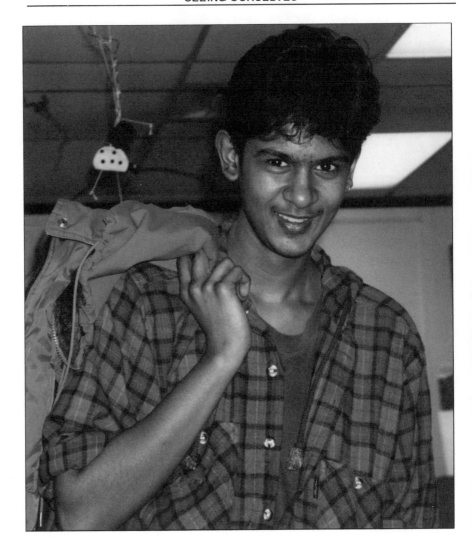

Questions:

1. How would you describe Canadian cultural identity? How is it constructed?
2. "Everyone living in Canada participates in Canadian culture to varying degrees." Explain.
3. Account for the existence or non-existence of a dominant ethnic subculture in Canada.

2

RACE, ETHNICITY AND CULTURAL IDENTITY

In Chapter One, we discussed race and ethnicity as characteristics by which individuals are identified in our society, and around which subcultures are constructed. Building on this, in the first section of this chapter we will examine some of the factors that determine the construction of culture and its expression at the individual level—an individual's cultural identity. Following that we will explore the role of race and ethnicity in peoples' lives.

Factors Influencing Individuals' Cultural Identity

Cultural identity refers to (a) the collective self-awareness that a given group embodies and reflects (e.g. racial, ethnic, gender groups) and (b) the "identity of the individual in relation to his or her culture" (Adler, 1977: 26). It is the latter aspect that is important to us here. We will explore the dimensions of cultural identity as "a functioning aspect of individual personality and a fundamental symbol of a person's existence" (Adler, 1977: 26).

Figure 2 illustrates some of the factors that contribute to the development of individual cultural identity. The construction of cultural identity is a complex process. Nevertheless, the chart is an attempt to bring clarity to the issues involved. These factors are not static, they change over time, with individuals' changing awareness of self, others and the social system, through interactions, and as individuals respond to social change. Apple contends that identity "is

Factors contributing to an individual's cultural identity (starting from the inner circle).

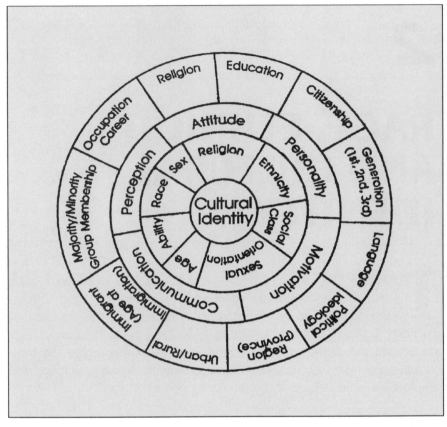

1. Individual's personal cultural identity determines lifestyle and behaviour. 2. Personal factors (social), mostly ascribed. 3. Psychological factors. Some are based on innate sources; all interact with the personal and social factors. 4. Social factors that are shared by group members. Many of these are institutions through which socialization takes place, culture is transmitted, or behaviour is determined. (Spirituality here refers to that which is an integral part of a person's life. In some cases it is referred to as religion.)

not necessarily a stable, permanent, united centre that gives consistent meaning to our lives. It too, is socially and historically constructed, and subject to political tensions and contradictions" [1993: vii].

Social characteristics like gender, race, ethnicity, ability, age and sexual orientation, together with factors such as education, citizenship status, political affiliation, etc., are likely to influence a person's attitudes, perception, personality and motivation. Socializing agents such as the family, teachers, peers, mentors, coaches, significant others and the society in which the individual lives, play a significant role in the ways in which these factors influence individuals and find expressions. When combined, these inter-related factors play a role in the socialization process, in the nature of the culture that is transmitted and constructed by the individual, and ultimately in the behaviour of that individual.

The following example by Moran Chui serves to illustrate this process and the significance of culture in the formation of her identity.

On Being A Second-Generation Chinese-Canadian

I am a 25-year old second-generation Chinese-Canadian female. My name means "Admired Lotus Lily." I was born in Belleville, Ontario. My parents are naturalized Canadian citizens originally from The People's Republic (of China) who met in Hong Kong. Because we re-located to Toronto when I was approximately 2 years old, I remember little of small-town Ontario. Practically my entire life has been spent in the big city; I have never left North America. And luckily for me, there is a stable community of my own ethnic background. I take great comfort in this.

"Chinese-Canadian," in my opinion, describes a person of Chinese descent living in a Western society, such as Canada. It has been difficult for myself and I am sure many others of my culture to assimilate into some of the dominant Canadian values. Take for example the family. My family is very important to me but no one actually realizes the obligations that I take on happily. Few of my friends and co-workers who are not Chinese-Canadian know that I am expected to support my parents in old age (and definitely not put them in an old age home!). It is that time in my career when moving out of Toronto may be advantageous, but I could never move out. Some people think it's because I am insecure but they just don't understand. I worry about my parents a great deal and moving out is not culturally encouraged for reasons other than marriage (if that!!). But before I finish making my point, it should be noted that I take on these duties and responsibilities willingly. I would feel tremendous guilt and pressure if I upset everyone in my family.

I can hardly communicate to my parents in their native tongue and I am not literate in Chinese. I do not see this as a liability but my mother does. She is concerned about the preservation of the Chinese culture. For this reason, she also frowns on intermarriage. My mother still complains that my third-cousin married a white Jewish male. She argues that it is because the culture will be lost within a generation but I do not see the difference between myself and my third-cousin's children. I must disappoint her greatly.

It has been hard for me to fit into the Canadian culture, and/or be accepted by other Chinese. I sometimes become paranoid and think that my cultural peers perceive me as a "wacko." This is probably because they may think of me as over-assimilated and assertive beyond their comfort zone. I don't fit the stereotypical submissive East Asian woman. My dress and accent do not give me away. In fact, I am probably not living my culture in many ways because I have assimilated much more than first generation immigrants. On the other hand, even though I do not readily mesh with my own culture, I do not possess the white privilege that many Canadians of European descent possess. They can mix right into the predominantly white culture at their whim; I will always have my skin colour and physical characteristics to set me apart. Metaphorically I sit on a fence and cannot be categorized or ordered into any group. First generation lower income immigrants naturally assume that I am totally Westernized and whites think that I am totally Chinese in my ways of thinking. In some ways, both points of view have grains of truth. But where do I fit? And where do I belong?

For a substantial part of my life I grew up in a predominantly European Catholic neighbourhood. It was hard to make friends because I was different, specifically because I was from a different race. That was the first time that I experienced racism. Not only was it among students from school who sadly picked it up from their parents but also from neighbours who did not like Chinese people. You see, our family was one of the first non-white families to move into the lower-middle class white neighbourhood. Many of those families have moved to the suburbs now. In fact, my neighbourhood is quite "yuppie-ized" and has a greater East and South Asian population now but I will never forget the feelings of ostracization and isolation that I felt then. Even as a law student (yes, there are Chinese law students!), I experienced a more subtle racism. During my articling interviews, many potential employers asked me if I could speak Cantonese because they have many commercial law clients from Hong Kong. At a Bar Admission presentation, I was told that I had an accent. In fact it was another woman, who incidentally was white, but I was the only visible minority present. After the seminar, a fellow law student noted that I did not have a Chinese accent, and that it was in fact a distinctly "Toronto" accent.

Often people will ask me "What are you??!!" or "Are you Filipino?" It really bothers me. I guess you could rationalize that I get mad because

people are prejudging me. But it goes deeper than that. Much deeper, I get angry because I expect people to know that I am Chinese and not Filipino. The differences are vast and I perceive myself as more culturally Chinese.

Sometimes I reflect and wonder what kind of Chinese I am. Am I a good person? Am I a bad person because I do not have the burning desire to go back and visit the lands of my ancestors? A lot of friends want to do this but I do not need to see "Mecca." Am I in denial about my ethnic roots? I often did and still do have problems telling people what professions my parents were in. My mother used to be a garment worker around the Spadina Avenue area in Toronto. It could be a mixture of shame of being from a lower class family. It could be the fact that I didn't want people to stereotype my parents or people of my race as people who only work in low-paying, back-breaking work. The image of the immigrant garment worker and immigrant restaurant worker are classic Canadian stereotypes. It could be because I wanted to disassociate myself and leap into a better class and I thought that the knowledge of my family background would hinder my chances. So many East Asians are ghettoized and fall into a vicious cycle.

Undergoing the constant process of evaluating perceptions we hold is crucial to personal growth.

The inter-relationship of everything that has occurred in my life, including the race, gender, and class issues, cannot be explained simply in this short essay. I end by saying that there is positive news in all this doom and gloom. I can accept who I am in the Canadian context. I am Canadian and I am proud! I can undergo the constant process of evaluating who I am, and evaluating the perceptions I hold. It is easy to be lazy. But I think in order for me to personally grow I must not be smug about how "liberal-minded" I think I am, how I know what racism is all about because I have experienced it. I must think twice.

Moran's experience reflects the identity issues of ethnic and racial minority Canadians. Moran discusses how much her ideas, values and aspirations are very much a product of Canadian culture, and at the same time influenced by her Chinese subculture. But as she notes, she has "assimilated" some of the dominant cultural norms and values. At the same time, she is very committed to her subcultural Chinese view of the family. She "willingly" accepts the "obligation" to support her parents, and would not wish to "upset" them. But, while she is comfortable with what is expected of her from her family and the Chinese community, she also demonstrates that there are limits. The responsibility of supporting her "parents in old age" is acceptable but she does not consider not being able to speak Chinese as a liability or an indication of cultural loss.

Moran also explores how being a racial minority affects her existence. She states that while she has "assimilated much more than first generation immigrants," and even though she does "not readily mesh" with her subcultural group, all this has not protected her from the stereotyping and racism that she has experienced throughout her life. This she attributes to the fact that she does "not possess the white privilege that many Canadians of European descent possess" since her "skin colour and her physical characteristics" will always set her apart. These experiences contribute to Moran's conscious definition of herself as a minority, and ultimately to her cultural identity. As Smith (1991) points out, the development of identity in minority group individuals entails dealing with the sense of initial rejection of one's ethnic group, to moving "from an early stage of unawareness and lack of differentiation to one of ethnic awareness, ethnic self-identification, and increasingly ethnic differentiation on the basis of contact situations" (p. 183).

The alienation, ambiguity and doubt that is voiced in Moran's essay: "But where do I fit? And where do I belong?" and "Am I in denial of my ethnic roots?" reflect the extent to which many ethnic minority individuals are trapped between the dominant culture of the society in which they live and their own subcultures. This dilemma is created as these people begin to come to terms with their "otherness" in a society that has rejected them but whose culture they have internalized. Moran's experience is not unlike that of Sun-Kyung Yi, a "Korean-Canadian," who in her essay "Split Personality" (1992) writes that she went through the process of acculturation into the host culture aware that only by so doing could she enjoy the benefits which Canada has to offer. Still, she declares that it is "difficult to feel a sense of belonging and acceptance" when you are regarded as an "other."

In writing about the relationship between identity and culture in his essay "Beyond Cultural Identity," Adler affirms that:

The psychological, psychosocial, and psycho-philosophical realities of an individual are knit together by the culture which operates through sanctions and rewards, totems and taboos, prohibitions and myths. The unity and integration of society, nature, and the cosmos is reflected in the total image of the self and in the day-to-day awareness and consciousness of the individual. This synthesis is modulated by the larger dynamics of the culture itself. In the concept of cultural identity, then, we see a synthesis of the operant culture reflected by the deepest images held by the individual (1977: 28).

Indeed, Moran's essay demonstrates the significance of culture and subculture in establishing an individual's sense of identity. Subcultures serve as a means of providing stability and comfort, mediating the ways in which the dominant Canadian culture constructs the group's cultural identity. The degree to which an individual identifies with her subculture varies depending on place of birth, social class, abilities, education and occupational expectations and achievements, interaction with members and non-members of her group, and her willingness to adapt to the main cultural norms.

Ethnicity plays an equally important role in the formulation of cultural identity for the members of the dominant cultural group. However, this group's situation is less problematic. Smith (1991) argues that while the ethnic identity development of the majority group individual is continually being validated and reinforced in a positive manner by both his membership group and by the structure of the society's institutions, such is not the case for members of many ethnic minority groups. Positive reinforcement frees the majority individual to focus on aspects of his or her life other than ethnicity (p. 183).

The following account by James is an example of one dominant group member's experience:

> The often-asked philosophical question "What is the meaning of life?" is very difficult to answer, but I believe that to answer this question we must first know who we are—our identity. For if we do not know ourselves, how can we begin to understand the meaning of our existence? To know ourselves is to be able to define our identity, who we are and the factors that contribute to our being the person that we are.

> I don't think of myself as having a "colour," and I guess that is because society does not highlight or stress this message to me every waking moment as it does to a person whose skin is not white. The message sent by our "first world" society is that the "civilized world" is white; I can't imagine the impact on a person who is not white. The formation of a person's identity will surely be influenced by colour and in the case of a person who is not white, this can cause a great deal of confusion (which might be termed as an identity crisis).

> I am an immigrant. I was born in Glasgow, Scotland, and my family immigrated to Canada when I was four. This would be my ethnicity, but I have no specific conscious attachment to the culture of my place of birth. Coming to Canada at a young age, I had not fully absorbed the culture of Scotland and so it was not very difficult for me to assimilate into Canadian culture. I did not have to suffer the potentially painful effects of acculturation because Canada was, and continues to be, in many respects very similar to Scotland. The neighbourhood that I first lived in was comprised of white working class families and I can't recall any people of different cultural backgrounds in the neighbourhood.

> While as a child I was never bombarded with messages of my Scottish ethnicity, I was still very much socialized into that culture. The friends of my parents were mostly Scottish (i.e. first generation here in Canada) and all white. And I grew up conscious of some of the negative perceptions that were associated with being Scottish. Some of these were being cheap, wearing a kilt, eating porridge, and speaking with an accent. There were occasions as a young person that I would not acknowledge my ethnicity because of the stereotypes associated with being Scottish (certainly the impact of what I perceived to be negative characteristics pales in comparison with stereotypes that people of other cultures are subjected to).

In high school, starting in grade ten, I played basketball with guys who were mostly from the Caribbean. While I did spend a great deal of time with the guys on the team I maintained other friends, which in part may have been due to the fact that none of the guys I played basketball with were in any of my classes (this was because they were taking trade classes and their regular classes were not at the advanced level). I spent about four years with the same guys from the basketball team. We would also go to parties together on the weekend, as I did with my group of mainstream friends. I went to all the school dances and liked the music that was being played. This kind of music was recognized or associated with black people.

Sports and recreational activities are an important part of Canadian culture, and serve as opportunities for cultural interaction and integration.

The way I dressed was "mainstream." I did not try to dress like the guys I played basketball with. There were very specific styles that were associated with particular cultural groups. I had developed two distinct circles of friends and felt comfortable in either circle. The two circles of friends were those who I played sports with (who were predominantly Caribbean) and those that I knew from grade school (who were mostly white). In high school I never used pejorative language and friends that did, I would distance myself from.

During high school I was not conscious of my behaviour until in a conversation a friend (who is black), mentioned that I "act black." This struck me as a very strange comment and my response to him was that I am not acting any particular way but just being myself. I inquired further as to what was it that he thought I was doing that drew him to his conclusion. He could offer no specific answer as to the specific black behaviour(s) that I exhibited.

The next time I heard a similar comment was by my college basketball coach, who said I played basketball like a black guy. This was easier for me to relate to because I could actually picture the meaning of what he had said. Now I did not make a conscious effort to play basketball like a black guy, I just played the way I learned. This learning took place with the guys who were black. I actually considered the statement the coach had made as a compliment because black guys were some of the best basketball players around.

My identity is never questioned, people automatically assume that I am Canadian, born and raised here. I am almost never asked where I was born; in fact many people are often surprised when I tell them I was born in Scotland. I am also never asked what kind of an accent I have, although when I visit Scotland I am often asked if I am American (which I take great offense to).

As a white person, I am never asked to be the spokesperson for all white people, a position that many minority people can easily find themselves in. I guess this is because most white people know that all white people do not think alike; but those same white people assume that people of other racial groups think alike.

Have I had privileges because of the fact that I am white? Well, because I understand how society works I would have to say yes. A more difficult question to answer is: What were those privileges that I received, aside from not being followed around in stores by a sales clerks, or receiving better service in a restaurant? I don't know. Did I ever get a job because I was white? I don't know. Perhaps this is the crux of the problem that whites have in accepting equity programs. It is that we "honestly" don't believe that we have ever had any special privileges purely because we are white. This demonstrates the urgent need for societal re-education.

Race and Ethnicity in the Social Construction of Identity

Race: A Social Construct

⌈Race is an arbitrary and problematic term that is employed in the classification of human beings⌋ Over the years it has been used to refer to (a) lineage (groups of people connected by common descent or origin); (b) subspecies (populations of people with distinct geno-types); (c) ethnic groups (e.g. Anglo-Saxons, Italian); (f) religions (e.g. Jews); (g) nationalities (e.g. Irish, Chinese); (h) minority language groups (e.g. French Canadians); (i) blood groups (e.g. Blacks; South East Asians); and (j) people from particular geographic regions (e.g. Mediterranean, Europeans) (Elliot and Fleras, 1992: 28; Li, 1990: 6). Such varied usage has resulted in race being seen as an objective biological and/or social fact which operates through independent characteristics (Omi and Winant, 1993). Further, there is the accompanying belief that there are personalities based on racial characteristics; and that inherited biological or physical characteristics are the most important individual and group traits.

Obviously, the meaning of race is not *fixed*—it changes based on historical period and context. The problem is clear: Who really belongs in these categories? Many people don't fit into any of the five colour-based racial categories (brown, black, red, yellow, white) that we use today.[1] Where would we, for example, place Arabs or people from the middle East, or people with combined racial backgrounds? Such a list would be quite long if we were to continue, but the point is evident: There is no clear, undisputable definition of race. Does that mean then that our references to different racial groups or identities is merely a means of manipulating and creating division among people? Do racial characteristics play a role in people's lives? Omi and Winant (1993) argue that "the concept of race operates neither as a signifier of comprehensive identity, nor of fundamental difference, both of which are patently absurd, but rather as a marker of the infinity of variations we humans hold as a common heritage and hope for the future" (p. 9).

---

[1] It is only in recent times that we have begun to use "brown," particularly in Toronto, to refer to people of South Asian origin. In the United States, in Los Angeles, for example, "brown" refers to Latin American.

Race is a socially constructed classification, and is therefore not determined biologically, but socially and psychologically.

Therefore, for the purpose of our discussion, "race" will refer to the socially constructed classification of human beings based on the historical and geographic context of individuals' experiences and is often the basis upon which statuses are conferred, groups are formed, agency is attained, and social roles are assigned. Consequently, individual and group identities and behaviours are a product of these factors. An individual's race is determined socially and psychologically rather than biologically.

Leo Driedger (1986), in writing about ethnic and minority relations, notes that Northern Europeans, the dominant population in Canada, tend to be very conscious of skin colour and often classify people accordingly (p. 284). Yet when asked to describe themselves, members of the dominant population tend to omit race as one of the characteristics, while minority group members, particularly Blacks, tend to identify race as a significant characteristic. As the dominant racial group, Whites tend to see their colour as the norm while identifying non-Whites in terms of colour. In fact, race is a part of everyone's identity.

The tendency to see race as referring mainly to racial minorities was brought out in one class when participants were asked to talk about themselves in racial, ethnic and cultural terms. One participant insisted that he was Canadian and therefore his racial and ethnic identity were irrelevant. When asked how he would feel if a Chinese and a Black person insisted that they were Canadian and therefore refused to identify themselves by their ethnicity, Rob responded by saying he would not be satisfied with their answers because to him, Canadians are people who look like him: "Chinese and Blacks are immigrants—they do not look Canadian." Another participant said to me, "I feel when you mention race you're talking about people of different ethnicities and countries."

Another common occurrence is to respond to the term "race" as synonymous with prejudice or racism. When asked to talk about race as it relates to their identity and behaviour, White participants tended to become defensive. They would respond, "I don't feel uncomfortable with Black people," or "Every time I've talked about race it's been about stereotyping or prejudice." Others write:

> *Greg:* As for my race, I am White, but I never really had to think about it before. I don't feel that it ever affected the people with whom I associated or talked to. My two best friends are Black and (Canadian) Indian. I was brought up in a family that didn't believe in prejudice and I'm proud of that. If I don't like a person, it is because of their personality, not their race or heritage.

> *Henry:* Concerning my race, which is Caucasian, I really don't believe that it has contributed enormously to my identity or behaviour. I feel this way because my culture is basically all Canadian.

> *Laurie:* I ... cannot see how my race influences or affects me. I have always been aware of how my ethnicity influences my ideals, morals, values and beliefs, and these personal elements have not changed. For me to say that race affects me would either show that I feel inferior or superior to other races, and this is incorrect.

Race affects how humans interact and form groups. Race is significant as long as groups are determined by physical traits, as long as these are particular attributes ascribed by their physical traits and as long as people react and respond to the existence of these physical traits. We must bear in mind that the social meaning of race takes precedence in the interactions and thinking of most people. Here, when we speak of race or racial group, we do not refer to biological categories, but most importantly, to the social meanings that society has given to race and the ways in which individuals and groups have internalized these meanings and acted upon them.

The following illustrates how Vanessa perceives the situation:

> I came to Canada from the Caribbean when I was 2 1/2 years old. All of my education has been in Canada. In light of this fact, being recognized as a Canadian should not be an issue for me. However, other groups have influenced me. In addition to my educational socialization, membership in a cultural youth group as well as my Black West Indian family were significant in determining the rate at which and the extent to which I would be identified as Canadian.

> Growing up in a Caribbean household, I learned the ways and customs of the old country. Without effort, I developed an authentic "Trini" accent by the time I was ready for Grade One. However, my teacher never really appreciated this sweet sound and enrolled me in speech classes. I learned to speak, dare I say, "proper English" as my teacher would have it. But rather than completely abandon this accent, I kept it and mastered how and when to turn it off and on at will.

> In the evenings at a cultural centre, I became familiar with the traditional dances of the Caribbean and Africa. There, I became acquainted with the arts and crafts as well as the folk tales of my ancestors. In the daytime, I studied about the Group of Seven, Sir John A. Macdonald, Peter Rabbit and the Brothers Grimm, while in the evenings I read about Anansi the Spider, Toussaint L'Ouverture and Sam Sharpe. Clearly, I had the best of both worlds growing up—a Canadian Black with knowledge of her ancestral past.

> So why is it that this Canadian, who is often seen eating fries and hamburgers and wearing jeans and a T-shirt, continues to shock White people when she answers "Canadian" to their question, "What are you?" After responding, I get a further question, "No, I mean originally?" It seems that if a person is non-White, regardless of how long s/he has lived here or indeed even if s/he were born here, White society never fully accepts them as Canadians. The assumption is

always that they are from somewhere else. Yet, a White person from Scotland who has lived in Canada for as long as I have would not get a raised eyebrow when s/he answers "Canadian" to the question "What are you?" No second question ever follows.

It appears that only when a person reaches the height of national or international fame is her/his ancestry ignored and s/he becomes Canadian. I think of Oscar Peterson, the jazz pianist, Lincoln Alexander, the Lieutenant-Governor of Ontario and, dare I say, Ben Johnson, the athlete.

These Black men seem to be accepted by White Canada as being Canadian. Unfortunately for Ben Johnson, we witnessed him fall from being a Canadian to a Jamaican-Canadian in the space of one weekend. This incident causes one to question how permanent and secure that title "Canadian" really is. And indeed, is it truly possible to become one as long as you look like me?

Andrew: *"I am bi-racial..."*

> *... If I were asked for a definition of myself, I would say that I am one who waits; I investigate my surroundings, I interpret everything in terms of what I discover, I become sensitive (Frantz Fanon,* Black Skin, White Masks*).*

I am given multiple names, told I am tragic and made to feel that I must choose to be either Black or White, or exist somewhere in the centre, benignly being told that it's the space of the "happy medium." I am bi-racial and frustrated because the pundits of mixed race children, who are usually not mixed themselves, believe in such a thing as "having the best of both worlds." On the same tip, I would not be stupid and naive enough to say that I live with the "worst" of both worlds, although in many ways I find this reasoning to be the easiest to rationalize when both my "worlds"—Black and White—look at me as some sort of abrogation in a world governed by what W. E. B. Du Bois called the "colour line."

My father is White, my mother is Black, and I am Black. For some this logic doesn't make much sense ... *you could pass for white you know* ... and it seriously troubles their minds ... *hey nigger, I'm talking to you* ... so much so that they want to probe my mind to find out how I cope with my fissure. Being seen as a "tragic mulatto" seems to be a perennial problem and fascination for some White and Black folk who want to ask, IS IT POSSIBLE FOR MIXED RACE PEOPLE TO BE BLACK? It seems that there must be a designated camp that I must call home, to be Black or White, or is "bi" the answer? In a world of television talk show mentalities I know people want to ask "aren't you confused?" Of course, I'd say yes, but who isn't in this world?

I've heard some people say that it is the coming together of people of different races, ethnicities, and cultures that will help eradicate some of the social dissention in the world, namely racism. Strangely, this philosophy, the miscegenists' dream, sounds like an inspirational jingo from singer Bobby McFerrin, "don't worry, think half-breed." I am not an optimist because some peoples' dreams are others' nightmares, including my own. Because of such thinking, I've grown increasingly suspicious and critical of my parents' marriage, wondering if they really believed that "love sees no colour" shit. It's not the love that I question, after all love is one of the last of the humanitarian principles still in existence, but their inability to see that baffles me. Did my father question his white skin and male privilege at the same door that my mother possibly hung her sentiments of self-hatred? And at the same time are there any coincidences of these related facts shaping the dynamics of their relationship? These are serious questions, as they should be, and I feel like I have every right to be suspicious of some, but not all, of the circumstances surrounding my introduction to this world.

As a child it is easy to take what you see for granted, so it didn't seem like such a big deal to have parents who were not the same colour. But there was something that I didn't understand until I started to seriously think about my father's world, the Eurocentric male one, presenting itself as the centre of all of that which is correct and normal, and my mother's as a sort of bastardization of the norm. Being a product of the centre and the periphery has a funny way of playing with your head and there's definitely not enough love in the world to save you from that sort of trauma.

Growing up I negotiated the world on the politically conservative White side and the liberal Black side. My mother, whom I once cussed in public and called "nigger," reminded me at one and the same time that I was not white but to always remember that my father was White. In the past couple of years my mother's reminders seem to come more frequently as I speak more openly about the social and political lives of Black people. To me this is supposed to serve as some sort of inhibitor to expressing part of me which I believe she has chosen to ignore.

My father, for the most part, chooses to remain silent on the issue of colour. Sometimes I'll receive a book or an article from him where the

Our parents or other relatives are often important links in the process of racial or ethnic identification.

subject or author is a Black person, which is some sort of acknowledgement that I am, to some degree, Black. We never have had any open discussion about the politics of race or identity; it is an area that I feel uncomfortable dealing with so we just continue talking about jazz, Black athletes, and jerk chicken.

Some people who are bi-racial are caught in a sort of world cut in two, an either/or scenario about who they are, how they should be, and what they should do. I would be a hypocrite if I said that I have eclipsed this sort of difficulty in my navigation through the mazes of the White and Black worlds. However, it is necessary to understand that hybridity creates a new space and I am a part of this space for which there is no set archetype. If I say I am Black it does not mean that I am everything that is not White. It is, at the same time, so simple and so complex: I love that.

Ethnicity: A Social Construct

The terms "ethnic population," "ethnic food," "ethnic music," are used often in Canada. In some cases, "ethnic" is used to describe Italians, Portuguese, Ukrainians and others. It is also used as a stereotype. The term "ethnic" is used interchangeably with "race" and "immigrant" to try to socially define or locate people.

Leslie: To me, ethnicity was something that belonged to people who differed from the so-called average White Canadian—differing perhaps because of language, accent or skin colour. Thus, I believed ethnicity was something noticeable or visible. I believe my ignorance regarding my ethnicity is because I belong to the dominant group in Canada. Because I am White, English speaking, and have British ancestry, I have only thought of myself as a Canadian. In essence, I didn't realize I had ethnicity because I did not differ from the stereotypical image of an average Canadian.

The common notion among Canadians is that ethnicity is based on how people choose to identify themselves and is presumably of no concern to society in general. But, ethnicity is not simply a matter of individual choice, members of society play a role in defining ethnicity. For example, class participant Jackie Stewart writes that when she tells people her name, some respond by saying "Grrrrrrreat day for motorcar racing!" She continues:

I must hear that line at least once a day. People tend to associate my name with the once-great racing car driver, Jackie Stewart. The last name, Stewart, is a dead giveaway that I am of Scottish origin or ethnicity. People generally don't ask where my parents are from because they recognize their Scottish accent. However, when I mention that I, too, was born in Scotland, they look at me questioningly and ask why I do not have an accent. Or, they ask why I do not have freckles, or pale skin with rosy cheeks. How am I to know?

Ethnicity gives individuals a sense of identity and belonging based not only on their perception of being different, but also on the knowledge that they are recognized by others as being different. Isajiw (1977) notes that in terms of ethnic cultural practices, individuals go through "a process of selecting items, however few, from the cultural past—pieces of ethnic folk art, folk dances, music, a partial use of language, knowledge of some aspects of the group's history—which become symbols of ethnic identity" (p. 36).

Recalling how he struggled with his identity, Stefan writes:

My ethnic identity is Polish. My parents were born in Poland and came to Canada in 1967. I was born in Toronto, Ontario a couple of years later. I saw my ethnicity as an advantage and a disadvantage during my lifetime. When I was younger, I didn't want to admit that I was Polish. Even though I was born here, I felt that admitting my ethnicity would be a barrier to joining the "in-crowd" or the "cool group" at school. I even skipped the Polish language classes my parents sent me to after school. As I became older, I realized I couldn't change my

ethnicity. I was who I was. I became more proud of my Polish background. It felt good to be part of a Polish community where you were able to participate in ceremonies and activities based on your Polish background. It gave me a sense of belonging to a group, a sense of identity, a sense of security.

Individuals with several ethnic identities are *free* to identify with all of them. However, individuals often identify most strongly with the one that forms the basis of their socialization at home or with their peers, the one that seems most acceptable by the dominant group in society, or the one by which others identify them.

Ethnicity, like race, is socially, politically and historically constructed, and is subject to the ambiguities and contradictions that are to be found in societies.[1] It is dynamic. Its meanings change over

> Ethnicity gives individuals a sense of identity and belonging, as it emphasizes their cultural uniqueness to others and reinforces it within their own group.

---

[1] In Canada, one of the ways in which ethnicity is constructed has to do with the "official" no-

time. Nevertheless, ethnicity serves to establish status allocation, role expectations and group membership. Marger and Obermiller write that ethnicity is "a form of social organization, the boundaries of which are flexible in various social contexts. Cultural features are only symbolic and serve to mark out particular group boundaries" (cf. Elliot and Fleras, 1992: 134).

In the following essays, individuals explore their understanding of ethnicity.

Damian: My cultural and ethnic backgrounds are very much Slovenian. More specifically they come from a northern province called Slovenija [in the former Yugoslavia]. My parents immigrated from there twenty-two years ago and I was born here in Canada.

My parents brought with them all of their beliefs, values and traditions. A big part of their life was, and is, a dedication to hard work and their religious faith. Throughout my life I have been taught to respect those values and accept those religious beliefs.

With regard to ethnicity, it ranges from the way I dress to the type of food I eat. For example, my parents hate to see me in ripped clothing. When I was a child, and even now, their ethnic values made them feel that I should be well-groomed all the time. I feel that now in my early adult years I carry a lot of those early impressions with me.

The work ethic is very important to me. I feel that I always make an attempt to do things well and with enthusiasm. This is one of the main cultural differences. Canadian culture dictates a more relaxed atmosphere to work. One of the strange things that I tend to do is slack off when in an environment of long-time Canadians, simply because of this attitude. In a predominantly Yugoslavian environment, I tend to work faster and a lot harder. In this way, I am more Slovenian than Canadian.

A central focus in my life is my religious faith. My parents and most of the province they come from are Roman Catholic. My faith has always been a basis for my attitudes, actions and beliefs. With respect to sex and morality, the church dictates a lot in my life. This causes many nagging conflicts. Popular Canadian values and beliefs with which I sympathize come in direct conflict with the teachings of the church. I must many times reach some sort of compromise. Abortion is a great example of such a conflict. While the church strictly rejects the idea, I

tions of "bilingualism and multiculturalism."

am not sure as to where I stand on the subject. I am, I feel, a little more open-minded than many of the older generation Slovenians in my community. That is part of their general character which comes from that deep-rooted faith they grew up with. The fact that I grew up with the many different viewpoints of my friends and their respective backgrounds means that I have a broader outlook. In conclusion, I can say that while I was born here in Canada, my roots are very much embedded in the Slovenian way of life.

It is common to find religion or religious affiliation as an integral part of a person's ethnic identity, values and behaviour. In such cases, ethnic culture and religious culture are not regarded as separate. For example, as Damian points out, his Slovenian ethnicity influences his values and behaviour but what is also central to his life is his religious faith. Religion or spirituality is a very integral part of some ethnic groups compared to others, particularly those of orthodox affiliations. However, with the increase in secularization and religious diversity in today's society, it is likely that the influence of religious origins on defining behaviour is diminishing. In the following essay, Mark, a Jewish Canadian, explains the role of religion in his life.

"Yes, I am Jewish. Is there anything wrong with that?" I cannot remember how many times I have said that sentence, but I know it has been far too often. I believe this problem arises because too many people classify others into groups based upon their ethnic backgrounds. When people are classified into different groups, each develops its own set of values, beliefs, and attitudes.

I would not consider myself a religious individual, nor would I consider my family religious. As the generations progress, the emphasis on religion decreases. When I was young, I was given the opportunity to learn about my ancestors, my heritage and my religion. My parents provided me with the guidance to learn what being Jewish is all about. I must admit I am glad to know about my background, yet I feel I place little emphasis on it.

Although I am not a religious person, nor do I come from a religious family, some attitudes and values remain of great importance to me. The one which stands out above the rest is to continue the Jewish religion by marrying within my own ethnic group. Even though one's religion is not of great importance to me, I believe it is important to keep the Jewish faith alive so that following generations may learn of their heritage as I did. By providing children with a definite religion at birth, they are able to know and understand where their ancestors came from. It is through this understanding that people are given a certain sense of belonging and are pointed in one direction. Because I am of the Jewish religion, that is the direction I hope my family will maintain, although I do not feel that my methods are superior to those of others.

DOMINANT-MINORITY GROUPS

The history of a society provides indicators as to the dominant-minority status of its different ethnic and racial groups. Kinloch (1974) points out that a characteristic of minority groups is that they experience oppression at some time in the country's development. Burnet (1981) further points out that minority groups tend to be vulnerable and subject to discrimination. Physical and social attributes, like race and ethnicity, then determines social interaction and involvement within the society. In Canada, the dominant ethnic group is Anglo-Saxon, and the dominant racial group is White. The remaining racial and ethnic groups can therefore be classed as minorities. Writing about the power of the dominant group and how that power is normalized, Ng (1993) points out that in Canadian society.

> European men, especially those of British and French descent, are seen to be superior to women and to people from other racial and ethnic origins. Systems of ideas and practices have been developed over time to justify and support their notion of superiority. These ideas become the premise on which societal norms and values are based, and the practices become the "normal" way of doing things (p. 52).

Just as race and ethnicity are a part of identity, so too is dominant-minority group status. Through socialization, "the lifelong learning process through which individuals develop selfhood and acquire the knowledge, skills and motivation required to participate in social life" (Mackie, 1986: 64), individuals acquire a sense of identity as members of the dominant or minority group. Those who belong to a group that strongly identifies with the dominant or minority group will ultimately come to think of themselves as dominant or minority group members, respectively. Individuals' cultural identities become linked with their historical experiences, values, ways of life and the social patterns that are part of their group life.

Individuals' cultural identities become linked with their historical experiences, values, ways of life and the social patterns that are part of their group life.

Acquiring an ethnic and racial identity and a dominant-minority identification, however, is not simple in contemporary Canada's pluralistic society. Individuals are influenced by many factors outside of their home and their immediate ethnic and racial groups. They are influenced by schools, churches, workplaces, media and other major institutions. Sometimes, it is in encounters with these institutions that individuals come to recognize the status of their racial and ethnic group. Dominant group members may come to realize that they have a privileged and prestigious position in society, and as a result, access to all the social, political and economic institutions within that society. They will also be assured that they can "get ahead" without compromising their identity.

Minority group members, on the other hand, may come to realize that to get ahead they may have to compromise their ethnic identity. They learn that "'if they wish to enjoy the rewards of employment, education or social contact with higher-status groups, it will be necessary to forsake their language and many other cultural attributes of their ethnic [or racial] groups" (Agocs, 1987: 170). This could also mean denying their ethnicity or race because these characteristics identify them as "different" or "inferior." They may reject their ethnic racial group experiences, or they may embrace their culture and work hard to change the negative perception or low status of the group.

In short, the dominant or minority status of ethnic and racial groups mirrors their position in the stratification system of the larger society. Through socialization, individuals internalize their positions, which in turn influences their identity and behaviour. In the following accounts, we see how, when writing of themselves as dominant (or majority) group members, participants reveal how individuals learn about their status, internalize it and act accordingly.

Lyn: *"I am a member of a majority group that has a great deal of power..."*

As a White English Canadian, how my values, behaviour and attitudes are influenced by my origins is directly related to the fact that I am a member of the single largest group, racially, ethnically, and to a large extent, culturally. In this short essay I would like to focus on how these racial and ethnic cultures reinforce each other and how combined together, they can mask a number of assumptions I have about my relationship to the society I live in and my acceptance of that society's norms. In essence, I want to show how the values, attitudes and behaviours of the cultures I belong to fit into a system of thought and action that perpetuates those cultures and the power they hold.

I would like to take discrimination as an example. My experience of the class system in Britain has made me aware of how differences in origin, in this case most noticeably defined by accent (in speech), have a direct relationship to the position a person may hold in society in terms of economic power, political influence and control over day-to-day life. What I learned as a teenager in the 1960s in North America, when issues of civil rights and discrimination were in the news, the subject of popular books, and certainly regularly in classroom discussions, reinforced my awareness of what influences a person's ability to be accepted in society—to succeed in the terms laid down by that society and also in terms of personal freedom.

But I am a member of a majority [i.e. dominant] group that has a great deal of power. So, for example, being racially White I may have an awareness of these issues, and I may condemn my society for its inherent racism, but it is White culture that I experience day to day and the very fact that discrimination is rarely an issue for me personally results in my own racial identity becoming an invisible thing. The powerful people within my experience, directly or indirectly—the politician, the employer, the teacher, the social worker—are invariably White. I know that my race will not be an issue with most of the people I must deal with, as I know we will have a commonality from the start. Being in the majority in all three origins, there is also a good chance that either culturally, ethnically or both, our backgrounds will be similar. Neither will I expect my values or behaviour to be an issue because I fit into the "norm."

It is in the idea of the "norm" that racial and ethnic cultures mesh to form a powerful image of what is accepted or expected. I see myself reflected not only in the powerful people I am in contact with but in the books I read in school, the movies I see, the people I read about in newspapers. My day-to-day experience of life reinforces all that I have learned: the language and behaviour I have been taught; the values I have been told are the most important; the attitudes inevitably that I am or am not conscious of. As a result, I begin to see no other and I then begin to measure other cultures by the standards of my own without being aware that I am doing so.

It is this lack of awareness, this assumption of the norm, that has the strongest ability to perpetuate all the other behaviours, values and attitudes of my group because it dictates what I do and do not perceive. It blocks my ability, then, to understand and appreciate other values, other cultures and to question my own. I see what is different, but I don't analyze the difference. And it isn't crucial that I do so because I do not have to adapt myself. My group has the power and I don't have to attune myself to any other way of living unless I choose to. And choice versus necessity has a strong impact on what I see and learn.

So my group, being dominant, has the power to define what is acceptable, what is most valuable in me and in doing so, to define what attitudes I am and am not conscious of. If I cannot see myself I cannot see others clearly; and if I cannot see others clearly, seeing myself becomes more and more difficult. The mask is never removed. In this way, the power of the majority group is maintained as their values, behaviours and attitudes become self-perpetuating.

Lorne: *"I was conscious of belonging to the 'privileged' class..."*

I am a male, born to White Anglo-Saxon parents and raised in a small town north of Toronto. The European heritage of our family is obscure. We assumed we were British, but there may be some German background as well. My mother has recently done some genealogical research into our origins and has found that both her ancestors and those of my father immigrated to Canada from the United States shortly after the Revolutionary War of 1776 and had lived in the United States for a considerable time before that. We have been in North America for nearly 300 years and in Canada since before it was an independent country, so our connections with Europe can be considered unimportant.

I spent most of my teenage years rebelling against what I perceived as the confines of my cultural heritage. I was conscious of belonging to the (supposedly non-existent) "privileged" class, and was deeply embarrassed about it. I saw smugness and complacency everywhere and was determined never to be a part of it. Like many others my age, I grew my hair long, not simply in an effort to appear different, but to mark myself as being outside of my parents' culture. This was far from rare, but I still consider it an important phenomenon. It was less a case of fashion than a conscious attempt by the youth of the day to define their own culture as visibly different as possible from the one into which they had been born.

I rebelled against both the church (of which my parents were esteemed and active members) and the public school system. I felt that the interest of the church lay more in making its members feel comfortably secure in their own goodness than in spiritual exploration. At school, I refused to be part of what I perceived as training for hypocrisy and my marks fell as I decided to educate myself as I chose. I was interested in politics and read avidly of the struggles and revolutions of oppressed peoples. Lenin, Castro and especially Che Guevara were my heroes. I wished that I had a struggle as important as theirs, something solid to fight against, a cause that belonged to me. I realize now that many of the things I thought at that time had a lot to do with my own search for identity. I felt that belonging to the majority was a barrier to my individuality, that I had no real traditions or culture of my own.

I have changed since that time. I am no longer embarrassed about belonging to the majority. I have found enough individuality within myself to assure me that, yes, after all I'm not just like everybody else. Through experimentation in different religions, both Eastern and Western, and association with people from different backgrounds and cultures, I have come to believe in the power of individuals to define themselves as outside of cultural boundaries and to reshape their beliefs in the light of experience. This belief has its own drawbacks, however, as I shall discuss shortly.

Since I have ceased to struggle so adamantly against my culture, I have often been surprised to find attitudes and ideas that could not have come from anywhere else. I am speaking primarily of unconscious prejudices and assumptions which surface when I least expect them to.

For example, I take many things for granted as natural rights. I am comfortable in society; I feel that there is nowhere that I am not allowed to go if I wish, and nothing that is not prohibited by law that I cannot do. I don't fear the police. I am not in danger of being the victim of racially inspired violence. The only barriers to work or accommodation are my own qualifications and my financial situation. To illustrate the unconsciousness of this assumption of safety, I will tell a little story:

When I was living in Vancouver, I decided to take a walk around dusk along the beaches near the University. It was early spring and still quite cool, so the beaches were deserted. I walked about five miles, enjoyed a magnificent sunset and returned home after dark. Some friends were there and naturally I told them all about my stroll. One of my friends, a woman, said that she felt very jealous that I was able to do something like that. At first I didn't know exactly what she meant. Surely she was healthy enough to go for a walk if she felt like it. Then I understood that she was speaking about fear. Momentarily, I felt defensive, as if she were blowing something out of proportion and making it partially my fault. Then I understood that she was perfectly right. She perceived something as simple as going for a walk alone after dark as a privilege which I enjoyed and she did not.

Another result of my heritage, and one that stems directly from the feeling of safety which I have spoken of, is the belief which I talked about earlier. That is that the individual is the author of his or her own destiny, that we make ourselves. This implies another lot of assumptions. Basically, it assumes that the only limits to our choices are of our own making. It does not take into account how an individual may be forced or coerced into situations they would not otherwise have become involved in. It does not take into account how institutionalized racism and violence might hinder the growth of self-esteem. And it does not take into account how living with violence and hatred changes everyone.

Despite this, I still find my little creed valuable to me. For while others may have valid reasons for not being able to overcome the negative influences in their lives, I have no such excuse. It is up to me to make myself the better person I know I can be.

In the next account, John writes about his experience of interacting with minority group members.

John: *"I tended to ignore non-WASP problems and cultures..."*

Upon meeting Virginia and Bill, both native Canadian Indians, and listening to their opinions, comments, ideas and insights as to why others react to them as they do, I realized that although I had preconceived notions concerning the Indians, I was more ashamed of the fact that I tended to ignore non-WASP problems and cultures, than of the fact that I did have some biases toward others.

I recognized, and they helped to point out, that as a White male in Canada I didn't have to be interested or concerned with the plight of others; my heritage almost guaranteed me success in whatever I set out to accomplish. They, conversely, were always aware of who they were and of the treatment this afforded them. All along I had taken my heritage for granted while others were not allowed to do so and reminded of this fact daily. I think more than anything else, this fact awakened me to a new reality.

And when dominant group members experience a minority situation, what happens?

Mike: *"A feeling of uncertainty came over me..."*

I felt that I had no prejudice towards any other person. I later learned

In multi-ethnic societies, minority groups often find themselves in political or ideological conflict with the majority.

the bias I had toward people of other races was in fact prejudice. I could see myself being more relaxed around people of the same colour and race as me. This occurred to me in mid-October while I was studying in the library in Bramalea.

I was sitting at a large table completely alone. A group of young Blacks came and entered what I felt was "my space." I can't remember their exact names but they chose to sit all around me. A feeling of uncertainty came over me and I began to get very nervous. I had never in my life experienced anything like this before. They could sense that I was nervous and they seemed not to be really concerned about what was going on. I don't know, maybe they were used to the integration with Whites but I sure wasn't used to being around Blacks, not alone anyway. I then realized how a minority group must feel when they are always surrounded by people who are different from themselves. It would have been just as easy for me to leave the situation I found myself in but I wanted to feel the real feeling that I thought minority groups experienced all the time.

Later that day I talked to one of the Black guys I work with and asked him if this is how he feels when put in the same situation. He said that he doesn't feel any hostility towards any majority group, just when he is singled out and put down because at such times he has no backing from people of his own race. I then could see what prejudice was, because after I left the library everything was normal and I was in my own environment as I always thought it to be. It was possible for me to return to the average White class I was so used to. Just for a few brief hours out of the twenty years I have been alive, I feel I experienced something new.

It seems that in every situation we (Canadians) find ourselves there will always be prejudice present. It is a fact that the society we live in has to become more aware of prejudice and racism. I found myself in a situation and was able to relate somewhat to how minority groups must feel. This could never be done fully because I will always be White, but learning of others has opened my eyes to see how racism and prejudice act as barriers to interaction between people of different races. I trust that from this learning experience, I will become a better person, more sensitive and understanding.

On Linguistic Minority Groups

We often encounter Canadian residents who have been here for many years yet do not speak English or French. In many cases, these individuals circulate within their communities where they are able to do business, shop, bank and interact primarily with members of their ethnic group. In some cases, schools and other government institutions even communicate with them in their own language. Many who ask how such a situation could occur tend to think that these people should speak English—they should not be catered to. There is a sentiment that providing information and/or translation services merely allows them to retain their language and not make attempts to become "Canadians." After all, "when in Rome, do as the Romans do."

For example, using their experiences as reference, two participants react to the inability of some Canadians to speak English:

Sandra: Are they really trying or do they want to keep to themselves and not assimilate into the Canadian society? If people come from another country with a different language and are unable to understand people in their new country, they should make an effort to learn the new language so they can be understood, feel more at home and become a part of the majority of the people. I feel very strongly about this as I went through it when I came to Canada 34 years ago. I did not understand nor speak the English language. I took English lessons and worked among the English speaking people because I wanted to learn our new language. I also kept up my Dutch language.

Sue: I am able to understand that, " ... a person's language is a symbol of their culture and therefore part of that individual's identity." However, in my affirmation I have to recognize the feelings of frustration and impatience I experience with those who do not speak English fluently. And perhaps most difficult to acknowledge was my insensitivity towards these people, when it is this very attitude I abhor in others who do not understand Sign Language as part of a deaf person's culture.

Ethnocentricity is evident in the belief that because one group, usually the dominant one, exhibits a type of behaviour, all other groups should do the same. While it is understandable that individuals will use their own experience and situation to evaluate other people, it is important to recognize the limitations in doing this. What is true of one person's or group's experience cannot be generalized to another. Furthermore, to build positive and effective interaction between ethnic and racial groups that reside in Canada, we must avoid being ethnocentric.

To understand why it is important to people to retain their original languages while residing in Canada, we must first understand the relationship between language and culture: "Language is a system of communication that involves the written or verbal communication of shared symbols" (Avison and Kunkel, 1987:51). Language allows us to send messages and exchange ideas with each other. It also plays a key role in the development, maintenance and evolution of a culture (Avison and Kunkel, 1987:51). The symbols that are defined in a language mirror the things, worldviews and values considered important to that culture.

As such, language is a symbol and an integral part of cultural and individual identity. Since language plays such a central role in a person's identity and development, it is a struggle for people to learn a new language, particularly one which will in time influence their sense of identity. It is like becoming someone new. Some linguistic minority members may want to embrace the English language. For others, however, the psychological impact of doing so might be too much to handle, and they may never be successful at learning the new language.

Summary

In this chapter we have examined how race and ethnicity contribute to the social, political and cultural construction of individual cultural identities. We have tried to demonstrate that race, ethnicity and cultural identity are complex concepts that are historically, socially and contextually based. These social relations are dynamic; they do not have consistent meanings over time. Apple (1993) refers to them as "place markers" operating in a complex political and social arena. The social meanings given to racial and ethnic identity are directly related to the dominant and minority variable, and also to many other variables. Social, cultural and political institutions, as well as individuals, help give meaning to these social factors, which in turn determine how individuals act upon these meanings.

The participants' essays illustrate the complexity, tensions and contradictions that are inherent in trying to identify people mainly by race and/or ethnicity. They also indicate the heterogeneity, the similarities and the differences that are to be found among the members of the various racial and ethnic groups, and the degrees to which their sense of cultural identity and their social interactions are influenced by ethnicity and race. We did not examine the role of racism, prejudice and discrimination in the social and political construction of cultural identities and the interactions of individuals. This is not to say that we do not see these issues as significant. Certainly, the social meanings are very much related to these mechanisms of cultural control.

Questions:

1. What is ethnicity? How is it different from nationality and race?

2. Compare and contrast the different ways in which race has been constructed in Canada over the years, and the way in which it is constructed today.

3. What impact would Canadian culture have on the identity-formation of a newcomer to Canada?

3

CONSTRUCTING IDENTITIES

One goal of any heterogeneous society is to seek to build and maintain positive race and ethnic relations, so that all groups can live and work together. To reach this goal, we need to know each other, not simply by reading about one another, but through effective interactions. This is best accomplished by first examining ourselves. Exploring and understanding how this process occurs for each of us individually gives us insight into and appreciation for others who might be different from ourselves. But, as important as the differences are the similarities we find between us, regardless of race, ethnicity and national origins. Nevertheless, as Scott explains:

> For better or worse, and perhaps without even actually realizing the possible consequences, most people wrap themselves in a protective cocoon of self-concept.

> Unlike nature's irrevocable cycle of life, however, humans often choose to remain with the familiar and forsake the butterfly-like flight into the unknown. I believe this protective cocoon of self-concept spans the racial, ethnic and cultural difference gap, and is a defence mechanism that is hard to penetrate.

> To ask the individual to be the instigator of the penetration can be a traumatic experience for some. For others, it can be an uplifting and enlightening experience.

> For the dominant group members, however, (and I place myself in this category) the racial, cultural and ethnic influence has never really come into play—in a conscious sense—as related to values and behaviour. Therefore, initially it is rejected as a mere concept better left

To reach the goal of ethnic and racial understanding, we need to know each other through effective interactions.

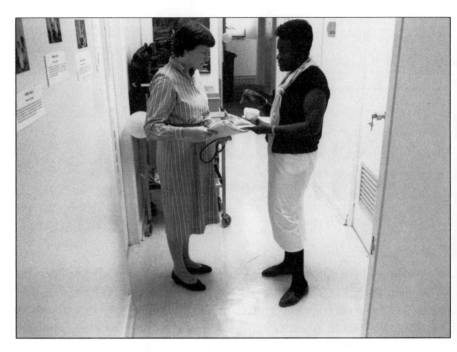

> to intellectual discussion, or more to the point, when the wells of discussion of sex and sports have run dry.
>
> When the enforced impetus of academic requirement is applied and more than the perfunctory scratching of the shell of self-concept occurs, the supposedly well-rounded individual can appreciate just who, why and what was [involved in] the moulding. [They can] better understand, and accept, the final product.

In this chapter, participants write about how their behaviours as well as their values and attitudes are a product or a reflection of their race, cultural, ethnic and national origins. Many of the writers admit to the difficulty of such a task. However, they recognize the benefit in this exercise.

The selected personal accounts in this chapter reflect how Canadians have developed their sense of self, and how their respective ethnicities, cultures, and races have influenced their lives. It is important for the reader to remember that these accounts are those of these individuals and therefore cannot be generalized to others, not even those of similar ethnic and racial backgrounds. There are many issues which may bear a similarity to others. The intent here, however, is not to profile ethnic, racial or religious group members, but to show the process of discovery and awareness that we must all undergo to become better acquainted with ourselves, and ultimately with other people.

Ethnicity, race, religion and nationality do not influence all individuals to the same degree. The influence of each characteristic varies according to the individual and her experiences. National origin may influence a person more if she is an immigrant, or if his parents are recent immigrants. Religion may have a stronger influence than race, language or ethnicity in some instances. It becomes clear that there is, for some, a degree of kinship between ethnicity and religion. In many cases it is difficult to separate them and therefore important to understand each.

John: *"I was the only non-African attending and I felt like I glowed in the dark..."*

I was born in Toronto, Ontario, to a mother of English nationality and a father of Canadian nationality. Both of my parents were born prior to World War Two and were raised in conservative, White-dominated communities. My mother's ethnicity is English. My father is of Scottish and Irish heritage, so my roots are completely centred in the British Isles. These roots and the values, ideas, thoughts and beliefs passed on to me from my ancestors have helped to shape me into the person that I am now. It is these origins, ethnic and cultural, as well as race, that have helped to influence my attitudes and behaviours.

I, like my parents, was raised in a predominantly White neighbourhood. There was one Japanese family and one Black family, but they were "Canadianized" and considered to be two different-coloured White families. Both families spoke English without a trace of accent, and were involved in all the community affairs and functions, and therefore did not pose a threat to the conservative upper middle class lifestyle. Had they spoken differently or exposed their racial or ethnic rituals publicly, I believe that they would not have been so readily accepted.

When I was about twelve, a Black family moved to our street and immediately the neighbours and my parents lamented, "There goes the neighbourhood." It was firmly believed that more Black families would soon follow and the area would be considered undesirable. Although my parents were raising me to believe that God loves everyone, that racial minorities have suffered great hardships and that we must try to understand them, it still wasn't right that they were moving into our neighbourhood.

About three years later, I met a young South African boy at school who soon became my best friend. We were inseparable. Although his skin was much darker than mine, I never really realized he wasn't White until I went to a family party. I was the only non-African attending and I felt like I glowed in the dark. All of a sudden, all the jokes about Negroes I had heard (and told) in school, all the prejudices I had acquired from family cocktail parties and all the snide remarks I had heard about "undesirables" came crashing down and confronted me. These people were friendly, polite, funny and, most of all, caring. I enjoyed their company and they enjoyed mine. It was really the first time I had broken out of the beliefs and values instilled in me by my parents and established my own.

I have lived and attended school in the United States as well as in Canada, and have seen quite a difference in the two cultures of these countries. I would say that I am influenced by both, and when out of one country, sorely miss its unique way of life. I know a lot of individuals who, when they think of the United States, think of loud and brash people, crime, commercialism and money. These elements can be found within the American culture, but I tend to notice the more subtle aspects. I think one aspect of the U.S. culture that has profoundly influenced me is patriotism. I don't mean parades and fireworks, but the feeling inside that you are proud of the country in which you live and of all the good things it has offered you and millions of others. I like the idea of the "melting pot". Although multiculturalism can be found in abundance in the U.S., I like the notion of people from all over forming one unified blend from hundreds of different "spices." I also like the credo "the land of opportunity", which I feel is at the core of American culture. The belief that, "with enough hard work and sweat and a little bit of luck, you can realize your dreams," seems to be woven into the fabric of the American culture and it is truly something which I apply in my life.

Through my parents' traditions and my early schooling, I retain a love and respect for the monarchy and the Commonwealth. I feel a kinship with other Commonwealth countries like Australia and a special unity with the people who reside there. I am glad that they form part of my Canadian culture.

Although I am now twenty-five years old, and have experienced many varied people and places, values and beliefs, I still find myself occasionally thrown back to my upbringing and the ideas to which I was exposed when I was younger. The night in Los Angeles when I broke into a cold sweat when I was asked the time by two young Black men on a deserted street is one example. My old stereotypes came racing back and I had to deal with them instantaneously. Another is the time I knew I had won a job only because I was White, male and of British heritage. I felt a certain smugness in the feeling that I belonged rather than that I deserved the job. This situation again illustrated to me how deeply I had been influenced by my racial and ethnic origins and how, although my heritage may be important to me, it is not necessarily the best but merely one of many.

I am proud of who I am and where I came from. Most importantly, however, I am proud of the person I am striving to be and of the diverse groups who continue to shape and improve me.

Paul: *"Where I am prejudiced is through all the stereotypes…"*

I was born and raised in Toronto. In our neighbourhood, if a new kid moved in, and he was White, and he didn't have an accent, and he didn't let on in any other way that he had immigrated from another country, he could be accepted as one of the gang. This was provided he could perform admirably on the field of sport and he and his parents didn't tell anyone where they were from until after he was accepted. Then it was "You're from South Africa? Neat!"

To be accepted at the public school I went to, located at the heart of a rich Toronto community, you had to be White, Protestant, very well off and above all, good at more than one of the accepted sports of the time: hockey (both ice and road), soccer, baseball or any of the track and field events.

Today, as a result of the events that have shaped my life, I am a bigot and a hypocrite. Don't get me wrong—I don't fancy myself as a redneck who goes around killing Blacks à la KKK, nor do I participate in Gay-bashing or any other type of physical outbursts aimed at any particular race or ethnic group. Where I am prejudiced is through all the stereotypes. Women and Chinese people can't drive. Pakistanis smell bad. Blacks are thieves and smell bad. Italians either build houses or kill people for a living.

Most of these stereotypes were fed to me over time by my parents and my older brother. I didn't know what the word stereotype meant then. I took these "phrases of wisdom" as truths and they altered my view of people. Prejudice is learned, not instinctive. I quote a song we often used to sing, written about my great-grandmother, Mrs. Murphy:

"Who put the overalls in Mrs. Murphy's chowder?/ No one spoke up, so she hollered all the louder/ 'It's a dirty, rotten trick and I could lick a Mick'/ Who put the overalls in Mrs. Murphy's Chowwwwwwwwwder?"

I remember asking my father what a Mick was. He replied, "a Roman Catholic." No further explanation was required as I knew they were the ones who didn't go to my school. At that point in my life, being Canadian was being White and playing hockey.

When I graduated, I went to a Junior High School. It was very different from what I had been accustomed to. After my first day, my father asked how it went. I said it was, "full of Niggers and Wops." I was not scolded nor corrected on my use of derogatory remarks. It was then however, that my Dad wanted me to go to an exclusive all boys school, but one thing kept me at the junior high—the girls started getting breasts. Besides, thank God, I still belonged to the clique that graduated with me from public school.

My friends and I got into a lot of fights in grade 7—ones that weren't our fault, we'd say. Looking back, I can truthfully say it was as much the fault of society as it was ours. There was not one non-White person at my public school and not one White person at our rival school. Junior high is where the two cultures clashed. I'm sure that there was as much racial discrimination going on at the other public school as there was at ours. Clearly there should have been some cultural integration.

In high school I met, and became friends with, a guy named Chris. We got along famously. The fact that he was Black didn't matter, except to my parents. They didn't like him. When pressed as to what they had against him, they couldn't, or wouldn't, reply. The fact that he was at the top of the class in nearly every subject and worked at school harder than anyone I'd ever met mattered little to them. It was then, at age 16, that I realized what bigots my parents were and I raised my rebellion against them. I grew my hair long, very long. I drank with my other friends, my White friends. I got my ear pierced. I got tattooed. I quit high school. I won't say this was all due to my parents' view of Chris, but that's what sparked it. If rebellions can be won or lost, then chalk one up for the kids. My parents came to really like Chris. Through the two years of the rebellion, Chris was the one friend that had stuck through it all. It was the day they looked past the Black and saw the person.

You can probably tell from the content of this paper that my youth and upbringing were the major influences in my life. I am still very much confused about what the Canadian culture is. As for my morals and values, I try to give everyone and everything a fair chance before passing judgement. The prejudices I have are not without basis. They are based on fact, life's experiences, or are a convenient way to blow off steam. When I say women can't drive, I am drawing a parallel between the number of times that I have witnessed driving infractions and which gender has committed them.

I have very few biases any more. The biggest influence on my life now is me. I no longer listen to others' opinions as gospel and now have a clear-cut sense of where my values lie. Culturally, I do, and enjoy, all the things that are typically Canadian: play hockey; eat salt & vinegar chips, and try to belong and socialize within all the other cultures that make up our society. I am a Canadian and very proud of it.

Joe: *"I was outside the cultural norm..."*

My parents emigrated from Italy in the early 1940s. They were married in Hamilton and that's were the family was raised. I am the youngest of four children.

I grew up in a decidedly non-Italian neighbourhood. The kids in the neighbourhood were a mix of Canadians, i.e. second, third, fourth generation British, Scottish, and Irish descendants; first generation Eastern Europeans; and perhaps one or two first generation Italians. This ethnic profile was, however, simplified according to the distinctions we used at the time. As far as my parents were concerned, the populace was divided in two: English and Italian. Anyone who didn't fit into either one of these categories (say, for instance, my Lithuanian friend) was viewed as innocently irrelevant to the basic societal dichotomy: English and Italian.

The ethnic mix became somewhat more complicated in elementary school because the school was at a distance from our immediate neighbourhood. Ethnic origins and ratios had been altered. It became a little more problematic to cram all those non-Italians into the English camp, but it was even easier to entrench ourselves into the Italian camp because we were readily identified as such both by school administration and other students. We were perceived as Italians. The predominant authority of the school was Irish and Catholic. The nuns and priests were Irish and Catholic, and we were the rather difficult but redeemable Italian Catholics. Belonging to such an identified and identifiable group gave rise to varied perceptions of identity. My "Italianness" could be causing me to suffer silent embarrassment one moment and defiant satisfaction the next. One thing was abundantly clear: I was outside the cultural norm.

The tables were turned rather dramatically in high school. The elementary school had been in a predominantly non-Italian area, but the high school was in an area where many Italians lived. Many of the students were from immigrant Italian families. It seems that the old English/Italian distinction wasn't quite relevant any more. It was time to start making much finer distinctions. We, my immediate clique and I, chose to carve out a new, unique identity for ourselves. We began to distinguish ourselves as the more advanced, sophisticated, anglicized Italians. Our group tended to deride the excesses of our less genteel compatriots while at the same time negotiating diplomatic relations with the English. The negotiations were fruitful, and permanent relations were established with a number of English cliques.

It is rather facile to proclaim that I always sensed something was wrong with this perception of who I was in relation to my world. During high school, however, I did develop a distinct dislike at being categorized as Italian or anything else. University was a welcome relief. Few of my peers went to university and though I still lived in the same city, I lived in a different world. I consciously avoided anyone who dragged me back to the English/Italian characterization of my identity. I sought refuge in the company of foreign visa students. They knew nothing of this, or did they? I suppose my friends from Singapore had their own notions of what it was to live in a former British colony.

At present, I choose to verify my "Italian-ness" against my parents. It's become a very personal, individual, individual identification. The connection is a specific one.

My ethnicity has been a significant factor in shaping my notion of self. Societal pressure has imposed its interpretation of who I am from the outside, and unexamined internal acceptance has reinforced this view. But all this is water under the bridge, isn't it? Surely this nonsense is buried in the past.

I have found that the insidiousness and subtle harm of ethnic and racial categorization is persistent. I can still feel the ghosts of "silent embarrassment" when British people reminisce about times gone by. Do they know that I feel uncomfortable? Are they conscious of the institutional baggage of their dominant position?

Until very recently, I have denied this whole issue and held to the opinion that all of it was, in fact, buried in the past. I rejected my own unease and dismissed suspicion of the cause of this unease.

As an ESL instructor, my association with recent immigrants has been instrumental in re-awakening my sensitivities to the issue. I can see the same type of ethnic and racial categorization being applied to the learners in my classroom. I can see them being constantly reminded

Ethnicity, race, religion and nationality do not influence all individuals to the same degree.

that they are somehow inadequate in their present form. If they don't change, they'll never move within the periphery of society. I am white and, despite any "Mediterranean" features, can do a pretty good job of disguising myself as part of the dominant group. I can fit; I can move in closer than the periphery. What, then, is a "more visibly" visible minority to do? Will a Black African or South East Asian ever be adequate? Will they ever fit in enough to move closer to the centre of society?

I do what I can to assure the learners in my classes that ethnically, racially, and religiously, they are adequate. I try to be a sympathetic listener who sees their frustrations as justified. I also try to use my membership in the administrative mainstream, albeit probationary, to act as a liaison.

Ethnic identification can be a psychological touchstone; ethnic categorization can be an unwelcome burden.

Katie: *"I consider myself to be a hyphenated Canadian..."*

Racially, I am White. My ethnic background is Ukrainian. Three of my grandparents were born in the Ukraine. They immigrated to Canada in the years prior to World War I. My maternal grandmother was born in the United States and her parents were born in the Ukraine. They moved to Canada from the United States at the turn of this century and were part of the group of Ukrainians involved in opening up the Canadian West.

Culturally, I consider myself to be a hyphenated Canadian: Ukrainian-Canadian. My parents, my brother and I were all born and raised in Canada. We practise Ukrainian culture as was passed on by my grandparents. In Canada when someone asks me what ethnic group I belong to, I say Ukrainian. However, when outside of Canada, I consider myself a Canadian.

How have these backgrounds affected me? I take my White colour for granted since we live in a predominantly White society. I am only conscious of it if I am with a group of Blacks or Asians or if I were to travel to a part of the world where there are few Whites (e.g. Zaire) or where it is an issue (e.g. South Africa.)

Canadian culture is more deeply ingrained in me as evidenced by the clothes I wear, the language I speak (English), and the everyday Canadian foods I eat. I have been influenced by the Canadian rat race for affluence and success, and the possession of various material goods that are part of the "good Canadian life" such as a T.V., a V.C.R., a car and furniture, etc.

I use my Ukrainian culture as a reference point from which I can observe other cultures and look for similarities between mine and theirs. I notice this every year when I go to Toronto's Caravan festival and visit the various pavilions.

As a second generation Ukrainian born in Canada, my family and I have assimilated well into Canadian society and, fortunately, no longer experience the discrimination that our great-grandparents felt upon first arriving here. However, I can empathize with other ethnic groups who are under Soviet rule (e.g., Estonians, Lithuanians, Afghans, etc.) and feel their dislike of the Russians. I can also feel for those who are being persecuted for expressing their wishes to be self-governing and speaking out against human rights violations. Ukrainians have long experienced domination which is the reason why so many are in Canada today and continuing to preserve their language and culture. Thus, I can better understand political prisoners around the world today. On the other hand, I have some understanding of Russians as both they and Ukrainians share the same devotion to tradition and, unfortunately, long speeches!

In the past year, I have become more interested in my Ukrainian heritage and I am presently studying the language since I was unable to learn it well as a child.

I did not know until recently how much my Ukrainian Orthodox background influenced me. We did not attend church regularly except for Easter, and I left the Orthodox church during my teen years. After attending different Protestant churches over the years, I decided to adopt the Anglican church since its liturgy more resembles that of the Orthodox church and it feels more like "home" to me. It was interesting to discover how much even my small church involvement in childhood influenced my present religious practices in an almost unconscious way. I celebrate Ukrainian Christmas as well as December 25, and Ukrainian Easter with my family every year. There are many other Ukrainian influences such as music, crafts, foods and other religious practices.

My cultural influences have made me more open to the differences in other cultures, especially European. I can feel more a part of them and assimilate a little more easily into Polish or Greek cultures, for example, whereas my "WASP" friends feel more awkward and different in comparison. However, I do feel different when exposed to non-European cultures such as Hindu or Central African, etc. I can understand why so many have immigrated to this country, especially when it has been for political and religious reasons.

Sarah: *"As a White person in Canada I feel confident and comfortable…"*

I was born in Montréal, Québec. My parents were also born in Montréal, to immigrant parents who arrived in Canada as young teenagers. They came from Russia, Poland and Romania. The cultures from these particular countries did not play a large role in my life. Until the age of thirteen I was surrounded by my grandparents and two sets of great grandparents. Yiddish was spoken at their homes. I did not learn how to speak Yiddish, but I did learn to understand some of it. This allowed me to understand quite a bit of the Yiddish humour, which was an important part of my life. Understanding was also a bond with the older members of my family, as they did not speak English.

In Montréal I was also exposed to the French language and culture. In the 1950s the French were expected to speak English even though Montréal was predominantly inhabited by French-speaking people. As English-speaking children we did not go to the same schools as the French children in our neighbourhood. We did not play together either and I regret that I lost the opportunity to learn another language and another culture firsthand.

Racially, I am White, like the majority of Canadians. Being White I am easily accepted and not subjected to prejudicial stereotyping (although once my name is mentioned this attitude often changes). As a White person in Canada I feel confident and comfortable.

As a child I was raised in a predominantly White, non-Jewish neighbourhood. There was one Black child in my class and we were often drawn together, possibly because we were both in the minority. I remember when I was twelve, my father and I were browsing through a bookstore and I found the book Black Like Me. It instantly intrigued me and my father encouraged me to read it. The book told of the experiences of a White man who changed his colour to Black and lived in the southern United States.

I can still remember the strong impact the book had on me. Being a naive pre-teen I could not believe that the Blacks were not allowed to drink from the same water fountains, use the same washrooms, or sit in the same sections of the bus as the Whites did. I will always be grateful that my father and I were able to discuss this book and reach a better understanding and respect for another race. I am pleased that my children attend a multiracial school and have had the opportunity to learn about other races and also share knowledge about their own.

My ethnicity is Jewish and this plays a very strong and important role in my life. Family ties have always been strong. I was brought up in a large extended family. This is also my children's experience. Perhaps this bond is the result of the years of persecution in other lands, which forced Jews to realize that the only real thing that mattered was the family. We could lose our homes and possessions—they could be replaced. But the families couldn't be replaced.

The ten commandments tell us to honour our parents and the Torah guides us towards maintaining a strong family unit. Children are most precious and I personally do not approve of abortion unless necessary to save the mother's life. This is consistent with the laws of Judaism which put the life of the mother first.

Charity or "tzdakah" is an obligation of every Jew. It is a "mitzvah" or duty to give money, clothes, food or time to those who need it. I belong to a women's organization that raises money for Arab and Jewish women and children in Israel. I also help the Canadian Cancer Society.

I value the State of Israel and I appreciate its existence. I have never visited Israel but I have a strong bond with it. During my parents' generation, Israel did not exist; perhaps if it had, my Mother's grandparents, aunts, uncles and cousins would not have perished in the Holocaust. Israel gives me a sense of security. Israel was the only country to come to the aid of the prisoners of the hijacked plane in Entebbe. During their forty-year history, the Israelis have welcomed Jews who have been expelled from Arab lands, fought to free Soviet Jews, and rescued the Jews of Ethiopia.

Synagogue is a central part of my life. All major events are tied to our shul—birth, bar mitzvahs, marriage and death. We observe the Sabbath and all the Jewish holidays. As a child, I attended Hebrew school and Girl Guides, which met at the shul.

As a Jew, I have had to live with anti-Semitism. I must face the incomprehensible fact that 6 million Jews were slaughtered by Hitler simply because they were Jewish. Fear, to a certain degree, surrounds me. There is always the fear that one day I might be forced to witness my children and family systematically being killed. This does not mean that I constantly live in fear in Canada. But I must remember that the Jews in Europe felt very secure that they truly belonged in their respective countries. When I was nine, I remember being punched in the stomach by an older boy I often played with. He yelled that I had killed Christ. I did not understand why he had suddenly turned on me. This caused me to feel fearful and suspicious of others. For the longest

We must all undergo a process of discovery and awareness to become better acquainted with ourselves, and ultimately with other people.

time when placed in a new situation, I did not offer the fact that I was Jewish. Years and maturity have made me confident in my Judaism.

While living in Kingston, Ontario, our family met many young people who had never met a Jewish person before. We opened our home to them and soon we were on very friendly terms. One evening, while working in a restaurant with two of my new friends, I was shocked to hear them say that they had been "Jewed." They explained that they had been shortchanged on a bill. I then explained the origin of the remark. Both women seemed shocked to learn it was a slanderous remark against Jews. This lead to many more discussions on Judaism. We remained friends for many years and I feel this integration helped build a greater understanding of our different ethnic backgrounds.

My behaviour is also greatly affected by Judaism. I celebrate all Jewish holidays. I believe this is a link to the past and to the future. I choose to live in a racially and ethnically mixed neighbourhood that also includes other Jewish families. I want my children to appreciate Canada's multiculturalism while still holding on to their Jewish identity. We belong to a Jewish community centre and Jewish service clubs. My children attend Hebrew school after their regular public school. While we do not keep kosher, we do not mix meat and milk, nor do we eat pork. I tend to dress modestly. Strict Jewish law would dictate that I wear a wig and that my arms and shoulders be covered at all times, but I choose to dress more in the Canadian style. Friday, our sabbath, is a time for family. We eat a traditional meal and often share it with visitors. We follow the rituals of lighting the sabbath candles and saying the blessings over the challah and the wine. I love to read and Judaism has always encouraged the quest for knowledge.

My cultural background is Canadian. As a Canadian, I value my freedom. I can choose what neighbourhood to live in, what school to attend, and where I work. I am also free to practise my religion. As I have previously stated, there are discrimination and prejudices in Canada, but we have a legal system to protect us.

I consider myself to be a very proud Canadian, but one who will always treasure my unique ethnicity.

Barbara: *"My ethnic background was a major part of my early years…"*

I am a Canadian Jew. I was born in Toronto in 1935 and have lived in Canada all my life. In this essay I shall try to explain how my racial, ethnic and national origins have shaped my attitudes and behaviour.

Both my parents were Polish Jews who immigrated to Canada in the early 1930s. They left Poland because they believed that they could lead richer and fuller lives in Canada. Apart from the fact that they spoke Polish, there was nothing Polish about them. They felt little warmth or affection for the country that had treated its Jews so badly.

I grew up in the College/Bathurst area [of Toronto] which, at that time, had a large Jewish population. Practically all my friends and classmates were Jewish. At the high school that I attended, ninety percent of the students were Jewish. Most of my parents' friends and relatives lived in the same area, and there was a great deal of visiting among them. There were four synagogues in the block where we lived, one of which my parents attended on religious holidays. The majority of stores in our neighbourhood were owned and operated by Jewish merchants. This environment made me very aware, at an early age, of my Jewishness.

While my parents were not deeply religious, they were certainly practising Jews. We observed the dietary laws in our home, and we celebrated the Sabbath and all the other major religious holidays.

While both my parents spoke Polish and Yiddish between themselves and with their friends and relatives, they made no effort to teach me either language. Unlike most Jewish children of my generation, I did not even attend Hebrew school. To my parents it was of paramount importance that I acquired a good command of English and that I did well in school.

The war years were very difficult for my mother. She was the only member of her immediate family to immigrate to Canada; all the others remained in Poland. Unfortunately, she lost them all: her parents, her six sisters and brothers and their spouses and children.

I believe that the enormity of my mother's loss instilled in me a deep and abiding prejudice along with the firm conviction that it must be resisted. I learned very early how evil, ugly and destructive prejudice can be.

I think that my experience as a member of an ethnic minority has also made me more sympathetic to the feelings and to the problems of new Canadians. I realize that non-White Canadians, unlike myself, encounter even more prejudice and discrimination. I can still remember when there was a good deal of accepted prejudice within Canada. Only thirty years ago, our political, social and economic institutions were virtually under the complete domination of the traditional White, Anglo-Saxon male population. In Ontario it was not until the 1950s that legislation was passed to give minority groups some protection from discrimination in housing, education and employment.

Partly because of my lack of religious conviction, and partly because of my lack of formal Jewish education, I am not a practising Jew. Although I maintain close contact with my relatives and my Jewish friends, I do not observe the dietary laws in my home, and I attend synagogue only on ceremonial occasions.

Obviously my ethnic background was a very major part of my early years and I have always had a strong sense of being Jewish. However, while I am a Jew, I am also a Canadian. In contrast, my sense of identity as a Canadian did not emerge until I was an adult.

When I attended school during the 1940s and '50s, the British influence was still very strong. We concentrated on studying English history and English literature. In common with Canadians everywhere, we sang "God Save the Queen" and flew the Union Jack.

Since then, my growing awareness of being a Canadian has reflected Canada's own growing awareness of itself as a separate and distinct nation. In the intervening years I have become more familiar with Canadian history and Canadian literature. I have travelled widely in Canada and have developed a deep affection for all its varied regions and people.

In the early years of my marriage we lived in Saskatchewan. This gave me a perspective of a very different part of Canada, and intensified my sense of being a Canadian.

During the past eighteen years I have lived with my family in an area with a significant racial, ethnic and cultural diversity. My children attended schools with young people from all over the world. I believe that this has been a positive experience for them; they learned at an early age not to think in racial or ethnic stereotypes.

As in earlier years, these changes have been achieved in a peaceful and democratic manner. In Canada, social change has been accompanied by relatively little violence and a respect for law and order. It is precisely this ability to solve problems in a healthy and constructive manner that I find to be quintessentially Canadian.

This legacy of non-violent change has made Canada such an attractive country for so many people. It is this very quality that makes me optimistic for this country's future.

Naomi: *"I have yet to understand what it means to 'look Jewish'..."*

I was born in Toronto, Ontario. Both my parents are Polish Jews who immigrated to Canada in the early '50s. The culture from Poland did not play a large role in my life.

My father is a survivor of a concentration camp. Unfortunately, he lost his whole family, his parents, 8 sisters and 3 brothers. My father lost his family in the horrifying war and as a result, I never knew my aunts, uncles and grandparents. My father felt it was important to share with his children his religious roots and his experience in a concentration camp. I think it is important to remember the Holocaust so future generations will not forget and will prevent such a catastrophe from occurring again. At a very young age I learned how evil and destructive prejudice can be. The message my father instilled in me was "Do not hate! Do not harm, and share with others less fortunate." So much of what I aspire to be as a person I learned from my wonderful father. To my father, establishing a new life and developing a family was of significant importance.

I was raised in a predominantly Jewish neighbourhood. Yiddish is spoken in my home. As a child, I remember asking what each word meant and now I can fully understand it but I cannot speak as well. The humour in the language is great and till this day I appreciate it.

My parents are not deeply religious, but we celebrate the major religious holidays. We do not keep kosher in the house. My home is more traditional rather than religious. Friday, our sabbath is time for family. My father says the blessing over the challah and wine and my mother says the blessing over the candles. We eat a traditional meal often shared by family and friends. My parents have a strong sense of family and community which was passed down to me and I hope I do the same.

I do meet up with prejudice. A very common response from people whom I meet is "What are you?" as a way to determine my racial background. I then proceed to tell them that I am Canadian. They would then ask me, "Where are your parents from?" I would say Poland, and they would then look at me confused and say things like "you are not fair and blond" (stereotypes of a Polish person). When they learned I was Jewish the response always amazed me when people expressed surprise and would say "You are Jewish!" As if it were a disease or something. And when some people think they are paying a compliment by saying: "We do not think of you as Jewish, you are different than most Jewish people I know." This is an outright insult of my ethnicity that I am proud of. Another typical comment was that I "do not look Jewish." Till this day I have yet to understand what it means to "look Jewish" considering there are Jewish people from all parts of the world.

I believe that my experience as a member of an ethnic minority has made me empathetic to the problems faced by new Canadians. I am aware that non-White Canadians are faced with more prejudice and discrimination than myself. However, my cultural influences have made me more open to the differences in other cultures.

Finally, having been born and raised in Toronto, I have had the privileges of access to good education. I value my freedom, I am able to choose what school I attend, where I live and where I work. I am proud of who I am and the person I am continually striving to be and the diverse individuals and groups who continue to shape and enlighten me. I believe that children at a very young age should be taught the differences and similarities of various cultures. As a result, we as individuals would understand each other more and realize that there are more similarities than differences among cultures and our country would be a better place to live in.

Ria: *"As an English-speaking White Canadian I fit into our society easily…"*

I am a Canadian citizen. That might not tell you a lot about who I am because being "Canadian" is an ambiguous term to describe the identity of an individual. Every citizen in Canada has their own unique background because Canada is a country of many races, ethnicities and cultures. Their lives are affected by these things and more, including social class and family life. In this essay I am going to explore how being a White, Dutch Canadian has affected my behaviour, attitudes and values.

I am a first generation Canadian with Dutch parents. My parents immigrated to Canada from Holland, their ancestral home. My parents belong to the Christian Reformed Church which first began in Holland and the two cannot be separated because they are so closely related. In the 1950s, my parents came here to build a life and raise a family. They followed the "work ethic" that most immigrants do, saving money and working long and hard. I was expected to do the same. A good person was one who was honest in his business and a hard worker.

My family grew up, like most other Dutch families, in the church. They all had a strong sense of family and community which I still feel with my friends and family. I have been influenced to respect the value of life, to do good for your neighbour and to live an honest life. I was also taught stewardship (the proper, responsible care of possessions), the "sacrificing" of pleasure for responsibilities, and not to waste. I uphold these values highly and respect those who do as well.

Another part of my Dutch heritage is the Dutch language. I am fairly fluent and find great advantage in that since I am interested in older people like my grandparents who speak Dutch. The older generation is rich in experience and wisdom that we can learn from. The Dutch's cosy homes show the value they place on family and home life, which I feel is important.

Being White in Canada means being in the majority and as an English-speaking White Canadian I have been fortunate to fit into our society quite easily. I feel accepted in society and its groups, and have had good opportunities for jobs while other racially different people have not. I can say that I feel a steadiness in my overall place in society. Being White has freed me of some prejudices and other racial challenges that others might experience here in Canada. One curious thing I admit is that I tend to look on other races with a mixture of sympathy for the joking they get, and mistrust because I don't know them or associate closely enough with them to fully understand their thinking and lifestyles. My ignorance is a hurdle.

Finally, having been brought up in Canada, I know the privileges of driving at an early age and of receiving a good education. I have had ample opportunities for jobs plus the freedom to reside any place I choose. Canada is an affluent western country full of freedom and choice, which I experience daily. After visiting Honduras, a country of poverty, I especially appreciate this country's affluence and freedom.

Jenny: *"We have chosen Canada because it is a free country and tolerates multiculturalism…"*

My family came to Canada from Hong Kong as landed immigrants two years ago. We are Chinese, born and raised in Hong Kong. Our parents were born in China, but they went to Hong Kong in 1949 when the Communists took over mainland China. We decided to leave before the Communists take political control of Hong Kong in 1997. We have chosen Canada because it is a free country and it tolerates multiculturalism.

We are adapting to the Canadian culture; however, in no way do we want to give up our own identity as a distinct ethnic group. We are proud of our ethnic heritage and we want our children to learn and uphold it. On the other hand, we are aware that it is important to learn the values of Canadians in order to integrate into the mainstream of the society. We feel ourselves at the crossroads, trying to find a good balance between the two value systems—the one we were brought up with, and the one we are confronting at the moment.

The majority of the Canadians are Anglo-White, and we are a Chinese-Yellow minority. We know that no amount of cultural adaptation can completely eradicate our racial distinction. We find that being a minority means we are in a disadvantaged position in political, economic and social standing. Nevertheless, we want to be good citizens here and we want to prove that we are worthy members of society.

I am writing this essay as an individual and as a parent. My racial and ethnic origins have bearings on my values and attitudes and manifes-

Learning the official languages of the dominant culture is one of the ways in which acculturation takes place.

tations in my behaviour in terms of what I do, what I plan for my children, and what I expect from them.

It is a common view among the Chinese parents here that they do not want their children to be like "bananas"—yellow-skinned yet white inside. I am a supporter of this viewpoint. I believe that it is important to retain our own ethnic identity through maintenance of the Chinese language, familiarization with the Chinese history, celebration of the Chinese festivals, and linkage with the Chinese community:

1. *Maintenance of the Chinese Language.* Language is an important means of differentiation for it distinguishes us from other ethnic groups. At home, we talk to our children in Chinese, and expect them to answer in the same language. We ensure that they can read and write Chinese by sending them to heritage school every Saturday.

2. *Familiarization with Chinese History.* China is an ancient country with thousands of years of cultural heritage. We want our children to be familiar with the roots of our culture. We expose them to story books and videos about the great deeds of the great men and women in Chinese history, and explain to them what we can learn from these celebrated people.

3. *Celebration of the Chinese Festivals.* The Chinese festivals, for example, the Chinese New Year, the Mid-Autumn Festival, and the Winter Solstice have special meaning because they bring all members of the family together and promote kinship and common bonds. We value these celebrations and encourage our children to participate.

4. *Linking with the Chinese Community.* By visiting Chinatown, attending events organized by the Chinese community, reading Chinese newspapers and magazines, and communicating with relatives and friends back in Hong Kong, we keep ourselves informed of the happenings in the Chinese community, and we expose our children to these aspects of the Chinese culture to supplement what we teach at home.

The Value of Learning From Confucius' Teaching

Here in Canada, we find that at the grassroots level, there is a general lack of seriousness towards work. At school, there is a liberal attitude towards students' academic achievement; and at home, there is little respect for parents and grandparents compared to that which exists in Chinese families. We would feel threatened if our children should pick up these attitudes, and to counteract them, we find it useful to emphasize the teaching of the great Chinese teacher and philosopher, Confucius. Specifically, these values are spelled out as follows: (1) the virtue of filial piety—the love and respect for a parent; (2) the virtue of industry—the need to excel through hard work; (3) the virtue of being an all-round educated person—the need to be trained in the mind and the body, for education is the foundation of a future career.

The Value of Learning the Canadian Culture

Being in Canada, I believe that it is equally important to learn the Canadian culture in order to live a meaningful life. At the moment, I believe in the importance of mastering the English language, learning Canadian sports, celebrating the Canadian festivals and enjoying family life:

1. *The Importance of Learning the Language.* I will continue to polish my English so that I can communicate well with people in the workplace; we want our children to learn both English and French so that they can do well in school.

2. *The Importance of Learning the Canadian Sports.* Sports have become part of the Canadian way of life, and a topic for conversation. We are learning how these sport games are played, and we want our children to be able to play hockey, baseball, soccer and learn skating, skiing and swimming.

3. *Celebration of the Canadian Festivals.* We celebrate the Canadian festivals such as Easter, Thanksgiving, Hallowe'en, and Christmas like other Canadians. I think this is important, as we want our children to be able to share and talk about the joy of these festivals with their friends at school.

4. *The Importance of Family Life.* I observe that most Canadians put a lot of emphasis on family life. Sunday is regarded as an important day for family gathering and religious worship, and the issue of Sunday shopping is attacked vigorously. Having been here for two years, I am used to the idea of going to church on Sunday morning, and spending the rest of the day with my family.

I observe that in one way or another, I am changing my behaviours and lifestyle. Though striving to uphold some of the values I have brought from my mother country, I am gradually assimilating the values of the Canadian culture. I am sure that in a few years I will subconsciously pick up more of the predominant values of the Canadian society.

Nadine: *"Being a ten-year-old and coming to this country was horrible..."*

I was born in Guyana, South America as were my parents. And as far as I know four generations before them were also born Guyanese. Therefore, my nationality is Guyanese, while my ethnicity is East Indian. My ancestors came from India. My original language is English.

Life in Guyana was very simple. I realized this when my family moved to Canada. I was ten years old when we came here, and the differences were clear to me right away. Where I was used to having mom at home, now she was working. Women back home did not work as much as here. I noticed both my parents to be very uptight all the time, which is something I never saw back home. Life over here was all work. They were always worried about house payments and all kinds of bills. They never owed anyone money in Guyana.

Being a ten-year-old and coming to this country was horrible. First of all I came half way through the school year in the midst of winter. Not only was it hard to adjust to school, but also the weather, my new friends and speaking English the Canadian way.

It took me a long time to get used to all of this. At home I was Guyanese in that I still spoke the same way and ate the same foods. But at school I tried very much to be Canadian. Somewhere along the way I decided I did not want to be Guyanese any more and that I was going to try the hardest I could to be Canadian, like my newfound friends, and disregard my Guyanese heritage. For a long time I wished I was White. Life just seemed simpler—you didn't have to lie or make excuses or even apologize if your skin colour was white. I really envied White people.

I did meet up with prejudice. I can remember taking the long way to school just to avoid running into people who would call me racial names. However, there were people that would say to me, "Well, you are White in the way you think and act." I used to take it as a compliment, but as I grew older I started to understand that there's not a more terrible thing a person could say to me. I think it's adding insult to injury when someone says that.

My Mom and Dad brought us up by Guyanese standards—very, very strict. The emphasis was on getting a good education and eventually getting a good career—absolutely no socializing. That was when I started rebelling. I wanted to go out just as all my friends did but I wasn't allowed. I was torn between the two cultures. By day I was at school being very much Canadian in the way I acted.

I used to get very depressed and hurt over this because my parents couldn't understand what I was going through. It was only when I was 19 that my parents started to let me go out. I felt a lot of resentment and hate for a long time towards my parents for this, but my four older sisters seemed to be better able to accept it.

My parents are both very hardworking people who always wanted the best for us. As my father has said to us so many times, "You can do anything or be anything you want in this country." That's why he brought us here—for a better life and I really do believe that. I live my life today by those words.

We were never religious. By tradition we are Hindu, as most Indian people take on that religion, but my parents never practised it. Therefore any religious beliefs I have are just from what I've learned over the years, and I do have a very strong belief in God.

Although Canada is multicultural, at times I am still very self-conscious of my colour. Mom and Dad have always taught us to be objective and to think about other people's feelings—to take people for who they are, not what they look like. So I can feel for all other minorities in this country. Not just in skin colour but anyone who is discriminated against for whatever reason. I can honestly say I know how they feel. And from being a minority, I've learned to appreciate all people regardless of race, creed, ethnicity etc. because I have been on the receiving end of it. Therefore, my skin colour coupled with my parents' influence has made me a better person.

I've adapted to Canadian culture very well but I still have Guyanese in me. I think I'm a bit of both. I dress Canadian, I eat Guyanese foods, my friends are Canadian and Guyanese.

The places I go to are very much Canadian—the bars I go to or the events I participate in socially. I've only gone out with White guys and this is a preference and maybe a prejudice. I can't explain it other than saying I've never been attracted to any other guys except Whites …

I now feel a great admiration for my parents for coming to a new country and starting all over again, and for being extremely successful in doing so. I now realize it was just as hard for them to adjust as it was for me. If anything, I feel ashamed for all the problems I caused them. I know I'm a better person for all they've taught me. There's a lot of love and respect for them on my part. I don't deny myself my Guyanese heritage any more; as a matter of fact, I am very proud of it.

In conclusion, I would like to say that I feel very privileged and lucky to be able to have two cultures. Although it was a struggle in the beginning, now it's a blessing. I have been given the opportunity to take what I like best from both …

Carol: *"I grew up thinking that Whites were superior…"*

Sixteen years ago I immigrated to Canada. It was in the early '70s when there was an influx of immigrants to Canada, especially from the Caribbean. I was born in the Caribbean island of Trinidad to parents of West Indian nationality. My father's and mother's ethnicity is African.

Racially I am Black. I have lived half of my life in Trinidad where the majority of the population is of African descent, and the second major group is of East Indian descent, interspersed with Chinese and Whites. Living there, where the majority of people were Black, I felt no threat to my self-esteem because of prejudice or racial discrimination. However, from a very early age, I learned that to be White or fair-skinned with long hair was much better than being Black. I grew up thinking that Whites were superior, prettier, richer, and never did menial jobs, because that's what I saw of the Whites I came in contact with in Trinidad.

This belief was inculcated in me from my parents who always spoke highly of Whites, showed great respect for them, and made remarks and comparisons which made them appear superior.

As I grew older and learned about the history of my race, I realized that this attitude my parents had toward the White race is a legacy which was passed on to my generation, dating back to slavery and colonialism.

Immigrating to Canada was an eye-opening experience for me because it helped to change my beliefs and concepts of White people. It has also made me more conscious of my race because I am now in the minority, and I am reminded of it daily. For example, when I listen to the news and read the headlines in the newspapers, if there is something negative about a Black person, I feel as though I am a part of it. I feel as though everyone is looking at me and thinking about me in the same negative light as that person who committed the crime. I feel as though I am on stage. Similarly, if there is something positive or good, I feel proud.

To an extent my race does influence my values and attitudes, because as a visible minority living in Canada, I feel that achieving success in anything means extremely hard work and struggle. As a result, I have placed a very high value on education, which I feel is one of the main tools to success. I am passing on this value of education to my children because I realize that without it their chances of success is almost nil. In addition, I am trying to instill in my children the value of being proud of their Black heritage. I am also trying to develop in them a self-esteem that would counteract the darts of racism, prejudice and discrimination which they will definitely have to face in this society. I am also making them aware of the fact that even though they are Canadians, their success and achievements can be attained only through working twice as much as their fellow White Canadians.

However, as I reflect on my values, behaviours, morals and attitudes toward life, I must also note that whereas culture, ethnicity and race are significant, I am to a large extent strongly influenced by my religion.

As a Christian, I try to apply the principle of love to my fellow men, by using the "golden rule": "Always treat others as you would have them treat you." Sometimes practising this rule becomes difficult when I am faced with racial discrimination, prejudice, or racial slurs. For example, I remember walking home from the bus stop one day, when some young men passing by in a car shouted, "You————nigger!" A mixed feeling of anger, devastation, and prejudice came over me. I had to quickly console myself by thinking that they were just ignorant strangers who don't know me, so I should ignore this remark. There were other incidents, like when my husband and I were looking for an apartment. We were told on the phone that an apartment was available. We made an appointment to see it and went there. The superintendent took a White couple to see the apartment, left us waiting in the lobby then returned and told us it was taken. We were living just across the street, so we walked home, phoned the same building and inquired, and were told by the same superintendent that the apartment was available. We got the message and started to look elsewhere. These and other incidents while job-hunting, and even things at school make it difficult for me sometimes to practise this principle of "love your fellow man" and the "golden rule." But over the years, I have learned to cope by practising this rule and ignoring derogatory slangs hurled at me, or racial discrimination and prejudice. Now, I do not feel the sting of racial prejudice as much as when I first arrived here.

In my daily life I try not to see people first through their colour or race, but as individual human beings. In spite of cultural differences, ethnicity, race or religion, we all share a common heritage as members of the human race, and we have the same basic human needs to be fulfilled, therefore we should not make ourselves feel superior or inferior to others.

Sometimes immigrants come to Canada because of a lack of poitical or religious freeom in their home country.

Being a Black Canadian who is a part of a minority group, I am aware that my ethnicity and race will always play a role in influencing my values and attitudes in life. However, because my religion is a way of life for me, it determines how much of society's values, behaviours and attitudes I assimilate. It, therefore, affects my main outlook on life.

Elaine: *"My experiences with discrimination differ from other Blacks…"*

My biological parents represented two distinct races. My father was born in Germany, and migrated to Canada with his family as a boy. My mother is a Black Jamaican, who came to Canada with her family in the sixties. My mother and father were never married, as a result of bigotry and ignorance within my father's family. They did not want any black blood "tainting" their aryan line. This early disownment caused me to feel uncomfortable with the fact that I was born White, and not Black like my family. I was not proud of my colour, and envied other mixed children who looked Black.

Although I was a White child, and in Jamaica a noticeable minority, I do not remember having any problems because of my colour. On the contrary, when I think back I realize that being seen with such a fair child was a status symbol for certain members of my family. And they frequently paraded me through their functions and friends. While in Jamaica, I played with children of many cultural roots, commonly mixed as well.

I came back to Scarborough to live with my immediate family before I started school. Here, my family continues to practise Jamaican culture. I remember a diverse cultural and racial representation among my friends and peers in Scarborough. I don't recall any children (including myself) being isolated and/or teased because of their race or religion. I am very thankful that from a young age I interacted with other cultures, and learned that we are all just people inside.

As I grew older, I discovered just how racially oriented and religiously sensitive our society can be. Although I rarely had to deal with prejudice directly, as I look racially part of the majority, I have witnessed many others being treated with varying degrees of cruelty. Paul [page 61] suggested that within his neighbourhood, if an individual (usually White) is from another culture they are accepted without discrimination only when they have already proven themselves. I have experienced this phenomenon personally (with white people), when it is revealed that my family is Black. Depending upon the degree to which they have "accepted" me, this information is greeted with fascination, awe, or discomfort. This is by no means limited to the White population. Many times I have been instantly recognized as a "sister" within Black groups when this same information is revealed.

My experiences with discrimination then differ from that of [others] who had to deal directly with it on a larger and different scale than me. They are visibly part of a minority group or community, while I am a member of the small non-visible minority.

There are many who try to believe that all people are the same. I do not think that. Instead, I believe that every individual is unique, and those differences should not be hidden, but exposed with pride. The key is not using these differences to degrade, but to appreciate variety, learn from diversity, and enjoy change.

Zena: *"As a member of a visible minority, I feel that my shortcomings will be attributed to my race, ethnicity, etc. ..."*

An immigrant Canadian, I am a part of the much talked about Canadian ethnic mosaic. I epitomize the diversity of this mosaic: an East Indian by race, born and raised in East Africa (a second generation African), a practising Shiite Ismaili Muslim and with a working knowledge of three languages (East Indian, Swahili and English). A Tanzanian national by birth, I left my country in 1971 as a result of political considerations for a four-year stay in the United Kingdom prior to immigrating to Canada in 1975.

It was during the sixties that Tanzania (known as Tanganyika then) and the other countries in the region attained independence from Britain. The colonial affiliation meant that up until 1970 the school system, the judiciary and other institutions were modelled along the lines of those in Britain. For example, the medium of instruction in schools and the predominant language of commerce and government was English. I was therefore brought up with an understanding and appreciation of British culture—the predominant culture I subsequently found in the U.K. and in Canada.

A strong part of what I am is the Ismaili community I belong to. The Ismaili faith, one of the 72 sects of Islam, takes the Islamic concept of religion as a way of life (i.e. unlike the strict Augustinian distinction between material and spiritual, Islam considers both to be equally important) even further. The community encourages and has developed major programs in education, social and economic development. Higher education, excellence in commerce and the professions is put at par with prayer as is enterprise with a conscience and self-help. My faith has instilled strongly in me the existence of God, and a balance between the pursuit of material things with prayers for the soul.

Culturally, I consider myself a Canadian Ismaili. This would not be different if I were asked this question on a visit to Tanzania or at JK (JK—commonly used abbreviation for Jamatkhana, the Ismaili prayer/community house). As minorities in all countries they reside in, Ismailis' first loyalty is to their countries of residence—there is no Ismaili code of conduct; they adopt language and dress code for the respective countries. As an "unhyphenated" Canadian I see myself as a citizen, sharing with other Canadians the same future, all equal and without special privileges.

As someone who left her country because of political reasons, I am able to appreciate the stable political environment, democratic values and institutions, and the various freedoms (of expression, religion, etc.) far more than Canadians who were born and raised here. This is reflected in my active participation in, and support of, civic affairs; e.g. the fact that I always vote in all elections, my membership in a political party, my open-mindedness in accepting various differing opinions, my interest in reading newspapers and in particular editorials and opinion pieces, and my support and respect for law and authority.

Similarly, I am able to appreciate the "high" standard of living in Canada, having lived in a third world country where electricity and running water were considered (and are still considered) luxuries. I place a high premium on education. It was a luxury "back home" both in terms of user fees and availability—Tanzania, with a population of 25 million, has one university.

Although I was born and raised in relative luxury, the poverty and lack of opportunities to most Tanzanians are permanent reminders that to most of the people in the third world, getting three meals a day remains a major preoccupation.

These "backgrounds" have also instilled in me a high regard for the work ethic and self help. Social security programs (medicare, pensions, etc.) do not exist in Tanzania or India (the country of my great grandparents' birth) and therefore this dependence on government is an alien concept for me. Although as a liberal-minded social democrat, I support the UIC and welfare systems, I would find it difficult to collect from these programs. Work ethic, pursuit of excellence and self-help are reinforced in all my background influences (nationality, ethnic and religious). As a parent, I expect to pass along to my children these values and related ones of thrift, and of carrying as little debt as possible.

Another major influence is my being a member of a visible minority which is frequently negatively stereotyped. The ignorance of my fellow Canadians as to the very many different peoples generalized as East Indians (a Tanzanian Ismaili like myself has as much in common with a Tamil from South India as a WASP would have with a Ukrainian— they are both White) is disappointing. I am frequently drawn into the role of an educator, explaining about different Eastern cultures and religious backgrounds.

Unfortunately, the only thing many Canadians know about the world's second largest religion (Islam has 1 billion followers) is the political violence and terrorism in the Middle East, which is like equating Christianity with violence because of the struggle in Ireland between Catho-

lics and Protestants. People lose sight of the fact that Moslems, like everyone else, can be poor or rich, tolerant or intolerant, honest or dishonest, illiterate or scholarly. In personal terms, this has cultivated a tolerance for other cultures, a desire to learn more about them and a sympathy for the negative stereotyping they might be subjected to.

Another fallout from this is that I try very hard to be a model citizen since, as a member of visible minority, I feel that my shortcomings will be attributed to my race, ethnicity, etc. A beneficial result of this (a sort of a "backward compliment") is that this makes me a winner since I try harder than I would have otherwise.

Hillary: *"I never did want to be White to fit in…"*

To my knowledge, I was born in Montréal, Canada, and was adopted by a White couple while I was an infant. As far back as I can recall, I noticed the difference between my family and myself. I was Black, they were White— it was an obvious difference.

In our neighbourhood, which was White and French, it was a setback to be English, and having a Black child living amongst a White family, willingly, was a major strike. There was no worse a household could do, it seemed. My family endured black cats in our swimming pool, broken windows and many ignorant comments and questions, such as, "Does she eat at the table with you?", from ignorant people who had trouble seeing a human being behind the colour of their skin.

I also encountered many racial slurs, but learned to be thick-skinned and quick-mouthed. I also realized that only an uneducated person voiced such ignorant and foolish things. Therefore, I ignored them. This was another trait I developed: to ignore people quickly and easily. My brother also taught me how to defend myself, he said he didn't want me coming home beaten up because someone didn't like the colour of my skin.

After many years we finally became accepted, since we posed no visible threat to the community. But by that time we had enough and were ready to move.

We moved to Ottawa when I was 12 years old. There weren't any Blacks in the neighbourhood, so I obviously hung out with White individuals in my age group. But I always knew and was proud to be Black. I was never ashamed of the colour of my skin, my heritage or my cultural background. Nor did I ever want to be White in order to fit in better with my family. If anything, I wished that they were Black.

" ... If I cannot see myself I cannot see others clearly; and if I cannot see others clearly, seeing myself becomes more and more difficult."

Growing up in a White family has been in a sense a growing experience, as well as a strange and difficult experience for me. People ask me frequently, "What is it like, growing up with Whites?" How can I answer that? I've never known anything else. Growing up among Whites has taught me to be open-minded. It has taught me about cultural diversity and about trust. Yet it has also taught me to distrust many Whites after individuals have proved themselves trustworthy.

As a youth, most of my friends were White and I had developed a broad interest in music. Now most, if not all of my friends are Black, and my interest has centred on traditional "Black" music. Such as R&B, hip-hop, rap, reggae, soca, jazz and the like. I have tried to know and understand all aspects of my culture.

At times I wished that I knew and lived with my natural family so that I would be enveloped by people that I could compare myself inside and out to (I went through a very difficult transitional period in my teens because I was slim and I wished I know my family to see if it was genetic, to hear advice, etc.), and relate to culturally. But I didn't. My family is White, and I love them.

SUMMARY

We can conclude from the preceding essays many things. That values, attitude, behaviours, indeed individuals' entire lifestyles, can be related to their race, ethnicity, religion, nationality and citizenship. Secondly, that to know yourself is that first step toward knowing others. As Lyn expressed it, " ... If I cannot see myself I cannot see others clearly; and if I cannot see others clearly, seeing myself becomes more and more difficult." Thirdly, that in addition to our Canadian culture, individuals also have an ethnic culture which is an integral part of their identity.

Finally, it has been pointed out that knowledge of our origin equips us with the social and psychological tools necessary to effectively interact in our society: "I continue to search deep into by background and culture, my childhood and upbringing, my old and new surroundings in order to find reasons for my behaviour and to search for answers."

Questions:

1. What are some of the factors that influence the construction of an individual's identity?

2. What is meant by "multiple identities"? Discuss how factors that combine to construct identity operate.

3. Is a person's identity development independent of others and ther context or situation in which he or she grows up? Why or why not?

4

SIMILARITIES AND DIFFERENCES: MAKING COMPARISONS

In telling about the process which was used in the exercise in which he compared his cultural identity, values and experiences with those of a German Canadian, Thomas wrote:

> To understand how our values and behaviour are affected by our background, it sometimes helps to also examine someone with different racial, ethnic and cultural roots. By comparing the two, we will be able to gain a better understanding of ourselves and those around us.

> But how can one tell if certain values and behaviour should be attributed to someone's ethnic background or simply their personal experiences? For example, if a person is materialistic, is it because this is a cultural trait or is it just the person's personality? For the purposes of my paper, any distinct trait of the subject which is also shared by other people of the same origin will be considered to be related to the person's cultural background and not individual experience.

> Another problem which arises involves the interview itself. The interviewer cannot simply ask someone to explain how their background affects their values and behaviour. The subject has to describe how he or she feels about something, and from these statements, conclusions can be drawn by the interviewer. Although I have tried to be as objective as possible, keep in mind that these conclusions are as I perceive them, and my perception is coloured by my own racial, ethnic and cultural roots ...

> Human beings are very complex creatures and it would take a lifetime

of study just to fully understand one individual. Not all of us will become sociologists in our lifetime, but if we are open-minded when it comes to dealing with people of different backgrounds, we will be able to better understand not only them, but ourselves.

It is this concept of learning about self and others that is the basis of the following essays. In them, individuals make comparisons between themselves and persons whom they interviewed. In their analyses, the writers attempt to show how their similarities and differences are related to such things as their racial, ethnic, cultural and immigrant experiences.

The writers are conscious of the fact that they cannot generalize about an entire cultural group from an interview with one person. In noting that generalizations cannot be made about her, and therefore neither about her subject, one participant wrote:

> I feel that I am not considered the typical member of my culture. Then again, does anyone fit the "norm?" Even though I am a WASP, I behave in a manner which many people refer to as weird ... I also must consider the fact that whomever I compare myself to probably does not entirely represent her cultural group either. Therefore, in interviewing someone from a different culture, I cannot compare my group to her group—it must remain person to person ...

Many of the writers were able to conclude that there are "far more similarities than differences among cultures." This is significant, for in many cases the writers expected to find that because of differences in race and ethnicity, there would be very few similarities. This finding indicates to us that while we may have different religions, play different games, and dress differently, the philosophies behind these various practices, and the role they play in our lives, seem to be the same. Furthermore, insofar as everyone experiences the Canadian culture and the corresponding values and aspirations, it is understandable that this will be reflected in most Canadians' lives irrespective of race, ethnicity, religion and subculture.

Tina: *"I began to notice how much some cultures are misunderstood..."*

While studying the Native Canadians, I interviewed a young lady named Sam. During our talk, I realized that we had some similarities and some differences in values, ideas and behaviours. In my attempt

to point out some similarities and differences of our separate values and behaviours, I began to notice how much some cultures are misunderstood. We should all stop thinking that our way is "best," and try to relinquish our ethnocentric attitudes.

The Native Canadians are a very religious group. As Sam shared some of the religious practices, it occurred to me that although the methods were different, the purpose and the meaning behind them were similar to my own practices. When an Indian goes on a vision quest, there are certain steps he or they must follow. First of all, a vision quest is an outing an Indian goes on to seek direction or to solve a problem. Before they can go out on the quest, they must first enter the sweat lodge to clear the mind and soul of evil or angry thoughts. They enter the lodge without clothing and they must stay until they feel that they have cleansed the mind. Often prayers of forgiveness are

Physical features are often the basis for people's judgements about race and ethnicity.

said. After leaving the sweat lodge, they must not tell anyone what went on inside. They then go in search for a spot in the wilderness that gives them a sense of tranquillity and there they stay for about four or five days, meditating. Once the vision quest is over and they return, they must not tell anyone of their vision, with the exception of the medicine man.

After listening to Sam tell me about the vision quest, it made me think of our Roman Catholic "core" weekend. The Catholic church started core weekends, but any denomination may attend one. Although the method is different in ways, the meanings are similar. A core weekend is supposed to free you of all your sins and make you more aware of yourself and your relationship with God. At the beginning of the weekend you have to make a promise that you will not tell anyone outside of the weekend what took place, with the exception of your priest or minister.

During this time there are healing services, meditation, prayers and confessions. The weekend usually takes place at a school or hall where the clocks and windows are covered so that no one is aware of the outside world—just themselves. We are given simple meals and there is little sleep. When you leave, you are under an oath of silence and you feel cleansed and spiritually fulfilled.

Both the vision quest and the core weekend are paralleled in many ways. In each of the practices the people are seeking guidance; whether from Sam's god or mine, everyone needs guidance in their lives. Both methods produce a cleansing of the mind and soul. In Sam's practice, this cleansing comes before the actual vision takes place, whereas in my practice the cleansing is the result of the weekend.

In both groups we find that cleansing of the mind and soul are very important for spiritual growth and awareness. Neither Sam nor I are allowed to share our experiences with anyone except a knowledgeable person like the medicine man or the priest. Only these people will truly understand and advise us properly. Both rituals involve prayer and meditation and a great awareness of one's self.

Another similar value between our two groups is the meaning of the medicine pouch and the hope chest. The medicine pouch is a very personal item to an Indian. Inside, it holds a part of their life. Over the years, Sam will collect items that create positive feelings for her and place them in her pouch. For example, while on a vision quest she saw a smooth stone and it gave her a powerful positive feeling, so she put it in her pouch. The medicine pouch is usually given to her by someone who is very special like her mother, grandmother or medicine man. Then, when she wishes, she will pass it on to her daughter or son. The contents of the pouch are unknown to all except the owner. The secrecy of the items is due to the fact that no one would understand the meaning or significance of the items and if seen they would lose their "power." The medicine pouch is very personal and sentimental only to the owner and those it is passed on to.

Equalling the meaning of the medicine pouch, I have my hope chest. My hope chest holds great personal value to me. Inside it I store parts of my past that I want to remember, like my first stuffed animal, my baby booties, and the start of my chinaware for when I marry. All of these items are very personal to me and no-one would get the same satisfaction of looking at them as I do.

My hope chest was given to me by my grandfather whom I love and admire and when the time comes, I will pass it on to my first daughter or granddaughter. Unlike the medicine pouch, the contents of my hope chest can be seen by others, although it's hardly worth it if they don't understand and know me. My hope chest holds great sentimental value for me, and for those yet to own it.

The personality of a person is held in both the medicine pouch and the hope chest. They reveal a part of each person's culture. By viewing each item in both the pouch and the chest, a person can determine what a person values. For instance, with the examples given, they might see that the Indian values nature, whereas the English-Canadian has more materialistic values.

Unfortunately, the difference I found between Sam and myself was the racial reaction from other people. When interviewing her, she told me of an incident where she was blamed because of her race. She was in school with the rest of the students who happened to be English-Canadians. When the teacher returned to class there was something missing from her desk. Immediately, without questioning anyone, she turned to Sam and blamed her for stealing the object. When Sam told her she didn't take it, the teacher then accused her of lying. Sam expressed to me that this wasn't the only incident where this had happened. Many times she has had to take the blame because of her race and ethnicity. She gets accused and charged without a fair trial.

On the other hand, being a White English-Canadian, I have had no trouble in that area. I've never received the blame without already having been fairly tried. I've seen it happen to other races like the

Blacks, the Mexicans and others, and until people are educated in different cultural histories, they will always use these stereotypes and prejudices against other cultures.

During my interview with Sam, I recognized some similarities and some differences in the values, ideas and behaviours between our separate ethnic and racial groups. Religiously, in my own way, I have similar spiritual wants as Sam. We both practise them differently but the personal fulfilment is similar. Both of us will go through our lives collecting items that are meaningful and special to us, and then pass them on to a loved one.

The difference that I saw was not a pleasant one. Both of us have to deal with racism but in different ways. Sam has to put up with stereotypes from the White people, and someday she hopes that things will improve; but there is still a lot of education needed, whereas I have to deal with being a racist at times. I, too, had my stereotypes about the native Canadians, but after my interview with Sam and research on Natives, I had a better insight into the attitudes and beliefs of the Canadian Indians. I think all people should follow this rule: "Do not judge lest ye be judged."

John: *"I was better able to see my own prejudices..."*

Upon meeting a person from a different culture, a daily occurrence in today's multicultural melting-pot environment, both individuals are superficially aware of the other's uniqueness. Skin colour, accent, and dress all form an initial impression of the "outer self" of that person, but very rarely do we get to delve into their thoughts, beliefs and value systems. This, of course, is where the true heart of the person beats. Education, traditions, family rearing and societal influences are all elements which help to shape and mould the human into the special being that he or she is and it is through the examination of these elements that we can gain valuable insights into our "ethnic" neighbours.

Quite recently I had the opportunity to meet and interview Bill, who is racially and ethnically a Native Canadian Indian. Before our meeting, I, of course, had predetermined certain facts and thoughts concerning him and I am sure he probably had done the same about me. We both, however, were in for an educational experience. Although we did have our inevitable differences, it was the similarities we shared that I found fascinating. Both of us, having been raised in Canada, would have had some similar experiences; however, even culturally we had some distinct parallels. It is the similarities and differences that I shall examine in this paper and I will maybe shed some insights into how these racial and ethnic differences and similarities allow us to appreciate each other's individuality.

Bill spent his early formative years on an Indian reserve in Northern Ontario and although he moved to Toronto before his tenth birthday, he considers the North to be his true home and the major influence on some of his thoughts and feelings. Conditions at the site were not very hygienic, and living quarters, he remembers, were generally more like upgraded cabins than houses. He recalls it with a sense of fondness, however, because of the remembered warmth of family memories. He stated his belief that family is very important to the Indians and that "family" included very close friends who were related by values and beliefs. He indicated that the exile a lot of Indians felt was due to the isolation of the reservations from the rest of the populace and this encouraged the close-knit supportiveness that was, in fact, necessary for him to function emotionally. He found separation from family very detrimental to the individual and was in awe when I related my family upbringing.

Although I had been brought up with the belief that the family unit is an extremely precious notion from which support, love and encouragement flow, my experience was somewhat different. I was raised with love and sensitivity but never felt the bond of which Bill spoke. To him, his family was his mainline, but to me it was quite often a group of people that I sometimes loved more out of duty than desire. Upon the examination of two other ethnically English families with whom I have had repeated contact, it seems that although the family is respected, it is also somewhat distant and not terribly demonstrative. Perhaps that can be attributed to the British upper class aloofness and the well-established boundaries of class and respect. Nevertheless, it seems to be prevalent in the three English families I know intimately. Conversely, Bill related that his family, and the Indian families he knew, were very close and expressed as much physical love as they did verbal love. Even though we both had a strong belief in the family, I came to recognize that while his was a physical reality, mine was more of a concept, and I envied him his ties.

Religion is usually a major influence on a person's development and values, as is lack of religion. Both Bill and I had been raised with the belief in an Almighty Creator and that this Creator should be revered and worshipped. In my religion, Christianity, the Creator is known as God while in Bill's the Almighty is referred to in Sioux tongue as

Wakan. Wakan differs very little from God; both created the Heavens and the Earth and all creatures great and small, and both are fervently worshipped by followers of the faith. It is the other aspects of the two religions that illustrate their differences.

Bill devoutly believes that every object found on Earth has an essence, be it a tiny stone or a mighty waterfall. He believes that all the creations are whole, and that any disharmony which ensues after an object is removed or destroyed should be righted by the return or replacement of a similar article. In his opinion, man should always be as one with the environment and sensitive to the natural aura of the Almighty's creations.

He doesn't feel that a place of worship, like the Christian church or the Jewish synagogue, is a necessity, because faith is an ongoing process and an individual should show this faith in daily settings and actions and not just obeisance on a given or acknowledged day.

My new friend went on further to say that it was his conviction most Indians adhered to the ancient beliefs, and through rituals like the "vision quest," a solitary, cathartic journey into one's inner space, helped to ensure new generations would be cognizant of the old ways and would ensure their continued existence.

I similarly believe that a place of ritual worship is not a prerequisite for perpetuating one's beliefs, but I am at odds with the dogma of my leaders. The High Anglican church states that church attendance is an essential part of faith, and it considers non-attendance and lack of involvement in the religious community unacceptable. While I carry forth my convictions, this is one aspect of the church with which I do not agree and therefore am considered somewhat unworthy in the eyes of the ministry.

The two of us discussed this notion, and Bill chuckled that the solution was obvious. Since I agree with most of the Indian beliefs on which he had elaborated, he jokingly argued that I should convert to "Wakan-ism." Although I can well imagine a devout Anglican blanching at the thought, after careful examination, I discovered that even after taking into account the varied differences, the two religions are more alike than I would ever have thought.

Even though Bill, in reality, is the "true" Canadian, my White, Anglo-Saxon, Protestant culture has made me, in the eyes of the majority of Canadians, the recipient of the "true Canadian" title. Because I am a White, English-speaking male from an upper middle-class family, I have never had to be concerned with how my ethnicity would affect job

Rituals are a significant part of any culture.

prospects, housing enquiries—in short, how others would view me. Because of my social and cultural identity, I am almost guaranteed success in any field I choose. This option is not always available to all members of today's "modern" society and Bill very ably illustrated this point to me.

Bill is considered a "half-breed"—he has an Indian mother and a White father, and consequently he has the physical attributes of both. His skin is a little paler than that of his mother, a true Sioux Indian, but nevertheless from a visual standpoint he is certainly far removed from Caucasian colouring. His hair, which tends to be straight, is jet black and certain facial features, although somewhat softened by his father's genetic influence, are evocative of the Indian stereotype.

I have referred to his physical features because he feels they have a significant impact on the treatment he sometimes receives. He told me that occasionally people would take a second look in attempting to determine his racial background. By himself, he said he encountered very little prejudice, but if seen with a group of Indian friends, the reactions were not always so subtle. Ladies clutching their purses a little tighter if the group came near, obvious sneers directed toward the group, and blatant slurs voiced just loud enough to carry, are all experiences Bill and his friends have endured. "I don't know what they think we are going to do," he relates to me, "but there often seems to be this tension in the air between US and THEM."

As he recounted certain incidents, I realized that although I had never behaved outright in such a manner I was guilty of harbouring certain similar misconceptions, and I almost felt like apologizing. I let him know this and he laughed. He said he expected people to have certain preconceived notions of Indians due to books, stories and films, and he had learned how to adapt to it.

He suspected any minority would agree with his view that adaptation and enlightenment would help to curb such petty ignorances and that, hopefully, in a time not too distant, the aforementioned situations would lessen and then cease to be altogether.

Upon conclusion of the interview, I began to reflect on some of the instances we had discussed. We are two human beings from extremely different backgrounds, yet there was always a common thread of agreement to be found in most of the topics on which we touched. Although I could never expect to fully comprehend his cultural identity, nor he mine, the opinions of one so far removed from my own upbringing were extremely enlightening. I was better able to see my own prejudices. Although I still tend to see things ethnocentrically from time to time, understanding my own and then another's culture, I believe, is the first step to breaking down some of the racial and ethnic barriers erected so long ago.

A respect must be engendered for the differences of our many cultural heritages, for it is only in this manner that we can learn from and grow with each other. An acknowledgement of our similarities should be recognized because norms, values and beliefs, although varied, are all based upon love, friendship and understanding. Only after a careful examination of a different culture, can we begin to see that although we appear dissimilar outwardly, there seems to be a sameness which is only evident if we make a conscious effort to discover each other's individuality within.

Lyn: *"As a member of the dominant group, I don't feel the conscious necessity of reaffirming my cultural heritage…"*

In this discussion of similarities and differences between my own ethnic culture, English Canadian, and the group which I studied, French Canadian, I would like to concentrate on how each group views its heritage, and the importance each group places on its culture. I would also like to discuss how each group views the preservation of that culture and how this is reflected in behaviours and attitudes. In doing so, I will make comparisons between the individual I interviewed and myself.

The individual I interviewed is a Franco-Ontarian and holds many of the values of French Canadian culture, one of the most important being the commitment to family. This commitment is also extended to include involvement in the close-knit Franco Ontarian community. Historically, these values have been strengthened by the position of Franco-Ontarians as a minority within the larger English culture.

Jacques has a strong sense of his own heritage and a sense of loss and isolation from his culture. Living in Southern Ontario, it has only been relatively recently that he has had access to French television or radio and the French community here is very scattered. His language is crucial to him, and, as to most French Canadians, inseparable from his culture. He cannot practise this culture unless he returns to his home town or visits other French Canadian centres. As a result, preservation of his language involves a day-to-day struggle. Because of this, he places a high value on that language and is very conscious of his own ethnic and cultural identity as distinct from English Canadians'.

Although I am an immigrant, I am of English birth and this places me firmly within English Canadian ethnic culture. I have been socialized to accept the high value placed on success in the public sphere, on material success and economic status, which are values that are emphasized more strongly than commitment to family and community. But it is through such things as economic status or power that English Canadian cultural identity is reinforced.

As a member of the majority (or dominant) group, I don't feel the conscious necessity of reaffirming my cultural heritage as I can practise that culture daily. It is reflected back at me in my day-to-day experience of society—in the institutions which surround me, for example. Although the preservation of ethnic cultural identity may not appear to be an issue, it is shown to be an important one by the ways in which the majority culture perpetuates itself through institutions such as political parties, schools and various media and by the strong reluctance to relinquish control over those institutions. The historical denial of official-language status to the French language is a good example of this.

It can be seen then that both groups place a strong emphasis on preservation of a cultural heritage they both value highly. The important difference lies in the assumptions and attitudes that surround those beliefs.

Jacques assumed his ethnic and cultural identity to be continually under threat of assimilation by the majority English culture. He had no occasion to use his language, and his ties were to the Franco-Ontarian communities of northern Ontario, but he had to work in the south. As a result he was both conscious of, and desired to emphasize, his identity, his "difference."

I, on the other hand, surrounded by my own ethnic culture, have tended to lose all sight of myself as having an ethnic identity. I and other members of my group preserve our culture by living it without being aware that we are doing so. I don't feel the necessity of emphasizing my "difference," and yet tend to be unaware of the "sameness" which surrounds me as actually having an ethnic cultural basis. This attitude in English-Canadian culture has resulted in a strong tendency to deny or ignore those differences. The attitude that we are really all the same comes from the assumption of what the same is—namely, like us. When the majority group denies or ignores the assertion of difference it is also denying the need for accommodation of those differences which could be threatening to their own cultural "sameness."

This highlights another important issue in the discussion of these two groups and how they view preservation of their respective cultures. Both groups consider themselves to be charter members of Canadian society. If we take this to mean that a charter group's institutions provide the basic structural framework for society, then it can be seen that only English culture has retained this status in Ontario. As a result, English Canadians assume this status to be valid almost without thought. The desire of the French in Ontario for official status appears as either irrelevant or as a vague historical issue because nowhere do English Canadians see evidence of this status. For the Franco-Ontarians, official status involves the very right to existence as a distinct cultural and linguistic group. It becomes a crucial issue of survival and far from irrelevant to daily life since their culture is not reflected in the language used or the priorities of government. Our tendency to deny understanding of this desire on the part of the French shows how easily threatened we can be. Sharing charter group status is acceptable theoretically, but in terms of "granting" legal status it somehow becomes questionable.

Both cultures, then, have the same intense belief in the necessity of preserving their cultural heritage and maintaining language and values while living day to day. The key difference here is in what is assumed; on one hand, the conscious effort made toward preservation of identity, and on the other the largely unconscious perpetuation of culture through which identity is preserved.

In comparing these values and ideas, the differences and similarities of the two ethnic-cultural groups, I have drawn on knowledge of my own group and conversations with Jacques. I could see that our differing backgrounds, relative to the culture within which we live, has had an effect on the relative strengths of those values and ideas and on how clearly we perceive their existence. This was very evident in discussing Franco-Ontarians, and perhaps it could be generalized to any other ethnic group living within a different majority ethnic culture. Acceptance and definition of differences can become crucial in the preservation of a distinct ethnic identity. Awareness of similar needs by the majority culture is also crucially important in preserving both cultures.

Maureen: *"I did not regard having two languages as a tool for survival..."*

For my paper I chose to investigate the French Canadians. Part of my investigation involved speaking with Charlotte, a French Canadian born just outside of Québec City. She is about fifty years old and is married to a non-French gentleman. They reside with their children in Brampton, Ontario.

This paper consists of similarities and differences between Charlotte and myself. Certainly there are others than those mentioned here, but I have chosen to highlight four specific areas—religion, language, education and politics. Please keep in mind that I have developed these views from my own interpretations resulting from conversations with Charlotte and while I believe I have relayed her beliefs, attitudes and behaviours accurately through comparison to mine, they do not necessarily reflect her interpretations.

My awareness and interest in the French people has grown immensely since studying the French Canadians through library research and spending time with Charlotte. During our conversations, the subject of religion surfaced more than once. Baptized and raised a Roman Catholic, she has, over the past three or four years, found herself drifting from the church. She clarified this to mean a physical separation—not spiritual.

She has been experiencing some doubt as to the necessity of weekly attendance at Sunday Mass, and feels secure with her decision not to attend regularly. For her, the continual love for God and her fellow man takes precedence over the obligatory Sunday attendance. She usually attends at Christmas and Easter with her husband, a non-practising Catholic. Charlotte displays no hostility towards the demands imposed by the Church, but simply feels she is fulfilling her obligation to God by other means.

Religion continues to play such a major role in the French culture that I was taken aback to hear her personal view. She acknowledged the importance of religion in her culture for the majority of francophones, but at the same time defended her stand as a personal conflict which she feels she is dealing with appropriately.

I, too, am a Roman Catholic and am presently practising. Being of Irish origin, it seems to follow that I am Catholic, but I do not feel I practise because it is a cultural trait. I don't feel I practise because I am Irish, but because the faith is fulfilling for me, and I enjoy partaking on a regular basis. So while we both acknowledge and appreciate our faith, we both follow different methods of practice.

Religion and language are two major aspects of the French Canadian culture. Charlotte is bilingual, I am not. There are certainly more francophones who have learned English than there are anglophones who can converse in French. It would appear that we both fit our cultural moulds in this regard. However, the French are accused of forcing their language on the non-French. It appears quite the opposite to me.

To date I have made several attempts to learn French with little success. Perhaps it is just too difficult for my simple mind, or more likely, I do not regard having two languages as a tool for survival. Charlotte does. Not only does she see the French language as an important tool in conjunction with English, but also as a preservation of her cultural heritage. She is proud of her ability to communicate in both languages and recognizes the advantages of these two languages not only here in Canada, but also for worldwide travel.

While Charlotte's views reflect the practical, the majority of her group regard the situation from a political standpoint—that French is one of two founding languages in this country and both should be spoken and understood by all, for a bilingual Canada.

We both appear to hold education in high regard as we are presently pursuing new careers through community college. It appears I am following a cultural behaviour shared by my society—that of furthering my education. The fact that the government's financial assistance encourages people like Charlotte and I to further our skills indicates the cultural similarity.

One other area worth of discussion is that of politics. Clearly our most obvious differences are those I am discussing in this paper. While we both are opposed to separatism, our knowledge and awareness of the Québec struggle and Canadian politics in general differ greatly, myself being the more ignorant of the topic at hand. Charlotte was able to cite Bill numbers and significant political dates, and could make quick references to names of importance because of her culture. Their struggle for distinct recognition throughout Canada plays a major role in their culture and Charlotte's political know-how is not uncharacteristic. I, on the other hand, fit my culture's mould to the tee. Because I am a member of the majority, English and White, I feel I have no need to

Cultural customs are passed through families, but these customs change over generations.

strive for recognition and pay little heed to the political world around me. This is nothing to be proud of, but certainly noteworthy and definitely a cultural norm.

Certainly we share more similarities than differences, partly because we are both White and both speak English. Despite our different methods of practising our faith, the fact that we are both Catholics plays an important role in shaping our values. As for our differences, they appear to stem from religion and language, two of the major cultural traits of the French Canadian.

Paul: *"I was, and for the most part still am, politely racist…"*

White Canadians vs. Black Canadians: an interesting title for an essay. It came about somewhat through my interviews with some Black Canadians. It mostly came from the person within me. Someone who has never shown his face on paper before. Someone I am ashamed to have as a part of me. That someone is a bigot.

This paper is supposed to show the differences and similarities that I as a White Canadian share with my Black Canadian counterparts. What makes White Canadians different from Black Canadians? Well, I think there is a problem with that question. Why should there be any difference, other than the colour of one's skin? The simple fact is that there is. So, let me also ask why are they different.

When told that we were researching Black Canadians, I can't say that I was overly enthusiastic about the whole idea. I was, and for the most part still am, politely racist. When interviewing them, I found them to be polite and eager to help but at the same time they were very non-committal. Maybe I'm being paranoid, or maybe I'm superimposing my own faults onto those of the Black Canadian, but I couldn't help but think that those whom I was interviewing were hiding something from me. I felt the tension in their voices and they seemed to be very careful in the words that they chose when speaking.

I interviewed a man named Trevor who was originally from South Africa. Trevor and I are very different. First, and foremost, he is very dark black and I am very white. Aside from our obvious physical differences, his whole life (e.g. his schooling, the way he was brought up, the foods he eats, the clothes he wears) has been nothing like my own. Trevor is a computer programmer, as am I. The more we talked, the more I came to realize that we are alike in many ways, too. The ways in which we are alike aren't as superficial as what kind of clothes we wear or how we grew up, but on a deeper plain. Our goals, for instance, are very similar. Career advancement, buying a home, getting married to someone; but aren't these the goals of most Canadians, regardless of race, creed or colour? Of course they are, and that's what I came to realize.

While I came upon my revelation, I learned a few things about myself that I didn't really want to know. First of all, that I think I am a bigot and secondly, that I am probably a White supremacist too. Strong words indeed, but not without basis. Don't get me wrong, I am definitely not proud of my last comment, it was just something I had to admit.

If I hold a prejudice against a racial group, I am a bigot, so says the Oxford Dictionary. It goes on to say that a stereotype is an idea or character that is standardized in a conventional form without individuality. If I laugh at a joke that uses a Black for its punchline, because I associate a stereotype with what has been said, I am a bigot. For example: "What do you call a Black guy in a new car? A thief." Funny, eh? No, the joke itself is not funny, but it makes reference to a stereotype about Blacks that they're all thieves, which I do find funny. Does bigotry come in varying degrees? I think it must. Although I would chuckle on the inside to the preceding joke, I find it hard to say anything bad about Black Canadians in public and stick up for them when comments are made in particularly bad taste. An example of this was not too long ago when a co-worker recited this joke: "What do you call a busload of Blacks going over a cliff with one empty seat? A crying shame." That kind of joke is not funny. It does not point our a funny stereotype of a certain race à la Newfie jokes, it is pure malice and cruelty against a specific group. The fact that it was Blacks mattered little. Am I a bigot? I don't know what I am any more.

A White supremacist, though? I think so, sometimes. When sitting with Trevor, he pointed out a few ways in which prejudice had bee used against him since coming to Canada. Among them are the same prejudices shared by most Black Canadians: finding suitable housing, finding a truly non-discriminatory workplace and striving for equality in almost every aspect in everyday life. For some reason though, when he grieved about having trouble finding a job, I secretly found happiness in that. I found a way in which I was superior to him because I felt that I could find another job at any time without too much difficulty. I felt that if it came down to him or me for a job, I would be certain to get the job, knowing the way society is. On the same token, I am a very competitive person. I often search out other people's faults and use them to my advantage when I can. I often make my job appear to be a more challenging position when comparing it to another's job and can always fall back on my large salary to dominate over another. I often lie to make a point and won't hesitate to point out faults in others to improve my position over them. This is not a confession, just a statement to alleviate myself from thinking I'm a White supremacist. So have I done a good job? Do I still think I'm a White supremacist? I really don't know what to think any more.

Trevor and I talked a lot about how he had been prejudiced against and by whom. As the conversation progressed, some hostility came out in his voice about certain groups, including Whites. This automatically put me on the defensive, and I started to defend the White person's position more and more. He made me feel as though I don a white cape and mask on the weekends or something. He was obviously upset about the way he had been treated at times, but I didn't know whether he was mad at me because I was born White, at himself because he was born Black or at society because it mattered. I chose the latter. As for myself, I am happy that I was born White, but don't feel I should be prejudiced against just because I was. I now see that this is how Trevor feels as well. So, this is not a Black Canadian's point of view, but one shared by all humans.

There is no reason whatsoever that anyone in Canada should be prejudiced against. I think I find fault in others to make myself seem a little bit better than they are. I think this competitive spirit within me is human nature and will not stop. I think discrimination against others based on their sex, race, creed or colour is something that is superimposed on us by authority figures and the media while we are young.

After talking with Trevor, I felt guilty for thinking that we were different or should be treated differently by society. I am confused about how I am supposed to feel about someone of another race. If I use a stereotype to describe them, how accurate am I being? I mean women still can't drive, but are all Blacks thieves and is this in good taste? I don't understand my role in society any more and am almost embarrassed about my whiteness when not in a White majority situation.

I think White Canadians and Black Canadians are very similar in almost all regards. We eat alike, we dress much the same, our tastes in music is not all that different. We even suffer from the same identity crises that society has placed us in, just in opposite corners.

Mark: *"Is there only one normal way of life?..."*

As I sat waiting to interview my friend Dave, I attempted to foreshadow his replies. Dave and I are very good friends, yet we have totally different backgrounds. I am a Canadian Conservative Jew, and he is a Roman Catholic Italian Canadian. Although our ethnic differences are tremendous, we tend to share many similar views on a wide variety of topics such as marriage, having children, and prejudice found in the working force and daily life. However, because of our dissimilar backgrounds, we hold opposing views on issues like family relations and religion.

Is there only one normal way of life, a pattern, a single direction that is decided for everyone to follow, or is each individual required to discover his personal lifestyle? When discussing our ideas, one dominant issue emerged—marriage. Dave has just recently become engaged. For myself, marriage has never been an option—I have never considered not getting married. In the Jewish religion, one of the most highly regarded and holy events is the joining of two individuals in the bond of marriage. I feel as if it is a prerequisite to a fulfilling life, as does the Roman Catholic church.

Dave does not deviate from this aspect of his ethnic group, although he does not see himself as a religious individual. We have both been socialized to marry one day in order to proceed with a normal way of life. From our separate family lives to our religious upbringing, marriage is considered a security to provide us with the strength to achieve future goals. I can remember as a child sitting in synagogue hearing the rabbi relate tales of the ceremonious marriages recorded in the Bible which, in turn, created the Jewish religion as well as many other religions.

As Dave grew up, he learned the beliefs pertaining to a Roman Catholic Italian and I learned of those which relate to me as a Jew. At the age of 23, Dave now views religion as being "very misleading, hypocritical, and no longer spiritual." He also feels it is too judgmental. Dave's parents were strict about following the laws and customs of his ancestors and passed them on to him. When Dave reached an age when he questioned why his parents did the things they did, the reasons were never explained to him. For Dave, the laws and customs remained his parents' ways and never truly became his own. Because of this, Dave does not feel any bonds with the Roman Catholic ways and, therefore, does not practise the customs at all, other than attending church twice a year to please his parents.

I must admit that I feel differently. As I was growing up, I attended a school on Sundays for two hours where I learned about the laws and customs my parents practised at home. At this school, many of my

Cultures do not develop without a high degree of co-operation and trust among members.

questions were answered. I have established a strong value for my religion. I have acquired values and ideas from my religion and have not disregarded the beliefs of my ancestors. I feel that is important to learn about one's background from a view that only a religious outlook can provide. Although I would not say that I follow the laws and customs of the Jewish religion strictly, I intend to pass on my knowledge to my children and provide them with the option to choose how religious they would like to be—as my parents have done for their children.

When we approached the subject of having a family, I felt there were going to be discrepancies. I have always looked forward to having at least two kids. Although having children is an individual decision, my strong family ties and my religion have played a large part in making that choice.

I believe I follow the norm which is wished to be carried out in both Judaism and Catholicism; however, Dave has deflected from the norm by not intending to have children. He feels it is a personal preference. He states that if he did choose to have a family of his own, among the prerequisites would be a mother who is willing to remain at home with the children, financial stability, and a strong relationship with his spouse.

Comparing our lives made me aware of the apparent differences which influence such a decision. Dave drifted away from his parents as he rebelled to establish his own identity. It was difficult for him to follow his parents' strict ways and abide by laws of the Roman Catholic religion which his parents follow closely. By understanding Dave's reasons, I am able to empathize with his feelings on this topic. Since his decision has been influenced by an unhappy upbringing and mine by one of happiness, it is evident as to why we hold different views.

As we are both Caucasian, neither of us has ever experienced prejudice based on colour; however, we have each experienced one form of prejudice or another because we are members of minority groups, Italian and Jewish. Dave feels that his surname is a cause of prejudice. His surname is very "Italian." When hearing such a name, or reading it on an application, people may immediately impose stereotypical views upon him. Such a factor may not seem relevant; however, when an employer is reviewing dozens of applications, every detail on that application is crucial information which forms an overall impression. At times, a name may destroy a chance to acquire a particular job if the employer is prejudiced.

The Jews have been discriminated against for as long as I can remember and are often victims of stereotypical views. Coming from minority groups has possibly contributed to our deep annoyance regarding this issue. Both of us refuse to judge people for what they are rather than who they are. Personally, I feel that there is not one person I have met in my 22 years who is without a single fault. If everyone dwells on each other's bad points, everyday life would be miserable for everyone. We live in an imperfect world.

It is very hard to relate Dave's behaviour and beliefs to his being Italian Roman Catholic. His ancestors came to Canada four generations ago and therefore, he feels absolutely no ties to Italy. He views himself as a Canadian. Dave feels that since his parents are Roman Catholic then he must be as well, although, as stated previously, Dave does not believe in his religion.

I, too, feel that I am more a Canadian than anything else. My final question to Dave was, "If someone were to stop you on the street and ask what your ethnic background and religion are, what would you answer?" He replied, "I would say I am a Canadian but if you were to go back and look at my ancestors, you would find that I am of Italian Roman Catholic descent."

Through much examination of Judaism and Roman Catholicism, I have attempted to understand the reasons behind the similarities along with the differences among different ethnic groups. In conclusion, one's ethnic group sets standards and provides direction for each individual member of that group. One's behaviour, derived from the values and ideas that one learns, reflects the amount one has diversified from the pattern set out for them and forms each person's lifestyle.

Sarah: *"Discrimination is something that I have never faced..."*

My subject's name is Mary. She was born in Hong Kong and immigrated to Canada with her parents and her brother and sister in the late sixties when she was still a young child. Her family eventually settled in the Brampton-Bramalea area. They were one of the first Chinese families in town. Today, Mary is studying engineering at an Ontario university. Now that Mary's basic background has been established, how does the fact that Mary is Chinese affect her values, attitudes and beliefs?

I asked Mary what she thought she valued most in her life. Her response was her family. In my opinion (and Mary agreed with me) this great respect for family in general, and for parents specifically, is a trait common to most Chinese. Children are taught from their youngest days that they must respect their elders for they have an obligation to them. Anything the children may do or achieve at any time in their lives is a reflection first upon the parents and then on the child. Mary feels that while there is a great reverence towards the parents, the parent-child bond is usually an emotionally distant one. Again, this distance can be attributed to the child's upbringing. They are taught to mask their emotions, to be stoic and hold all feelings in, for emotions can make one vulnerable to others.

Commenting on the fact that most Chinese people work in fields such as business, engineering, math, and sciences, Mary believes it is because these are all fields in which emotions, for the most part, play no part. These positions would be ruled by the head, as the saying goes, and not the heart. Therefore, because the Chinese believe that emotions should be restricted, it would make sense that they should prefer these jobs rather than positions in such fields as the arts.

Closely related to the issue of respect for parents and elders is the view of marriage. Mary's view of marriage is in accordance with my understanding of the "typical Chinese" attitude towards this institution. Marriage is not to be entered into lightly—it is a serious matter. In the past, most marriages were arranged; however, Mary doesn't hold to this view. She believes in marrying for love.

In the union of marriage [in Mary's view], there are different roles for men and women. The man is the master, the breadwinner and the decision maker. The woman's prime duty is to serve the husband and to provide and take care of the children. Although Mary is spending a great deal of time, money and energy on her education, as soon as she marries she will commit herself to this role of a dutiful wife.

Interracial marriage is definitely frowned upon. The reasoning behind this is that if a person were to marry a non-Chinese, that person would be an outsider and would cause problems and strife within the family. This could lead to a break-up of the most important institution, the family. On the night I first called her about the interview, she was involved in a family problem. Her parents had discovered that she was dating a non-Chinese. Mary was forbidden to see him. When I last spoke with Mary, this matter was still not resolved. This incident has caused a great strain in Mary's relationship with her parents, but she doesn't feel that she should have to date only those who are Chinese. However when I questioned Mary further, she said that in all likelihood, the man she marries will be Chinese.

Upon examining my own values and beliefs about similar topics (family and marriage), I found that basically my beliefs are similar to Mary's, but there is a degree of variance. For instance, in my family, there isn't such a rigid set of rules or a demand for respect. There is respect among the members of my family, but it has not been ingrained in me through repetition of proverbs and lectures day after day; rather, it has occurred naturally.

Also in my family, the roles of various members are not so pronounced. Both my parents work, so both are breadwinners and both are caretakers. My mother does not have one set role, neither does my father. Unlike Mary's parents, they cross over between the typical "husband" and "wife" duties.

Another way in which my beliefs differ from Mary's is my view of marriage. I do not believe that the role of the wife is merely to serve the husband. I believe that if the wife wants to work, she most certainly should do so. Mary does not feel it is right for the wife to work outside the home. Inter-racial marriage is something that Mary feels is not for her, even though dating outside of her race is okay in her opinion. I feel that both dating and marrying outside of one's race or ethnicity is acceptable. Normally, being a member of the dominant group, the idea of interracial marriage might never occur to me. However, I dated someone of a different race for several years. Just as Mary's parents frown at the idea of dating/marrying outside of their race, so did my parents. Neither set of parents wanted to risk the weakening of the family structure if it were to be infiltrated by someone with potentially different values and ideas.

Discrimination is something that I, being a member of the dominant group, have never faced but I imagined this might not be the case for Mary. Had she faced any discrimination? When this question was

Although celebrations can teach us much, we need to combine them with critical reflection as well.

posed, Mary's response was a very quick and almost defiant "No!" When pressed further, however, she grudgingly admitted that perhaps in the past there had been discrimination. She feels not only that discrimination shouldn't occur but she maintains that it doesn't. Several statements, such as the previous one, led me to believe that perhaps Mary was trying to deny the existence of discrimination by the use of such blanket thoughts and ideals, such as "everyone should be treated equally" rather than dealing in reality. Mary says that discrimination doesn't exist, and yet I have seen her exhibit prejudice herself. For example, she often makes derogatory comments about other Chinese, she avoids contact with other members of her race and ethnicity, and she actively tried to associate exclusively with members of the White majority.

Mary thinks of herself as Canadian and not as Chinese. However, it is undeniable that Mary's values and beliefs stem from her Chinese background, just as mine have stemmed from my WASP background and upbringing. Whether one chooses to accept it or not, the fact remains that values, ideas and beliefs exist in a causal relationship to one's race, ethnicity and cultural history.

Debbie: *"Initially, physical contrasts cannot be overlooked…"*

One group that constitutes a small but important part of the Canadian population are the Mexican people. Based upon my interaction with Gerardo, a recent immigrant from Mexico, I am now able to draw comparisons between us that are essential before a better understanding of our similarities and differences can be acknowledged.

During our first meeting, our racial differences were quite obvious to both of us. His olive skin and dark hair are noticeably different from my fair complexion. Initially, these physical contrasts cannot be overlooked. Being part of the Canadian White racial majority, I admit that I tend to be somewhat judgmental of people who are racially different. All my life, I have been taught to believe that racial contrasts are indicative of cultures that oppose my own. However, my affiliation with Gerardo has fortunately developed my awareness of this critical and unwarranted perception. I now realize that this ethnocentric viewpoint is overflowing with unnecessary prejudice and discrimination. Although we are different racially, Gerardo and I have much in common.

First of all, our values appear to be the same when analyzing the importance of the family. Gerardo's Mexican background has taught him to value his family members highly, and to treat them with reverence and respect. Similarly, my British ethnicity has been influential in the same way. Like Gerardo, the relationships I have with my parents and siblings are important to me for similar reasons. Consequently, this shared value reflects upon our behaviour. When interacting with family members, we both agree that we are intentionally more patient and compassionate because of their importance to us.

However, this value is not identical in all aspects. When comparing the structure of our families, it became evident to us that the amount of importance we place upon each person within the family unit differs. This disparity appears to have been influenced by our different cultures.

Within the Mexican culture, the mother is the dominant family figure. Mexican people believe that the "woman's" place is at home so that she can raise the children and maintain the household. The mother is the parent who provides authority and support to the children. For all these reasons, Gerardo respects his mother enormously and values his relationship with her.

Contrarily, the relationship I have with my father is more important to me. Within the (British) Canadian culture, the father is still the dominant figure in the household who provides authority and support to the other family members. My own family continues to recognize this traditional role. Consequently, my culture has influenced my feelings of tremendous admiration and respect for my father. Thus, the relationship I have with my father, over any other family member, is the most important to me.

Some differences between Gerardo and myself can definitely be attributed to our different cultural backgrounds. However, this viewpoint in no way affects the corresponding amount of importance we place upon the "family unit" as a whole.

Another similarity between Gerardo and myself is our belief in the work ethic. Success is also highly valued by both of us. However, cultural and ethnic differences have again developed certain variances regarding our individual perceptions of work and success.

Gerardo does not value work for its financial rewards. His ethnic background has taught him to appreciate his job for the stimulation and enjoyment it provides, rather than for the money. It appears that the Mexican culture does not consider financial prosperity to be indicative of individual success. For this reason, he is not overly concerned with his salary. Personal satisfaction with oneself and secure relationships with family and friends are far more important to him.

Unlike Gerardo, my British ethnicity has taught me to believe that one's job is irrelevant if one's pay cheque is substantial because success can be achieved with financial gains. Additionally, my Canadian culture has also been influential in fostering this particular belief.

Consequently, these different attitudes have affected certain aspects of our behaviour. I tend to be far more aggressive and competitive than Gerardo because I want to succeed financially. In contrast, Gerardo is more relaxed and less assertive because financial gain is not a priority for him. Gerardo and I positively agree that these opposing ideas can be attributed to our different ethnic and cultural backgrounds. However, even though our interpretations of success are vastly different, it still remains a value that we both consider to be tremendously important.

In summation, it is fairly obvious how influential our backgrounds have been regarding the development of our individual values, ideas and behaviours. I realize that I have only skimmed the surface of the various similarities and differences that exist between Gerardo and myself. However, in making the comparisons, we have both acquired a better understanding and acceptance of each other, as well as feelings of kinship and mutual respect. Just as importantly, we each gained tremendously valuable insights about ourselves as individuals.

Barbara: *"We both come from cultures where the family is very important..."*

For this essay I interviewed Maya, who has been my friend and neighbour for eighteen years. Maya is a Hindu who was born in Delhi and has lived in Canada since 1960. I am a Canadian Jew who was born in Toronto and I have lived in Canada all my life.

Hinduism is not a rigid religion. Hindus worship many deities and there are many differences among people, villages and families. There are several sacred texts and many Hindus use idols or pictures in their worship. Maya has a prayer room in her home, where she goes to pray and meditate.

Maya worships her guru (teacher) as the highest deity. He leads a very simple life and spends his time in prayer and meditation. Her husband also worships the same guru, and they visit him in India once or twice a year for lengthy periods of time. She hopes that one day she will be able to emulate his lifestyle. Maya does not attend a temple, because she feels that she does not need a temple to practise her religion.

She believes in reincarnation. A person who leads a holy life is reborn as a better person, and so on until the soul reaches the ultimate, a state which her guru has reached. Maya also believes in an omnipresent God, with which the perfected soul lives in intimate and perpetual contact. Since her guru has reached the ultimate, his soul will be released to God when he dies.

My impression has always been that Maya's religion is very important to her and that it is a very private and very personal part of her life. Her religion also has a quality that is quite foreign to my thoughts and feelings. In contrast to the idols and polytheism of Hinduism, Judaism is a monotheistic religion which does not permit the use of idols in worship. The sacred text for all Jews is the Torah, which like the texts Maya worships (the Ramayana and the Bhagavidgita) was written by many scholars.

I am not a practising Jew; I have not believed in God since I was a teenager. Even though I was raised in a traditional home, I became an atheist. I think that this happened because I do not need a god to live a satisfying life. Being an atheist also means, that unlike Maya, I have no deity to turn to for advice or solace, and must depend mainly on my own inner resources.

Just as there are many different ways of being a Hindu, there are also many different ways of being a Jew. Even among the three main subgroups of Judaism, there are many individual variations. Also, like

Hindus, Jews are usually born into their religion, although both religions accept converts.

The central tenet of Judaism is to be a good person. However, there is no institutionalized system of rewards and punishment; Judaism believes that reward and punishment essentially come from within the person. Judaism teaches that goodness is reward enough and that, while a wicked person may appear to go unpunished, being bad is sufficient punishment in itself. Because of the emphasis on being a good person, people who make a contribution to society have always been highly regarded among Jews. I have always been attracted to work I consider to be socially useful.

Unlike Maya, I do not believe in an afterlife. There is no well-developed concept of Heaven or Hell in Judaism; Jews seem to be mainly occupied with this life. Since there is no afterlife, Jews believe that it is important to do one's best in this life.

I do not know how widespread the degree of asceticism practised by my friend's guru is among Hindus. As far as I know, it does not exist among Jews, and certainly it was never a part of my life and thought. There are a few Jewish rabbis and scholars who spend a great deal of time studying the Torah. However, this type of learning does not seem to have a high priority among Jewish people. While they value a good education, it is a secular education that is highly prized because an educated person can lead a richer life and can contribute more to society.

In spite of her high regard for her guru's lifestyle, Maya takes great pride in her home and her possessions. She readily admits this, but considers it a weakness that she must try to overcome. For me, as for most Jews, the acquisition of worldly possessions and comforts is highly desirable and a legitimate reward for hard work.

Both Maya and her husband speak Hindi as their first language and that is the language they use within the family. Both their children speak Hindi well and the family has made many trips to India, where most of their relatives live. During these visits, both children were taught to read and write Hindi, and both can do so fairly well. However, outside their home both children speak only English and also have a fairly good command of French.

Maya thinks that it is unlikely that her children will speak Hindi to their children. While her children enjoy visiting India and feel comfortable there, they both regard Canada as their home. For Maya, however, there is a strong possibility that she will eventually return to India. She says that while her mind has accepted Canada, her heart is still in India.

In contrast, both my husband and I were born in Canada and English is the only language we speak. Unlike other non-English speaking minority groups, Jews in Canada have never had a language to pre-serve. Most of them came from Eastern Europe and had no wish to speak the languages of the countries that most of them despised. However, I do envy people who are fluent in more than one language, because I feel that it adds richness and colour to a person's life.

Unlike many members of other minority groups in Canada, Jews have had no wish to return to their countries of origin, and would not have been welcome if they had returned. With no language or country to call their own, Canadian Jews have been only too eager to learn English and to adopt Canadian customs and habits. Unlike Maya's family, we spent most of our holidays travelling Canada and the United States.

Like most Jews, I feel not only a strong loyalty to Canada, but also an enormous sense of gratitude that my parents and grandparents immi-grated to Canada. While I have never wanted to live in Israel, I do support a Jewish homeland as a haven for Jews.

Maya and I both come from cultures where the family is very impor-tant. While Maya has raised her children to be aware of and appreciate Indian culture, she understands that in an open society doing this may create difficult choices for her children since they wish to remain in Canada. In contrast, I have had to make the type of choices that Maya's children are making. My children, in turn, accept without ques-tion that they may choose freely from the many lifestyles that Canada has to offer.

Since neither Maya nor I need the support system of an organized religion, we have never found it necessary or even desirable to live in an area where there are large concentrations of people from our own ethnic groups. Her children and mine have had the opportunity to grow up with children from many different ethnic groups.

Like myself, the only prejudice that Maya has encountered has been the occasional remark. Because I do not have a Jewish name and I do not "look Jewish," people occasionally make anti-Semitic remarks in my presence. In spite of these minor expressions of prejudice, we both feel comfortable in Canada and have friends from many backgrounds. Overall, we have great respect for the British cultural base on which English-speaking Canada is built.

We were surprised at the similarity of our attitudes on abortion, divorce, heritage language classes, affirmative action programs, refugees, intermarriage and capital punishment. I think that there are several reasons why Maya and I share so many of the same views despite our different backgrounds. We both belong to ethnic groups that have become integrated into Canadian society and have assumed positions of leadership in many areas. Our religions allow for many differences; and we have experienced the many social changes that have occurred here.

In my long and close association with Maya we have both found our similarities were far deeper and far more important than our differences.

Jackie: *"Because I have not experienced such hate I cannot understand how he felt..."*

The religion that has always interested me the most is the Jewish religion, but I wondered if it is solely a religion, or both a religion and a culture. I interviewed David, 38. When I met him I distinctly remember saying to myself that he looked Jewish. I must confess that I followed the stereotype that Jewish people have dark hair and a big nose. It was my first experience meeting a Jewish person and I was terribly ignorant about his religion and his ethnicity. Thank goodness he has a sense of humour.

David is Canadian-born but his grandparents emigrated from Russia during the Russian Revolution. David considers himself a second generation Jewish-Canadian of Russian descent. David also believed that his religion and ethnicity were the same. I explained to him that I was Scottish-Canadian but my ethnicity was Scottish. He still believed that his religion and cultural background were one, as his family never had strong ties with Russia. I argued his point and reminded him that although I was primarily brought up in Canada I still was a product of a Scottish upbringing and that likewise, he must have some Russian influences in his life. He disagreed. David also believes that the Jewish people consider themselves an ethnic group. He tried to explain to me that because the Jewish people never had a true homeland until 1948 and were from different countries, they joined together as one. I am still having difficulty understanding this, but David truly believes it.

I was born in Scotland in 1962 and as a family we immigrated to Canada in 1966. Although the Canadian culture has been a great influence on my behaviour, I still consider myself to be Scottish. I take great pride in my ethnic background as well as great pride in being Canadian.

David was brought up in a small town community in Northern Ontario where his family were the only Jews. The rest of the community was made up of French Canadians and Anglo-Saxons. This experience was a major influence on his behaviour as an adult, and a factor in how he feels about himself today. He vividly remembers the neighbours making comments to his parents that they had known a Jew once, or that they had never met a Jew before. As a child he felt this to be disconcerting as he was made to feel different than the other kids.

I never had that problem growing up in an Anglo-Saxon middle-class neighbourhood. I was never made to feel I was different or that I had to prove myself to fit in. But David seems to have experienced this kind of judgment most of his life. Once, when he was six years old, a young boy came up to him in the park and called him a "dirty Jew."

Without showing any anger he turned around and called the boy a "stupid peacock." I could not see the comparison at first, but David went on to explain that the other children laughed at the other boy more because they did not understand what a "dirty Jew" was but they knew that a peacock was a bird. He walked away from that situation learning a great lesson—that he should not listen to silly names like that but that he should feel comfortable with himself and his religion. I found the story sad but David laughs about it. I guess because I have not experienced such hate I cannot understand how he felt.

David feels that his strong family upbringing has helped him feel secure with himself and his life. His family taught their children that they had the freedom of choice to do with their life what they wished. His interpretation of success is an outcome of his family's philosophy. He sets his own goals which in turn are measured only by himself. He has no desire to "keep up with the Jones" and I can only wish that I could have that kind of outlook on success.

I feel that I am always under pressure to succeed. When my parents moved to Canada, they dreamed of giving their children a better life, including education, cultural experiences, etc. That is a hard thing to live up to. I am envious of David's philosophy but am not sure why there is this difference. It could be because my family, when living in Scotland, was lower-class, while David's family have been in the middle-class for several generations.

David's Jewish culture influenced him greatly until he left home at 25. When he moved into the Toronto work force, he felt that it was no

Role models are essential if we are to present career possibilities to young Canadians.

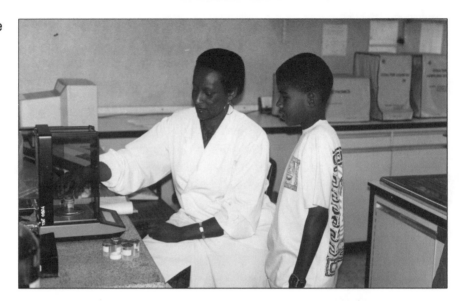

longer necessary to practise his religious beliefs or traditions until he had his own children. He believes strongly in his faith but does not feel it necessary to go to the synagogue weekly to prove to others that he believes.

I have no substantial religious background. My grandparents were Catholic but no longer believe. My parents felt it was my choice to decide if I was to be baptized or not. I sometimes envy the religion that David grew up in because it seems to strengthen a person. I guess I will always feel that I have missed out on something. David feels it is very important to educate his children about their religious roots as it gives them the pride in their culture, which he feels is an important part of a healthy upbringing.

There are many Scottish traditions that my family still follows such as Robbie Burns Day, [eating] Haggis and the wearing of the Kilt on special occasions. We still believe in many superstitions that have been passed on through generations. We feel this bonds us to our ethnic background, but David thinks differently. He describes two kinds of traditions: timeless traditions, such as the family unit, and traditions that do not apply any more, such as only marrying Jewish women to preserve the "race." It is ironic, but he admits that this tradition is a perfect example of discrimination. David feels that the Jewish religion and traditions go hand in hand. He feels times are changing and so must traditions; but religion must stay intact.

I have always had a strong work ethic that I believe was the outcome of my strict upbringing to succeed, but I sometimes push myself too hard and end up not enjoying what I do for a living. But this can also be a motivating factor, as it pushes me towards more education, which in turn can give me a brighter future. David believes that doing a job well and enjoying it is all that matters. He is an engineer for a large manufacturing company and admits that although money is important to him, he would not do a job just for the money. My family has always put great importance on how much money someone makes. I tend to go along with David's philosophy over my parents'.

David feels his family and religion gave him his first moral footing but he also felt his peers had been a greater influence on him. My strong moral beliefs were definitely an outcome of my family's teachings. I found it odd that I had no religious background and yet my morals and values were just as strong as those of a person who came from a strict religious background. For some reason I always felt that a religious person would have stronger morals than I, but now I can see that this is not the case. I must say I feel good about learning this.

David celebrates Christmas in the same spirit as I celebrate Thanksgiving—not in the religious sense, but as traditions and an opportunity to get together with family and friends.

"Through education at an early age, children should be taught about the different cultures that exist in Canada. They should be taught the differences and the similarities of these cultures and then we will probably see that there are so many more similarities than differences." This was a most profound statement David made when we were discussing discrimination.

I cannot say that I have been discriminated against because of my Scottish ethnicity, but possibly because of my sex (female). Never has my ethnic background been held against me or stopped me from doing something I had set out to do. David cannot say the same. Before he admits to being discriminated against, he admits quite freely that he discriminates against others. I was quite shocked, as most people feel uncomfortable admitting this. David feels that he can sense if a person is discriminatory by nature, and in turn discriminates against that person. Not in action, but by sitting in judgement. He admits that if a person doesn't live up to his standards he has no time for them. He hates this aspect of his behaviour and does try to change it, but he has come to terms with why he thinks this way.

He still feels that he sometimes has to prove himself twice over to be accepted by the majority. In university he hung around solely with Italians because he felt that he did not have to prove himself and that he could relate to their faith and strong upbringing. He felt he did not have to waste his time on people who judged others on their religious or ethnic background. He is fortunate that his parents gave him the confidence and strength to walk away from the ignorance of others. But he admits that perhaps these experiences of discrimination have made him discriminate against others. David's family believes in "an eye for an eye."

I have never been discriminated against. Neither I nor my family have ever felt this direct hatred from others, so how can I possibly begin to understand what people who are discriminated against feel. Anger? Hatred? Or an eye for an eye? I mentioned to David that seeking revenge on others who hurt you can only cause war, but if you turn the other cheek, things may pass. He is quite stubborn in this belief, although he admits it is not always the right way.

I believe David's strength and security is an outcome of having to fight for what he wanted and of keeping his head high when someone passed a racist comment. I respect him for handling the situation as he has. I believe because I have had a lot of things handed to me throughout my life and never been ridiculed, it has made me a weaker person emotionally than David—not that I want the anger he has experienced, but if I could experience some, it may make me appreciate myself more and allow me to conquer my fears.

It was difficult to think of other significant differences. Religion is an obvious difference. But I am not sure if it is a significant one—I had a strong, close family unit. There is our difference of interpretation when we talk of success. But I would think that had more to do with economic status and social class rather than culture. Obviously there are dietary differences and traditional differences, but I do not think these differences are significant in shaping our behaviours.

There are many similarities. I would not have thought this, being as naive as I was about the Jewish culture. Beliefs about education are the same. Our work ethics are similar. The family is the most important entity in both our lives. Both our homes are always open to friends and those in need. We are both honest and open-minded people.

If everyone in this country could do a report on a culture and recognize that there are far more similarities than differences among cultures, our country would be a lot better off. So would the children of tomorrow, who may yet be ridiculed and teased, who may grow up unsure about themselves in a country they call home.

Doug: *"I was able to tap information from this person who had been through so much..."*

Tsung, 25, is a Vietnamese refugee who fled Vietnam with most of his family in 1979. Now the family runs a small corner grocery store. They have assimilated into the community quite well and are liked by their neighbours.

Tsung's parents are Catholics from the southern part of Vietnam. He, in turn, was raised as a Catholic and has plans of bringing up any children he may have in the Catholic faith. Tsung's immediate family is of extreme importance to him. Having seen what war is like and what it can do to otherwise well-disciplined and civilized people, Tsung leaves no doubt about his sincerity. The family is a tightly-knit unit that shares just about everything.

I mentioned to him that in my family, individuals keep many of their problems, especially emotional ones, to themselves. Tsung summed up his situation neatly by saying that because his family had faced death so many times in Vietnam, the family became closer; and once they were free of Vietnam, they felt a moral obligation to help each other overcome any obstacle. Although I know my parents love me, in my family, to come out and say things of that nature is considered unnecessary. I feel intimacy is lacking in my family. There is a degree of feeling ashamed or embarrassed to say that you love or care for someone. Tsung claims these tensions or apprehensions just do not exist in his family. He explained that a family that has been through hell and back like his just cannot have those problems.

Tsung and his family celebrate all the holidays that Canadians do and also many of the traditional Vietnamese holidays. Although Christmas is associated with happiness and sharing, it also holds an element of grief for them. One of Tsung's older brothers defected to the North Vietnamese army one Christmas Eve and Tsung has heard from him only twice. Christmas gift giving, according to Tsung, is very personal and done with the utmost sincerity. In my family, gift giving is just something that is done. My brother buys me something so as not to feel guilty; I, in turn, buy him something.

Tsung was not very surprised to hear that I do not attend church. He informed me that if he did not go to church every Sunday and pray that he felt guilty. I asked why he felt he needed to be in church, specifically on Sunday, to pray. The question seemed to catch him off guard. He finally answered that his parents do, so he does. He never really questioned going to church, it was just something that people did. I suggested that the Good Lord was there, 24 hours a day, and all one had to do was talk and He would listen. I also insisted that one did not have to be dressed to the nines to talk to God; that if I wanted, I could talk to Him in the shower, while I was changing the oil in my car, or just about any time or place. As long as I was sincere in my thoughts, they would be heard. Tsung seemed perplexed at the simplicity of my statement as if he expected me to become more technical at any moment. He confessed that my thoughts were worth examining, but maintained that he would still attend church every Sunday.

I asked what he thought about communism and I was quite surprised to hear that he accepts it. He personally does not care for it but accepts it nonetheless. This acceptance of communism became more understandable to me as he explained his version of why North Vietnam would wage war for thirty years to rid itself and the rest of the country of capitalism. Why, he asked, should anybody want to live in poverty all their lives, be worked to the bone in their own country, only to see the fruits of their labour line the pockets of the French land and factory owners? He believes that the North Vietnamese had the right idea when they wanted the French out of the country, but it saddens him to see that they turned to the Soviet Union for help. After hearing Tsung's version, I have to confess that I agree with him 100 percent. If I were to grow up in the conditions that Tsung described to me, I think that I would be compelled to do something about it as well.

Tsung mentioned that he has not experienced any racism towards him and his family, but he does admit that he thinks others feel sorry for him. This bothers him to no end because if you feel sorry for someone, he explains, that gives the notion that nothing can be done to help the individual, that the situation is hopeless, and the person is eternally bound in his predicament. Tsung says he does not want anybody feeling sorry for him; instead, he wants them to accept him and his family as they are.

My final question to Tsung was if he had any personal prejudices or if there was a particular type of person he disliked. He answered that he did not, and when I told him that I thought he might be hiding something, he simply repeated his initial statement, and I left it at that.

I came out of the interview feeling satisfied that I was able to tap information from this person who had been through so much, and was quite willing to share his thoughts with me. The man is religious, smart, carries his own thoughts, and his family means more to him than anything on the face of the earth. I only wish that my family was as sincere and devoted towards each other as Tsung's.

SUMMARY

With few exceptions, all the participants stated that while there are differences between themselves and the interviewees, the similarities "were far deeper and far more important than [the] differences." As a result, one person suggested that:

> A respect must be engendered for the differences of our many cultural heritages for it is only in this manner that we can learn from and grow with each other ... Only after a careful examination of a different culture can we begin to see that although we appear dissimilar outwardly, there seems to be a sameness which is only evident if we make a conscious effort to discover each others' individuality within.

Many of the writers were "fascinated" with the discoveries they made. They talked about being able to "now understand some of the feelings," ideas, values and aspirations of the people they interviewed:

> In a way I find it amazing that our [different] backgrounds have led us to pursue the same career ... It was fascinating to share our thoughts and be able to tie them in to our ethnic, cultural and racial backgrounds. Perhaps if more people shared these conversations we may be able to achieve more harmony and understanding of Canada.

Having interviewed some minority group members, these participants gained insight into the disadvantages that minorities experience and their struggle to retain their cultural identity and gain acceptance, particularly from dominant group members.

> In discussing Franco-Ontarians, and perhaps this could be generalized to any other ethnic group living within a different majority ethnic culture, acceptance and definition of differences can become crucial in the preservation of a distinct ethnic identity. Awareness of similar needs by the majority cultural [group] is also crucially important in preserving both cultures.

Racism was seen as one of the unpleasant differences between minority and dominant group members:

> The difference that I saw was not a pleasant one. Both of us [the writer was Anglo-Canadian; the subject a Native Canadian] have to deal with racism but in different ways. Sam has to put up with stereotypes from the Whites, and someday she hopes that things will improve, but there's still a lot of education needed. Whereas, I have to deal with

being a racist at times. I too had my stereotypes about the Native Canadians, but after my interview and research, I had a better insight as to the attitudes and beliefs of the Canadian Indians. I think all people should follow this rule: "Do not judge lest ye be judged."

Questions:

1. To what extent would you say that exposure to another culture or subculture is able to provide insight into our own cultural identity?

2. Is exposure or interaction with other racial or ethnic groups enough to provide insight into the culture of that group?

3. What is your view of those students who believe that they have gained heightened awareness of another person's struggles in our society, simply from having interviewed them?

5

PREJUDICE, RACISM, DISCRIMINATION AND SOCIAL INTERACTIONS

Institutionalized Racism and Canadian History: Notes of a Black Canadian

By Adrienne Shadd

It always amazes me when people express surprise that there might be a "race problem" in Canada, or when they attribute the "problem" to a minority of prejudiced individuals. Racism is, and always has been, one of the bedrock institutions of Canadian society, embedded in the very fabric of our thinking, our personality.

I am a fifth-generation Black Canadian who was born and raised in a small Black farming village called North Buxton, near Chatham, Ontario. North Buxton is a community comprised of the descendants of the famous Elgin Settlement of escaped slaves who travelled the Underground Railroad to freedom in Canada in the 1850s. As a young girl growing up in the fifties and sixties, I became aware of the overt hostility of Whites in the area when we would visit nearby towns. Children would sometimes sneer at us and spit, or call us names. When we would go into the local ice cream parlour, the man behind the counter would serve us last, after all the Whites had been served, even if they came into the shop after us. Southwestern Ontario may as

Researcher and author Adrienne Shadd, specializes in African-Canadian history and culture.

well have been below the Mason-Dixon line in those days. Dresden, home of the historic Uncle Tom's Cabin, made national headlines in 1954 when Blacks tested the local restaurants after the passage of the Fair Accommodation Practices Act and found that two openly refused to serve them. This came as no surprise, given that for years certain eateries, hotels and recreational clubs were restricted to us, and at one time Blacks could only sit in designated sections of movie theatres (usually the balcony), if admitted at all. Yet this particular incident sent shock waves through the nation, embarrassed about such evidence of racial "intolerance" going on in its own backyard.

Somehow, this kind of racism never bothered me. I always felt superior to people who were so blind that they could not see our basic humanity. Such overt prejudice, to my mind, revealed a fundamental weakness or fear. Although, instinctively, I knew that I was not inferior, there was not one positive role model outside our tiny community, and the image of Blacks in the media was universally derogatory. Africans were portrayed as backward heathens in the Tarzan movies we saw, and Black Americans were depicted through the characters of Step 'n Fetchit, Amos 'n Andy, Buckwheat of "Our Gang" fame, or the many maids who graced the television and movie screens in small bit parts. (Black Canadians were virtually non-existent in the Canadian media.) I used to wonder if it could really be true that Black people the world over were as poor, downtrodden, inarticulate and intellectually inferior as the depictions seemed to suggest.

At the age of ten, we moved to Toronto. In the largely White neighbourhood where we lived, I was initially greeted by silent, nervous stares on the part of some children, who appeared afraid of me or at least afraid to confront me openly. Later, as I began to develop an awareness of the Civil Rights and Black Power movements through my readings, certain friends would respond with a frozen silence if I brought up the name of Malcolm X, or, for that matter, the latest soul record on the charts. Looking back, I can see that things ran fairly smoothly as long as the question of race could be ignored, and as long as I did not transgress the bounds of the artificial "colour blindness" under which I was constrained. This, apparently, was the Torontonian approach to race relations.

I share these reminiscences to illustrate the different forms which racism has taken over time, and in varying locales in Canada, whether in the form of overt hostility and social ostracism as in southeastern Ontario, or in the subtle, polite hypocrisy of race relations in Toronto in the sixties.

But how, you may ask, do these personal experiences represent examples of institutionalized racism? Do they not depend on attitudes which vary from individual to individual? Are not our Canadian laws and policies very clear about the fundamental rights of all people to equal treatment and opportunities?

The problem with this line of thinking is that it fails to recognize how powerfully attitudes and behaviour are shaped by the social climate and practices around us. If the only image you have of Black women is derived from the one on your pancake box, then there is something wrong with the media portrayal of racial minorities. If there are no visible minorities in the boardrooms of the corporate world, and few in positions of influence and authority in the work force, this sends a message far more potent than the Human Rights legislation set up to create a more equitable distribution of rewards and opportunities. When generation after generation of school children continue to be taught only about the accomplishments of White Europeans in Canada—mostly men—the myth that this is "traditionally a White country," as I heard a reporter say the other day, will persist, unchallenged.

The selective recording of some historical events and the deliberate omission of others has not been accidental, and they have had far-reaching consequences. Blacks and other people "of Colour" are viewed as recent newcomers, or worse, "foreigners" who have no claim to a Canadian heritage except through the "generosity" of Canadian immigration officials, who "allow" a certain quota of us to enter each year.

But this myth that Canada is a "White" country is insidious because, on the one hand, it is so ingrained in the national consciousness, and on the other hand, so lacking in foundation. There is a tendency to forget that Native peoples were here first; Blacks, first brought as slaves in the 1600s and 1700s, were among the earliest to settle on Canadian soil; the presence of the Chinese is traced to the nineteenth century. If fact, people from a wide variety of races and nationalities helped to build this country. Unfortunately, this reality is not reflected in our school curricula.

The long Black presence and contribution to Canada's development continues to go unacknowledged. People are surprised to learn, for example, that ten percent of the Loyalists who migrated to British North America after the American Revolution were Black. Their descendants, particularly in the Maritimes, have been living in quasi-segregated communities for over 200 years. Blacks were one of the largest groups to enter the country during the nineteenth century when 40-60,000 fugitive slaves and free people "of Colour" sought refuge in Canada West (Ontario) between 1815-1860.

Standard textbooks never mention that in 1734, part of the city of Montréal was burned down by Marie-Joseph Angelique, a Black female slave, when she learned of her impending sale by her slave mistress. Most Canadians are not even aware that slavery existed in this country. Women's history courses fail to acknowledge that the first newspaperwoman in Canada was a Black, Mary Ann Shadd, who edited a paper for fugitives between 1853-1859 in Toronto and later Chatham, Ontario. Heartwarming stories such as that of Joe Fortes, a

Barbadian-born sailor who came to British Columbia in 1885 and subsequently, as the lifeguard of English Bay, taught three generations of young people to swim—such stories are all but forgotten. Fortes is considered a true Canadian hero to those who are still around to remember him, but it seems that many younger British Columbians believe Fortes was a White man. And did any of you know that the term "the real McCoy" was coined after the inventions of a Black man, Elijah McCoy, born in Harrow, Ontario in 1840?[1]

Today's students, Black and White, look to the United States for information regarding the Civil Rights movement, unaware that a gripping saga occurred right here in Ontario. In the forties and fifties, organizations such as the Windsor Council on Group Relations, the National Unity Association of Chatham-Dresden-North Buxton, the Brotherhood of Sleeping Car Porters, and the Negro Citizens' Association of Toronto fought segregation in housing, accommodations and employment, as well as racist immigration laws. Much of the anti-discrimination and human rights legislation that we now take for granted are a direct result of the struggles which these groups waged.

Certainly, these few bits of information alter our perception of what has traditionally been taught in Canadian history textbooks. At the very least, they lead us to question the prevailing assumption that Canada was settled and built strictly by White Europeans. The educational system could be at the forefront in dispelling many of the myths and stereotypes which fuel racist thinking today. Instead, it aggravates the problem by channelling disproportionate numbers of Black children into low-level academic courses and ultimately, dead-end positions in life.

The point I am making is that racism is not simply a phenomenon which afflicts the minds of individuals and causes these individuals to perform discriminatory acts. Racism is something which afflicts an entire society; it is ingrained and reinforced in all the major and minor institutions of the society. Even in the most seemingly "objective" of undertakings, such as the writing of our national history, racism has operated to exclude minority groups from the historical landscape, thus rendering the accomplishments of these minority groups invisible, and therefore insignificant.

---

[1] From his mechanical work on railway engines, McCoy invented a lubrication cup or graphite lubricator used on locomotives. This invention made it unnecessary to stop the machines for oiling, hence saving 7 minutes per 100 miles of travel. Between 1882 and 1940, 45 patents were awarded to McCoy, all but eight pertaining to lubrication devices for heavy machinery.

Second, racism is not something which simply affects its victims in various adverse ways. It also benefits all those against whom it is not directed, by affording certain privileges. Just remember that for every visible minority who is denied a position because of his/her colour there is a majority group member who is awarded that same position because of his/her colour. Many well-intentioned White Canadians fail to recognize that their lifestyle and position in society is based on a system of class and race privilege. Of course, men enjoy additional privileges based on their gender.

Rather than focusing energy on helping the victims of racism, some of these people should examine the problem from the standpoint of their own situations of privilege. Perhaps in this way, more creative solutions to inequality can be initiated in the light of this kind of alternative outlook.[1]

On a more personal level, even the most subtle and polite forms of racism can be detrimental, especially as they affect children. In my own case, when we moved to Toronto I was made to feel different, alien, even though no one specifically referred to my racial origin. It is a feeling which has never fully left me and perhaps explains why to this day I do not feel comfortable in the company of a group of White people. And when some Whites think they are paying Black people a compliment by saying "We don't think of you as Black," as my sister's friends have told her, this is not just a misplaced nicety—it is an insult. We are not seeking "honourary" White status.

Before we as a society can liberate ourselves from the grip of racism, we have to acknowledge that it exists, and that it is not something which has been blown out of proportion; neither is it the figment of some people's imaginations. If we can do this much, we will at least have moved out from under the heavy shroud of self-delusion and deceit. That in itself would be a refreshing step forward.

---

[1] Canadian feminists have been grappling with this issue with limited success in the last few years. White, middle-class women, who have always dominated the movement in terms of leadership and theory, are beginning to realize the necessity of pro-active strategies in ensuring that women from all racial, ethnic, and class backgrounds are represented in every facet of the women's movement. By proactive, I mean strategies which actively recruit women from different backgrounds. In a few instances, they have had to "step down" from their positions of power so that women of colour could take the lead, as was the case during the organizing of International Women's Day 1986, when the theme was "Women Say No to Racism."

Introduction

In her essay, Adrienne Shadd talks of racism as being "not simply a phenomenon which afflicts the minds of individuals and causes these individuals to perform discriminatory acts." She goes on to say that "racism is something that afflicts an entire society; it is ingrained and reinforced in all the major and minor institutions of the society." She cites personal experiences in which individuals showed negative attitudes toward her, and talks about the "derogatory" images of Blacks which are depicted in the media. She also tells about being discriminated against by "the man in the local ice cream parlour who would serve them last, after all the whites had been served; " and about "certain eateries, hotels and recreational clubs" that were restricted to Blacks. Further, she states that in "even in the most seemingly 'objective' of undertakings, such as the writing of our national history, racism has operated to exclude minority groups from the historical landscape, thus rendering their accomplishments invisible, and therefore insignificant."

Shadd uses the word racism as opposed to prejudice—is there a difference? She alerts us to the different forms of racism: individual, institutional and structural. The question is: Is this difference important? Is racism based on individual attitudes? How does racism relate to discrimination?

In this chapter, we will explore these questions in order to: (a) expand on the notion of ethnocentrism, ethnic prejudice, racism and the accompanying issues of stereotyping and discrimination; (b) clarify the difference between prejudice and racism, and between the different forms of racism; and (c) present class participants' experiences and their suggested possibilities of elimination.

Ethnocentrism

It is very common, and indeed quite normal, for a person to use his or her knowledge and experience to evaluate another and thus impose a set of expectations. This practice, however, often leads to ethnocentrism, in which we operate on the notion that everyone in our society, irrespective of racial and ethnic background, should "speak like us," "live like us," and "participate in all the same activities as us."

Ethnocentrism refers to the tendency to see things from the point of view of your own (sub-)culture, and to position your cultural symbols as being somehow preferable. It can also mean assuming that what is true of your (sub-)culture is also true of other cultures (Carroll, 1987: 22). Ethnocentrism, then, can be seen as an uncompromising allegiance and loyalty to one's own (sub-)cultural values and practices as natural, normal, and necessary.

It might appear harmless to think that the (sub-)culture of one's group is preferable. Problems arise, however, when individuals establish expectations based on this assumption, and begin to use their cultural "standards" as a frame of reference for interpreting and evaluating the behaviour of other groups. Elliott and Fleras (1992) point out: "Not surprisingly, these groups are rated inferior, backward, or irrational. It can be seen that although favouritism towards one's own group can promote cohesion and morale, it can also contribute to intergroup tension and hostility ... [and] to a proliferation of stereotypes about outgroup members" (p. 55).

Prejudice

Over time, the word prejudice has come to mean an unfavourable attitude based on uninformed judgement (Haas and Shaffir, 1978: 24), or having preconceived opinions which are assumed to be true before having been tested (Driedger, 1989: 350). Elliot and Fleras (1992) define prejudice as a set of biased and generalized beliefs (stereotypes) about outgroups derived largely from inaccurate and incomplete information. It "involves that attitudinal component of identity formation, boundary maintenance, and intergroup relations." These faulty and inflexible generalizations contribute to a frame of mind which makes it difficult to evaluate minority groups "in an impartial, objective, and accurate manner" (p. 335).

The word bias is often substituted for prejudice. While biases can be both positive and negative, ethnic prejudice is usually a negative attitude. It is an unfounded, irrational, rigid judgement involving emotions, attitudes and subjective evaluation. Typically, such attitudes, predispositions or pre-judgments are not reversed or changed, even when new information is revealed.

The tendency to categorize and make pre-judgements may be seen as necessary since the human mind needs to organize the stimuli with which it is bombarded. We need to select and store only some of the many experiences and "facts" available in order to effectively react or respond to them. As we acquire new experiences and information we tend to assimilate them as much as possible into the categories that have already been formed. This enables us to identify related objects and retrieve information quickly (Driedger, 1989).

Depending on the experiences of a particular individual, this clustering or categorization will involve some degree of emotion. A person may feel more negative about some experiences and related persons than others. Some categories are more rational than others, but the process permits human beings to slip easily into ethnic prejudice. Erroneous generalizations are sometimes made and, indeed, some categories may reflect not merely feelings of dislike, but feelings of actual hostility. And, while social distance from others may be the result of a desire to maintain a separate ethnic identity, it can also stem from negative attitudes (Driedger, 1986).

RACISM

Racism is the uncritical acceptance of a negative social definition of a colonized or subordinate group typically identified by physical features (i.e. race—black, brown, yellow, red). These "racialized groups"[1] are believed to lack certain abilities or characteristics, which in turn characterizes them as culturally and biologically inferior. This is often how discriminatory or unequal treatment towards these groups is legitimized or justified. Elliott and Fleras (1992) define racism as "a doctrine that unjustifiably asserts the superiority of one group over another on the basis of arbitrarily selected characteristics pertaining to appearance, intelligence, or temperament" (p. 52). In his definition, van den Burghe (1967) identifies the link between race and racism. He refers to racism as "an ideology which considers a group's unchangeable physical characteristics to be linked in a direct causal way to physical or intellectual characteristics, and which on this basis distinguishes between superior and inferior racial groups."

Ng (1993) refers to racism as "common sense" or a "taken-for-

---

[1] Racialization refers to fact that social significance is attached to the physical differences, i.e., skin colour, of these groups (Satzewich, 1991). In the Americas generally, and Canada in particular, the first group of people to be "racialized" were the Aboriginals. This was part of the process of colonialization.

If we don't work
to stop racism,
who will?

granted" way of thinking which can be incoherent and at times contradictory. She contends that conceptualizing racism, like sexism, in terms of common sense draws "attention to the norms and forms of actions that have become ordinary ways of doing things, of which we have little consciousness, so that certain things 'disappear from the social surface'." Quoting Himani Bannerji, Ng continues: "racism becomes an everyday and 'normal' way of seeing. Its banality and invisibility is such that it is quite likely that there may be entirely 'politically correct' white individuals who have a deeply racist perception of the world" (p. 52).

What is most salient in the way in which racism is conceptualized is not the biological or physical differences between the groups but "the public recognition of these differences as being significant for assessment, explanation, and interaction" (Elliot and Fleras, 1992: 55). A key component of racism is power, not in terms of the "everyday" influence one individual might have over another, but influence that is supported by economic, ideological, political, social and cultural conditions of the society. In this case, power is seen as a regular and continuous part of everyday human existence, sustained by established laws, regulations and/or policies, or by accepted conventions and customs. As sociologist C. Wright Mills (1956) argues, only those with access to the command of the major institutions in society can truly have power.

Racism operates in different forms, and at different levels. Expressions can be wilful, deliberate, conscious. Or they can be indirect, unintentional, reflexive and unconscious. These expressions are reflected in individuals' attitudes and belief systems or in institutions' and society's policies and regulations (see diagram 3). To elaborate, *individual racism* is the negative attitudes that individuals hold regarding others. It is an ideology—a set of ideas and related beliefs held by a person who may or may not act on them.

Dobbins and Skillings (1991) explain that racism operates only in cases where individuals, because of their membership in a particular racial group, have access to power in and are able to enforce their racial prejudices:

> *In this sense, although people of colour can be on the receiving end of racist acts in this society and frequently hold prejudices about members of the dominant group, as a group they lack power to enforce or act on these prejudices. For this reason, it is said that people of colour do not act in racist ways unless they are acting as agents for the dominant power structure (Dobbins and Skillings, 1991: 41).*

Recall that "white Europeans" (Philip, 1992), and more particularly, "white European men, especially those of British and French descent" (Ng, 1993) are the ones who, because of their ascribed or inherited status in our society, possess power.

Institutional racism, sometimes referred to as systemic racism (James, 1993; Elliot and Fleras, 1992; Arnold et al., 1991), exists where the established policies, rules and regulations of an organization or institution systematically reflect and produce differential treatment of various groups within that organization or institution, and society generally. These regulations "are used to maintain social control and the status quo in favour of the dominant group" (Dobbins and Skillings 1991: 42). There is a reciprocal relationship between institutional and individual racism. The racist policies and practices of institutions are developed and implemented by individuals who, because of their training and allegiance to the organization, understand that they must adhere to the norms (including the role relationships) and sanctions to maintain the "order of things."

The third form of racism is referred to as *structural racism*. Other writers refer to it as cultural racism (Henry, 1994; Anderson and Frideres, 1981), institutional racism (Philip, 1992; Elliott and Fleras, 1992; Satzewich, 1991; Lee, 1985), or systemic racism (Arnold et al., 1991). For our purpose, like Hughes and Kallen (1974), we will call it structural racism. Structural racism refers to the way in which the

Three dimensions of racism.

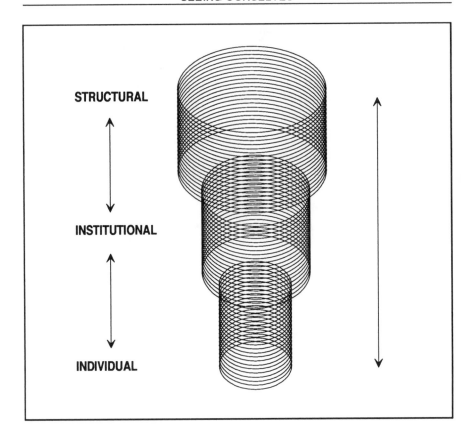

STRUCTURAL

INSTITUTIONAL

INDIVIDUAL

rooted inequalities of society operate to justify the allocation of racial groups to particular categories and class sites. It explains how the ideas of inferiority and superiority, based on socially selected physical characteristics, and which are to be found in society's norms and values, operate to exclude racial minority group members from accessing and participating in major social and cultural institutions, and the importance of one groups' cultural heritage over that of another. Hughes and Kallen (1974) suggest that it is structural racism which is particularly relevant when examining racism and discrimination in Canada. They contend that because of structural racism, minority group members are denied access to the qualifications, education and skills necessary for full participation in society (106).

Other types of racism mentioned in the literature are: "red-neck" racism—what some refer to as the "old-fashioned racism." It is characterized by its overt, conscious, deliberate, and highly personal attacks (including derogatory slurs and name-calling) on those who are perceived as culturally and biologically inferior (Elliott and Fleras, 1992: 58). Polite racism, the way in which Canadian racism is often depicted (Philip, 1992; Henry, 1978), refers to "the deliberate attempt to disguise racist attitudes through behaviour that outwardly is non-prejudicial or discriminatory in appearance" (Elliott and Fleras, 1992: 59). Finally, the "new racism" described by Elliott and Fleras (1992) as "disguised and sophisticated" reflects a conflict of opposing values within individuals. More precisely, it is "a contemporary expression of racial hostility toward racial minorities that goes undetected by conventional measures." Within Canadian society, this form of racism is seen to be "an ambiguous and disguised response to the growing presence of increasingly assertive racial minorities" whose activities and demands are criticized as a threat to national identity and social harmony (Elliott and Fleras, 1992: 62).

Ethnocentrism, prejudice and racism are attitudes and ideologies to be found among individuals that affirm dominant group members as superior and racial minority group members as inferior. The systems of ideas and practices that have been developed over time to justify and support the notion of superiority, "become the premise upon which societal norms and values are based, and the practices become the "normal way of doing things" (Ng, 1993: 52).

Power is the critical component within which the exercise of ethnocentrism, prejudice and racism operate. Specifically, institutionalized power embodied in values, norms, regulations, laws and practices of society and institutions operate to the benefit of dominant groups over the minority groups.

STEREOTypiNG

The concept of the stereotype was first used by Lippmann in 1922 to refer to the manner in which ideas, images and habits are accumulated, shaped and hardened. The term was adapted from the printing industry of the time, in which a "stereotype" was a metal plate with a uniform matrix of type which is moulded so that printing is standard and unchanging. For the social scientist, the concept of the social stereotype refers to "a highly exaggerated picture, the intervention of supposed traits, and the formation of incomplete images leaving little room for change or individual variation" (Driedger, 1989: 343).

Taylor (1991) delineates stereotypes as people's perceptions or beliefs about others rather than ideas based on factual information. It is characterized by shared beliefs—a set of characteristics believed by large numbers of one group to be true of another. They are poor judgements of others since in applying characteristics to entire groups involves over-categorization and over-generalization. This tendency to categorize and generalize about racial and ethnic minority groups is often accompanied by a strong belief in the "correctness" or "truth" of the stereotype and a disregard for fact. Stereotypes sometimes emerge from a person's encounters and experiences (good or bad) with members of other ethnic or racial groups.

Stereotypes serve first to categorize, organize or simplify the amount of extremely complex information that we receive in order to reduce it into manageable units. And when little or nothing is known about a group, stereotypes "fill in" the missing information, thus providing an organized perception of the group. Second, stereotypes satisfy the need for individuals to view themselves positively. Individuals tend to have perceptions and cognitions of their environment that re-enforce their positive self-image. If individuals' attitudes toward their own group are extremely favourable and attitudes toward an outside group are less so, this indirectly reinforces their view that they are good people.

To the extent that stereotypes refer "to people's perceptions and beliefs" and contain a "kernel of truth," they can serve a useful purpose when used to understand cultural differences and similarities. They can be guides to behaviours and can play a role in intergroup relations. Indirectly, they can help in defining one's self and social status (Taylor, 1981: 155). When stereotypes refer to a group's majority attributes in a positive way, the consequences are socially desirable insofar as "the particular intergroup stereotypes satisfy the desires of both groups involved, and where intergroup interaction is not characterized by destructive forms of conflict" (Taylor, 1981: 163). But as Driedger reminds us:

> *The assumption that when we know the facts about another person or group, we will act on those facts is not necessarily true. Reason does not always prevail: emotions often impose positive and negative evaluations. When images of others become rigid, like the printer's stereotype, and when they produce the same reaction automatically without further examination, then we have a social stereotype (1989: 344).*

Discrimination

Ethnocentrism, prejudice and racism are attitudes and ideologies; discrimination is the action which results from these attitudes and ideologies. It is "the process of putting negative cognitions into practice" (Elliot and Fleras, 1992: 56). Specifically, discrimination can be defined as "applied prejudice in which negative social definitions are translated into action and political policy, the subordination of minorities and deprivation of their political, social and economic rights" (Kinloch, 1974: 54). There are typically four denotations of discriminatory treatment: differential, prejudicial, disadvantageous, and the denial of desire (Driedger, 1989; Hagan, 1987).

Differential treatment is the difference in treatment of one group by another. This form of discrimination is said to exist when members of a given group who meet all the necessary requirements to participate in activities within the society or institutions are denied the opportunity to do so. They are "not treated in conformity with the nominally universal institutionalized codes" (Hagan, 1987: 338). Insofar as differential treatment is applied to produce equality of results or outcomes, then the context—i.e. the social and historical situation of the groups, must be taken into consideration. For as pointed out in our discussion of racism, inequality in power and access to resources produces unequal outcomes, hence differential treatment will be required in some cases to produce equality of outcome.

The behavioural expression of prejudice is bigotry and infers that differential treatment, or perpetrators' behaviours, are premised on malice or malevolent motives. The complexity of this form of discrimination is identified by many researchers. For example, Hagan (1987) notes that it is difficult to infer motives from behaviour, and that prejudice can be a consequence, as well as a cause, of discrimination. "Additionally, historical processes can presumably create self-fulfilling prophecies that may eventually conceal the conditions that created them. For example, patterns of differential treatment can create attitudes of resignation and acceptance on the part of recipients that eventually make moot the possibility of their prejudicial origins" (Hagan, 1987: 342).

Some of the clearest forms of discrimination with which we are familiar are those in which individuals are denied equal opportunity, and are not free to compete in our democratic society for the rewards to which they are entitled—their "rights." This occurs, for example, when members of ethnic and racial minority groups are abused verbally; when they are targets of "ethnic jokes" or "racial jokes"; when they are

subjected to literature which represents them in a hateful and derogatory manner; and when they are harassed, their property is vandalized, or they are attacked physically. This is referred to as disadvantageous treatment. It is defined as the treatment which occurs when individuals are placed at some disadvantage that is not merited by their own misconduct. It may be characterized as the "effective injurious treatment of persons on grounds rationally irrelevant to the situation" (Driedger, 1989: 351).

Hagan (1987) denotes discrimination that involves "denial of preference" as denial of desire. This is to be differentiated from cases in which particular individuals or groups voluntarily choose not to participate, or take advantage of opportunities in society because they wish to remain in the security of their subgroup (e.g. Hutterites and Aboriginals) (Dreidger, 1989). Individuals who seek full participation and equality are presumed to be discriminated against if they are unfairly denied access to, and opportunities in, education, jobs, housing, etc.

In sum, discrimination is the unequal treatment of people or groups through the granting or denying of certain rights. In the case of minority groups, these treatments often are based not on individuals' abilities and skills, but on characteristics such as skin colour, language, accent and other physical traits. Discrimination involves differential treatment where restrictions are placed on the aspirations of some members of society, such as in their desire to live where they choose, or their desire to work at any job for which they are qualified. Finally, disadvantageous treatment, such as jokes, name-calling, physical attacks and ejection from a community, are clearly types of discrimination.

Like racism, discrimination operates at different levels and consists of a complex set of ideas and actions. Researchers indicate that although there is a causal relationship between ethnocentrism, prejudice, racism and discrimination, they can vary independently under certain conditions. As Elliott and Fleras point out: "Fear, threats, sanctions, company policy, or good sense may encourage individuals to compartmentalize their prejudices and divorce them from every-day action" (1992: 56). Also, like racism, discriminatory practices are known to be inherent in the economic, political and social structure of Canada.

The genocidal practices against Aboriginal peoples, the enslave-ment of Africans, the treatment of Black Empire Loyalists, the Chi-nese "head tax," the continuous travel edict that prevented South Asians from entering Canada, the failure to give entry to Jews during the 1940s, the incarceration of citizens of Japanese heritage during World War II, the failure to remove restrictions on non-white immi-grants until the early 1970s, high unemployment and underemploy-ment among racial minorities[1] and settlers are all structural and institutional discriminatory practices. These are part of Canadian his-tory and inform our socialization, ideas, attitudes and behaviours. There is no question then, that discrimination is rooted in our society and we are all affected by it either as objects or unwitting perpetu-ators and collaborators. As Henry and Grinzberg (1985) noted, dis-criminatory acts are not isolated to a "handful of bigots." They are to be found, not only in individuals' actions, but also in the barriers which exist in society which deny certain people access to opportu-nities. Through discrimination, certain groups of people are able to maintain their positions of privilege, largely at the expense of other groups who are deliberately or inadvertently excluded from full and equal participation in society.

Ethnocentrism, prejudice, racism, stereotyping and discrimination are not merely a result of ignorance or misinformation, but are mechanisms which are rooted in the inequalities of society, and promote and sustain existing social relations among racial and ethnic groups. These exist often not as the result of individual acts, but as "a consequence of rules, procedures and criteria that all together have a discriminatory effect, *regardless* of motive or intent" (Philip, 1992: 158). Therefore, any analysis or discussion of these mechanisms must necessarily take into consideration the structural framework within which they exist. To ameliorate them requires more than "exposure" to racial minority group members, having them as friends, or hearing

---

[1] See Dei, 1994; Philip, 1992; Shepard, 1991; Ng, 1993; James, 1990; Driedger, 1987; Anderson and Frideres, 1981; Bibby, 1976; Billingsley and Muszynski, 1985; Commission on Equality in Employment, 1984; Head, 1975; Henry, 1978; Henry and Grinzberg, 1985; Hughes and Kallen, 1974; Ramcharan, 1975; Special Committee on Visible Minorities, 1984.

about them in schools or through the media. It requires structural analysis, critical self-reflection and systemic change. The essays that follow represent students' attempts to undertake that analysis and reflection so that they become "educated" about not only how our society works, but also about themselves.

What participants had to say about Ethnocentrism, Prejudice and Racism

Ryan: *"Individuals who do not wish to assimilate can leave…"*

I am in some way prejudiced. I feel that individuals who do not wish to assimilate to our society's rules and regulations can hop back on the boat and leave. We live in a country where individuals need to work as a team, as one mass—we don't need sore thumbs.

I have a problem with the Pakistan Sikhs. They come to Canada to seek a better life but instead they remain prejudiced against others. They march down our streets saying, "bring my mother over, save her from persecution." These individuals need to realize that they are part of a Canadian society. If they refuse to conform they will not last very long. They are in a new country now and are called Canadians. I don't want to hear all about your country's problems, because you ran away from your country's problems.

We need people who will work as Canadians. We need people who will work with Canadians. We need people who will work to be Canadians. We need people who will fight for Canada. Prejudice will weaken the bond between Canadians.

Individuals who wish to come to Canada are welcomed if you are qualified with a needed work trade. As a part of a growing society, it is up to all those new individuals to assimilate and conform so that people around you can relate to you and you to them.

Terry: *"They suggest we are being prejudiced…"*

It is my opinion and that of many others that Blacks carry too much of a chip on their shoulder and they are too quick to scream prejudices. In working at a track and field centre, I have had much contact with Blacks and have had a chance to observe Black behaviour. What I have noticed is that many Blacks have a very hostile attitude. They are constantly trying to manipulate everything. Since most of the athletes at the centre are Black, the roles are reversed and the White staff is in the minority. If something does not particularly please them, they suggest that we are being prejudiced. There have been a number of occasions when I have asked both Black and White athletes to comply with rules and have been called prejudiced and a few other choice names by the Black person, while the White person does as I ask without incident. The Black athletes are intolerably rude and unfavourable. I must say here that this is not always the case. I have met many rude White people and many pleasant Black people. Generally though, Black aggressiveness tends to be greater than aggressiveness in Whites.

Geographic location can determine what type of work is available and general working habits. In the case of Black immigrants, they have traditionally worked in tropical plantations and unskilled labour because that is what is available to them. Their educational system is much different from ours. This lends itself to lower-skilled labour according to Canadian standards, leading to increased difficulty in job placement and advancement, low paying jobs and manipulation into scab labour for Blacks. The hot climate of Black native lands such as Jamaica and Africa requires the Black race to be somewhat "laid back" and more relaxed. Lighter work and longer breaks are required in a regular work day.

Black social habits also differ greatly from Canadian customs. "Hanging out" as it is called, is a form of leisure, and sexual promiscuity is much more accepted. Unfortunately, when one "hangs out" in Canada, he is the target of criticism and often regarded as a troublemaker. When it comes to drugs and alcohol use, it is a fact that Blacks are more likely to become addicted. This is not because they use the substances more than Whites but rather because their body systems are different; they have lower levels of tolerance.

Janine: *"If there were laws against my religion I would feel violated..."*

When we were discussing the Sikhs, I questioned what I would feel like if there were laws against my religion in a place where I lived. I would feel violated if I were living in India and told that I could not keep a Bible in my home or carry it outside if I were going to a church meeting. Although I thought this through, my ethnocentric attitudes could not allow me to agree with the Sikhs carrying daggers, their religious symbol, in Canada.

Christine: *"A great friend but I would never marry him..."*

Two main topics which were of particular interest to me were prejudice and stereotyping. Dave, whom I consider a close friend of mine, is half Black and half White. His skin colour is very noticeable, but because we are friends, I thought that there is no possible way that I could ever be prejudiced or racist. After learning the definition of prejudice I realize I was and still am, to a degree, racist.

Certainly Dave is a great friend but I would never marry or even get romantically involved with him because of his skin colour. I am definitely displaying racism. I still don't understand why the colour of one's skin is so important to people when it is their personality that should matter. But my background is from a strong White Roman Catholic family, holding very close to the traditional views of White women marrying White men and Black women marrying Black men.

Brenda: *"Would you marry someone of another another race?..."*

Recently, a friend and I were discussing the issue: "Would you marry someone of another race and/or ethnicity?" Of course, there is no quick and clear-cut answer to this question as many matters must be taken into consideration. At first, we both agreed that people are people, and just that, whether Black or White or Yellow or Red. When we thought about the possibility that we have been raised culturally different, a few doubts surfaced.

My friend told of a former boyfriend. In his culture, women are only placed on this earth to satisfy man's every whim. This caused a great many arguments, and even though they were both willing to try to adjust their cultural differences, it was too difficult a problem for them to deal with.

After this I became more critical of my self-righteous attitudes. I began questioning whether or not I really could marry a person of a different race and/or ethnicity. Even if I could accept this man for who he is, would I be able to cope with the stares and criticism of others? There's much more involved than a simple, "Of course I'm not prejudiced!" Parental acceptance is very important in our society. I know for a fact that my parents would not have wanted me to marry someone of a different race or ethnicity. I concluded that marrying someone of a different race with a different cultural background is not for me.

I was told that this thinking was racist and prejudiced. I felt very wronged. I thought that I only saw people for who they are inside. I thought I would be friends with someone who was of a different race or ethnicity, without even taking that fact into consideration, but marrying someone is a different matter. It is not the same as being friends. I now realize that this thinking is just as prejudiced as any other.

Angella: *"I have a hard time feeling sorry..."*

One thing I found out about myself, which I am not particularly proud of, is that I am racially prejudiced. I had always understood the meaning of prejudice to be an uninformed judgement or negative attitude towards a person or group of people. I have always had a very bad attitude towards Native Canadians, but it was not an uninformed or misleading opinion. I grew up with Indians and my attitude towards them developed over a number of years. I feel that the Canadian Government is creating an inferior race of people by giving them everything. I have a hard time feeling sorry for people who are not willing to help themselves.

I am fully aware of the fact that the White man took their land, and they do deserve some kind of compensation, but there has got to be a better way for the government to deal with the problem. I realize that their culture is one of hunting, fishing and living off the land, but there is not enough land and resources to support all the Indians for the generations to come. It is unrealistic to think that they can live the way their ancestors did.

I know that I am being ethnocentric and that I expect them to change their values and beliefs, but it is hard to look at their situation clearly. I mean, when a community can tell it is pay day on the reserves by how many Indians are passed out on the streets downtown, you become a little skeptical of the way the government is handling the situation. I honestly do not think that I could ever change the way I view Indians by trying to look at the situation from their point of view. My opinion is set from many years of having to deal with these people and I guess now when people ask me if I am racist, I have to say yes.

Donna: *"Whites are biologically superior..."*

Racist attitudes cannot be changed overnight when they have been a part of me for twenty-one years, but I am more aware of the feelings that others have. Although I maintain the belief that Whites are biologically superior to Blacks, I appreciate now that Blacks, like all racial groups, are people who, like me, have feelings and bleed red blood.

Focusing on difference can also be prejudiced and racist

The above accounts may illustrate clear cases of racism, prejudice and/or ethnocentrism. But things are not always that clear. Take Kim, for example. She writes:

> I don't remember any Black people in the little town where I grew up until I was about ten years old. However, I do remember the first day they arrived at our school. Most of the kids stood around and stared; for most of us, it was the first time we had ever seen Black people. The first day there the teacher asked them to tell the class all about themselves. The two boys were twins and had just moved to our community from England. They were both very nice and by the first recess that day they had plenty of friends. After all, they were very much like us. They liked the same sports, they had the same hobbies, and they liked the new country they were living in. It was very hard not to like them, they were so nice.

Kim assumes that because they eventually came to like the two boys, neither she nor her classmates displayed any prejudiced behaviour. Note, however, that the race of the two boys was considered an obstacle. They had to prove themselves to be "very much like" the other children. Significant are Kim's comments that "they liked the same sports, they had the same hobbies, and they liked the new country they were living in." What if these two Black English boys had not?

Having prejudiced attitudes is certainly not exclusive to Whites. For example, Nadine, a young Guyanese-born Canadian of South Asian descent shows the conflict and contradictions that she experiences because of her prejudice.

> *"It's OK for me ... because I am a minority..."*
>
> I guess the most difficult part of the class was dealing with my own prejudices. Being a minority I never perceived myself as being racist. But I would never consider going out with a guy of any racial-ethnic background other than White English Canadian. I call it preference but in effect it is racism. I say this because I have been approached on numerous occasions by guys from different backgrounds and admit-

tedly I am very snobby. I don't give myself a chance to find out what they're like; I snub them because of their colour.

I tell myself it's OK for me to be this way because I have been on the receiving end of racism. But I am just as guilty as the racists I have faced in my time. I don't like feeling this way or having this prejudice. As a matter of fact I get extremely upset if one of my "White" friends makes a comment of sorts about a guy of a different race, yet it's probably something I would say.

I am not prejudiced against people in general. I have friends of all different nationalities, races, etc., both male and female. But when it comes to a boyfriend-girlfriend relationship, then I am racist.

A friend of mine recently asked me what I would do if my daughter (now 2 years) came home with a Black guy (or any other race). I blatantly responded I would kill her. I am very ashamed of this prejudice, more so because I am a minority. But it's just the way I feel. I've tried long and hard to find the source of this prejudice but I've yet to come up with the answer.

The most shameful part in all of this is how mad, hurt and upset I get when I find out other people around me are prejudiced. I am a hypocrite for the way I feel towards these people, because I am no better. For the prejudices I have I should be able to understand why other people are prejudiced. I guess it all comes down to the fact that I think it's OK for me because I am in a minority. I realize this does not justify my behaviour but it's what I tell myself to make me feel better. Believe me when I say it's an ongoing conflict within myself that I am trying to resolve, or maybe one day truthfully admit.

Participants Write About Stereotyping and Discrimination

Evidently, stereotyping and stereotypes are rarely in anyone's best interest. It could mean a misrepresentation of the person or the impossibility of being accepted as an individual. For those who practice stereotyping, it might be convenient, but it could also rob them of the opportunity to know groups and individuals more accurately and more intimately. Many participants indicate that "speaking with someone from another culture on a personal level gave us an opportunity to see beyond stereotypes."

Speaking with someone from another cultural group on a personal level gives us an opportunity to see beyond stereotypes.

Annette: *"I realized that my opinions were based on ignorance..."*

The research project on ethnic and racial groups really opened my eyes. On researching the Old Order German Mennonites, my biased opinions surfaced. I viewed them as "Bible thumpers," peddling their religion whenever given the chance. I also thought they were very serious people, who lived strict, unhappy lives. But what I perceived them to be like was very far from the truth. Upon completion of my research, I concluded that the Mennonites were very happy people who loved their way of life and kept to themselves. I reflected back to my previous convictions and asked myself why I had thought the Mennonites to be the way they were. After thinking this over for some time, I realized that my opinions, as well as my previously mentioned perceptions, all boiled down to one thing: ignorance. I was accepting and passing judgement on things I knew nothing about. My preconceived notions, I realized, had come from other equally uninformed people and existing stereotypes.

Jason: *"Stereotypes are not facts..."*

Stereotypes exist for every group that organizes itself as a culture, and of course the Chinese are no exception. The stereotypes which we held prior to doing this project were ones such as "All Chinese are brains," "All people who work in the 7-11 stores are Chinese," and, "If you want your laundry washed really well, take it to the Chinese." Needless to say, these are stereotypes and not facts. However, by examining various data and history, it is possible to see where these stereotypes have originated.

Regarding intelligence: Chinese frequently do well in school, not because of a higher inherent intelligence, but due to their motivation and to the emphasis and value placed on a good education. There is a great deal of pressure from within the family to succeed at anything undertaken since all achievements and failures are reflective of the family as a whole.

The belief that Chinese hold only menial jobs may exist because in the past there were not very many professional Chinese in Canada. Why? The Chinese were prohibited in the early 1900s from holding certain professional positions. This has changed now—Chinese occupy positions at all levels. We found that these and other such stereotypes could quite easily be dispelled by actively examining them.

Ray: *"Hockey is dominated by the white race..."*

I, and many Canadians, enjoy the great game of hockey. When you think of hockey you automatically think Canada. Hockey is dominated by the white race and there are several theories to explain why this is so. The theory that I tend to believe is the fact that every N.H.L. hero has belonged to the white race. They have served almost every Canadian-born white with a role model to look up to and dream of being just like him.

The black race has dominated every other sport, except hockey, and they tend to be very agile and quick on their feet. The game of football, soccer, baseball and track and field all deal with running and the black race has done exceptionally well in all of these sports.

Another important similarity is the fact that sports like soccer, football, basketball, etc. are all played in warm or room temperature, temperatures typical to their home climate. White people of Canada are used to the cold climate and enjoy many winter sports and pastimes.

Black people have also been stereotyped into sports that have been areas of achievement by past black athletes. The black race has had no role models in hockey, and therefore, few young boys show any real interest. Also, prejudice has been a major factor. Due to a common stereotype of black hockey players not being exceptional they don't enjoy the same opportunities from their instructors and coaches.

Himraj: *"All I wanted was the opportunity to play..."*

Racism has affected me personally since I can remember. Opportunities I felt were lost [occurred] because of my skin colour and nationality. I love hockey and have been playing since I was younger. One memory in my mind that still exists is the feeling of name calling and repeatedly being told that I couldn't play hockey because I was not white. I was repeatedly made fun of and laughed at as I was usually the last one picked for the teams. I grew up in a white neighbourhood, and as all the kids played hockey, I began practising the game hoping that one day I could play with everyone else. After a couple of months I became better as I was faster and much smarter than the rest of the guys. I was asked to play for higher calibre teams as I excelled in the sport. I was always working hard but was still made fun of by the opposing teams. My teammates learned to accept me but when another minority played on another team they taunted him with the same names used against me from the other teams. All I wanted was the opportunity to play and be treated like everybody else. I finally learned to work harder and shield the comments from my head. Unfortunately I would go home and feel how cruel and mean some people can be. One comment I will always remember is "you can never skate because your ankles are too weak."

RAciAl JokEs

Racism, ethnic prejudice and ethnocentrism are often displayed in jokes. The fact that statements or stories about racial groups are seen as "things to be laughed at" indicates a basic disrespect and/or a lack of information.

Dan: *"I believed non-Whites were inferior…"*

Throughout the course I was constantly confronted with my prejudices. I had a racial joke for every ethnic group we discussed and I am now aware that the reason I found the jokes so funny is because I believed that anyone who was non-White was inferior.

Andrey: *"It is only a joke man, take it easy…"*

Friendships are opportunities in life that can be both happy or sad. I grew up in a neighbourhood of many white children. I remember times were I would be rejected from attending parties because of my colour. I would usually get picked on as I was called many names about my colour and nationality. I even remember a time I was not permitted to enter someone's home because of the fear that I may steal something. As time moved on I simply learned to interact with different types of people. Most of my friends now are white and I love them like brothers. Unfortunately they tend to sometimes make fun of racial groups like the Chinese, Indian and Blacks. I am sad when I hear this type of ignorance I bring it up and explain that this type of behaviour is not right but wrong. The response I would get is that "it is only a joke man, take it easy." I feel that I expect more from these guys but my presence doesn't help. I feel sometimes they forget my nationality and think that I am white. I feel that the problems with my fiends are ethnocentrism and racism. They see racism as a joke and do it for amusement. Try to see it from a minority's point of view and it is downright stupid.

Minority Group Members: Their Feelings and Reactions

How do members of minority groups, who experience racism, stereotyping and discrimination, feel about these issues? Their responses range from frustration and discomfort to hurt and anger depending on their experiences and struggles for acceptance.

Judy: *"I was really offended…"*

Whenever a question was asked, a White person would start by saying "I'm not prejudiced," and continue to answer. I was really offended by this, because it was obvious that they were being prejudiced and just couldn't admit it.

Natasha: *"I was hurt…"*

After discussing prejudice I started thinking about the majority White race. How easy life is for them, never being stereotyped, but just taken for who they are—individuals.

Then I wondered what it would be like if I were White. I soon decided I'd rather stay as myself. I believe I'm richer, more cultured (for having both Canadian and Guyanese experiences) and more appreciative of life in general because of my colour and from where I came.

Although facing prejudice is a horrible experience, I feel minorities have something over the majority group. I feel we are more objective and appreciative because we know what it's like to be discriminated against. White people will never know and for that reason will always take life for granted.

In class discussions I remember thinking how prejudiced my classmates were. Nothing that would be admitted up front, but underlying prejudice was there. I also thought if our teacher were White, reactions would probably be more open. I was hurt a few times in class because of racial comments or preconceived notions that my classmates harboured about minorities. I guess it hurt me because these people will never know what it's like to be discriminated against simply because of their skin colour.

I also thought that they were ignorant of what people were really like. But what hurt me more was they never gave people a chance. They just kept their beliefs and never bothered to find out differently.

Hakeem: *"Hearing an ethnic joke makes me self-conscious and uncomfortable…"*

On interacting with my White friends and White people in general, I am never consciously aware of my colour unless an ethnic joke or remark is made. Then I become very self-conscious and uncomfortable.

Mark: *"Anger flows through me…"*

Many of my friends are not Jewish and often take part in racial humour. This does not offend me since I know it is done in jest. Such things as "I hear there's a sale on at ———, don't all Jews like bargains?" or "You have a big nose, you must be Jewish!" are often part of their repertoire. If I hear someone speaking in a negative manner about Jews and I sense they mean what they are saying, then anger flows through me. I can vividly remember one time standing in line at a movie theatre with a few friends and having pennies thrown at us by another group of guys. They screamed at us, "Come on, Jews, pick them up. Come on, you dirty Jews!" I felt so much anger and hate for these people, I just wanted to kill them. I let it pass because I was always taught not to fight unless it was for my own protection. To this day that incident stands out in my mind. Since I have experienced discrimination because of my faith, I have become much more aware of the feelings and the problems which arise when people judge others according to stereotypes.

Donovan: *"I was not truly a black person..."*

Stereotypes have been around for countless years, and their damage to the reputation of minority groups is incredible. In my essay I will focus on the stereotypes that have affected blacks, and in particular myself. Now, from experiences in my life I can put a finger on many stereotypes that have affected me personally but I'll only focus on two for this essay.

One of these stereotypes is that "All blacks are good athletes." It is easy to see how this stereotype came about, simply because of the black domination on the playing field of many of today's most popular sports. But this is indeed a stereotype. Because of these things a whole group of people are categorized as being better athletes. Now from my personal experiences, I did not excel greatly in sports and because of the stereotype of being superior in sports because I'm black, I felt inferior and embarrassed. I felt as if I had to play sports because it was expected of me. When it was found out that I was not as good as "every other black person" I felt I was less than them.

This also led to the opinion that blacks were not good in school, only in sports. This has not affected me personally, but has led to many blacks believing that they could not be as smart in school as the rest of the students, which of course is not true.

Another occurrence in stereotyping blacks I have experienced is that all blacks have natural rhythm and are really good dancers and they are born like that. I was not always that good a dancer and to this day am still not that great. But because I wasn't good at dancing, I was again made to feel inferior as a black person because of my lack of dancing ability. This made it seem to me that I was not truly a black person because of my inabilities. The sad thing is that so many blacks and not only whites believe in these stereotypes. This only hurts the entire black community as they believe that sports is their only hope in life and education is unimportant because sports comes easier to them and it is just simply expected of them. This leads to stereotyping black people into a group who are superior in sports but lacking in school because they actually believe that they are naturally better at sports because they're black. Stereotypes like the ones I mentioned in the preceding paragraphs have a terrible effect on the black population as a whole. Once caught up in a stereotype it is hard to cut loose from the belief that these false truths are not indeed true. If the people continue the stereotypes of today's world, the only people who will be hurt are themselves.

Finally, in an article in which he explains his process of becoming a "regular Canadian" Ajit Adhopia (1988) recalls that after making "so many sacrifices to transform my family from strange immigrants to true-blue Canadians," he still experienced racism. In his article "Prejudice and Pride," Adhopia illustrates that skin colour, more than cultural practices, often underlie racist treatment. He writes:

My new Canadian identity was shattered on a Sunday afternoon when I was sitting in my car waiting for a friend ... Three or four boys in their early teens walked toward me. A blond, blue-eyed boy looked straight into my eyes and yelled "You f ... Paki." His friends burst into laughter. They did not run, they just walked away leisurely ... Back home I was too angry and embarrassed to share the experience with my family. My anger turned into deep depression and for weeks I pondered upon a question: "Where did I go wrong."

Finally, it dawned on me. In my effort to become a regular Canadian I had missed one important thing—I forgot to change the colour of my skin. Darn it ... The young blond boy who thought he was insulting me is responsible for giving me the new awakening to my own cultural roots. My life is enriched, I am self-confident, I have a new dimension to my character ...

Behind Prejudice and Stereotyping: Theorizing About the Sources

Cecilia: *"It is our ignorance..."*

Just as many may be frightened of, and avoid contact with, our own senior population, because it forces an awareness of our mortality, we fear and avoid people of other cultures and/or races because they make us painfully aware of our ignorance. It is ignorance that fosters prejudice, and until Canadians can allow themselves to learn to know those considered different, they will continue to be guilty of the cruelty that is so much a part of prejudice. Would it help to think of ourselves as immigrants in a strange land? I think not, for it would be difficult to imagine being a victim of those things we tend to deny the very existence of.

Janice: *"Blame the Victim..."*

It was interesting to see the amount of emotion involved in our discussions of prejudice and racism. It seemed a strong indication of how many of us feel defensive about our prejudices. Speaking of my own ethnic, racial group—White, English-Canadian—I think that this discomfort often leads us to deny the source of it, which results in the creation of a kind of "blame the victim" situation. Uncomfortable with our prejudices and our ignorance of other cultures, uncomfortable with the perception that we are in some ways privileged by our Whiteness, we shut out not only the issues of prejudice, racism and discrimination, but also the people and cultures who raise the issue in our minds. Rather than face the discomfort or conflict, we avoid that which will bring it out. So, we deny that racism or discrimination still exists. We see our culture not as a product of our racial and ethnic identities, our heritage in a sense, but just as a normal way of life we needn't question.

Helen: *"We put each minority to the test..."*

It is interesting to note that my attitude appears to change with society's. The longer a minority group is here, the more tolerant we become of it. At one time the Blacks were strongly discriminated against; before that it was the Italians. At present the Sikhs seem to take the brunt of discrimination. Looking at the situation from that perspective, it appears we put each minority to the test. "Are they good enough to be part of our country?" Yes, they are. I sincerely say this now, but my realization of categorizing is difficult for me to accept and even harder to write down.

Kevin: *"Had no prejudices..."*

When some of my classmates made it known that they had no prejudices and then went on to express their ideas or opinions which contradicted their original statement, I began to question my own prejudices. I have always felt that I was unbiased, just as my classmates felt themselves to be. However, I have now come to the conclusion that deep inside everyone of us is a little bit of fear about a certain race or culture which gives rise to reservations. These reservations usually give rise to unjust assumptions or pre-judgements.

Debbie: *"An exception among my perceived stereotype... "*

All my life, I have been encompassed by certain "significant others" who freely exhibit prejudice and discriminatory attitudes to those people who are racially and culturally different. I feel that my interaction with Gerardo, a member of the Latin American community, was extremely valuable as it helped me to consciously recognize various characteristics about myself. As he informed me of the continuous discrimination and prejudices he is repeatedly exposed to because he is a member of a minority group, I felt that he was exaggerating. I like Gerardo very much, and I could not fathom why he felt so strongly about this belief, and additionally, I could not believe that other people were not responding positively towards him. He is a very personable, intelligent, compassionate young man.

Yet looking back upon this, I admit that I was regarding Gerardo with an outlook appropriately referred to as "cognitive dissonance." He was an exception among my perceived stereotype of the Latin American people, as he had married one of my closest friends. Therefore, my positive perceptions of him were actually based upon their marriage and not upon any knowledge I had of him as an individual. We are friends, but I believe this relationship would not exist if it were not for their bonding. I highly doubt I would have taken the initiative on my own. I am thankful for our interaction now, however, because I feel that I will be far more open-minded in the long run, and my initial stereotype has greatly diminished.

The writers through their comments have suggested that racism, prejudice, stereotyping and other negative attitudes and actions perpetuate because of ignorance, avoidance, fear, and discomfort with people who are different and whom we might not know. Furthermore, denial that racism and prejudice exist also perpetuates these attitudes and the resultant behaviours.

Eliminating Prejudice and Racism: More Than Having Friends Who Are . . .

Awareness and a willingness to look at more than skin colour is crucial to the elimination of both prejudice and racism. People must admit that prejudice and racism exist if they are going to deal with these issues. We must go beyond the common notion that merely by having friends who are Black, Chinese, Portuguese, Native Indian, etc. we have become free of prejudice. Much critical and painful self-analysis and self-awareness appear to be preconditions for working toward confronting and overcoming our racism, prejudice and the accompanying problems. In practical terms, interacting with the people who are targets of prejudice, racism and stereotyping proves to be one more healthy way of becoming more informed.

Annette: *"Try not to be so quick to judge..."*

I encountered a few difficulties in doing my research. I was uncomfortable with the thought of conducting an interview with a Mennonite. I wasn't sure how I should act around these people, or what to say to them. I had never seen a Mennonite person, never mind talked to one. I wasn't so sure that I wanted to either. Why, when doing the research had I thought that all my preconceived notions, attitudes and prejudices were gone, but now that it was actually time to come face to face with a Mennonite person, had they returned? As long as these people existed only on paper, they did not pose a threat to my views and beliefs. I then realized that it is much easier to say that we are not prejudiced than it is to actually not be.

Once the interview was over though, my fears vanished. They were real people, made of flesh and blood just like myself, but with different views and beliefs. They were nothing like I had perceived them to be. They were happy, loving and warm people. I was somewhat embarrassed by my previous thoughts and was glad that I had the chance to gain the valuable insight that I did towards the Mennonites' culture.

I feel that my attitudes, biases, emotions and prejudices have changed somewhat. Now I try not to be so quick to judge other people when I know nothing about them. I've learned that the colour of a person's skin, the way they dress and the rituals they practise are not a full indication of what that person is like.

Awareness and a willingness to look at more than skin colour is crucial to the elimination of both prejudice and racism.

Jason: *"Accept differences…"*

When I interacted with people of Chinese background, I found that I always double-checked what I was about to say before I actually verbalized it. I didn't want to say anything to offend the other people. I was being much more careful in these conversations than I ever would be even with a stranger with the same background as mine. I also didn't want to say something that was really stupid, for example, the way some people in the United States ask Canadians if they live in igloos. I wanted to present myself as having a bit of knowledge about their culture.

I think, as the conversation progressed, we both felt more comfortable with each other, and finally, were able to relax. We then were talking as two people, not as a Chinese-Canadian and a Canadian. But would we ever be able to "be ourselves?" After all, isn't our culture a large part of what we are? How can we completely be ourselves in a different culture? It's similar to having a lot of private jokes within a group. When in another group, these jokes are meaningless. Sure, wonderful relationships can be formed, but there's still a part that can't be shared and understood.

I tend, now, to agree with the statement that we are all racist. We do see people in different colours (i.e. Yellow, Black, Red, White). How we behave from this point on, determines to what extent we are prejudiced. If we dwell on this fact, and cannot see past the skin and find the real person, then prejudice becomes a problem. If, however, we can accept that difference and continue on forming relationships, then I think we are aware of our prejudices and are better able to cope with them.

Simon: *"There are good and bad people..."*

Looking back to before I initiated my investigation of Sikhs, I must admit that my feelings and attitudes towards Sikhs were very negative. There was a time when I didn't even want to look at one, let alone have any kind of interaction with them. I based all my opinions I had of these people on one poor experience I had with one Sikh in the past, a taxicab driver. What I realize now is that cab driver could have been Black, Sikh, White, Yellow or Purple. The point is that there are good and bad people existing in every culture. That driver could have been White and treated me the same way as the Sikh did. Because people don't like a particular minority group, they are quick to judge members of the group when they do something wrong. Time is not taken to acknowledge that no one is perfect, regardless of what subculture they belong to.

Kevin: *"Prejudice needs to be addressed and explored..."*

I believe that interaction and experience are the best teachers. Whether a one-on-one interview or a class debate, delicate topics or situations such as the subject of cross-culturalism and prejudice need to be addressed and explored personally for it is only through these methods that true emotions and consequently value examinations occur. Personal growth and development are possible only when such a confrontation exists.

It would be very easy for me to say that my prejudices and racism have been vanquished and that I have complete empathy for racial minorities and an understanding of their current situations, but I can't. Many ethnic idiosyncrasies still continue to anger me and I do still find myself generalizing a characteristic of one to a culture of many. The difference in my viewpoint now is that I am aware of my ethnocentrism and this, I believe, is of crucial importance.

Lenore: *"Requires 'putting yourself in their shoes'... "*

Being an educated "White English Canadian" has made me readily accepted here in Canada, whereas immigrants and other races who are Canadian-born have a great obstacle to overcome, i.e., prejudice. I, too, had my stereotypes and prejudices towards specific cultures.The easiest way of trying to overcome these mental actions, is to put yourself in their shoes. Imagine having to conform to a different culture, having to speak the language and till trying to remain an individual. I couldn't do it, so why should I expect any other person to.

There is still so much for me to learn about cultures and people. Customs, values and beliefs are specific to each one. Within each culture are individuals with individual personalities; there's never a "typical" Black, White, Chinese, etc. No one should have to live with discriminations, stereotyping, or racism. Only through education of the "ignorant" will this problem begin to lessen.

Leanne: *"Seeing racism in ourselves as something that is learned... "*

There were times during the discussion of racism that I felt a sense of relief. I had come to recognize that a difficult issue can be talked about and it is through discussion and taking risks that learning is made possible. I had come to think that racism itself wasn't the problem. What was reinforced for me, through these discussions, was the belief that it is the refusal to accept the racism that is there in all of us that is the far greater problem. Understanding it, seeing it in oneself as something that is learned and also denied by the larger society, is a way I think to lessen its strength. By denying racism because it makes us uncomfortable we only perpetuate it. I think that acceptance of our own tendency to remain within our own racial group and culture, and to deny differences because we are uncomfortable with them, is the first step toward changing those tendencies. This leads us toward learning respect for and acceptance of other races and cultures.

Angie: *"A little knowledge..."*

I think racism will always be around. Everyone is afraid of the unknown or something different. I don't think you can make a person non-racist, but you can educate them; a little knowledge goes a long way and eventually will cause acceptance. I believe this as I have come a long way from the way I was treated in 1974, when I first came to Canada, to 15 years later in 1988, where I am treated differently.

Respecting and accepting differences is an important step in forming positive realtionships.

SUMMARY

By way of concluding, let us look at some of the comments made as participants reflect on their attitudes, philosophies and actions after discussing the issues of prejudice, racism, ethnocentrism, discrimination and stereotyping.

Jody: *"Two different teachings..."*

"Jesus loves the little children; all the little children of the world. Red and yellow; Black and White; they are precious in his sight. Jesus loves the little children of the world."

This song, which I sang in Sunday School as a child, never gave me the message that was intended! As Southern Baptists we sang about people being equal but never believed it. People were only equal if they were White. When reflecting back over our discussions, I realize that I received two very different teachings as a child. My Christian faith taught me the love of all mankind, but my society taught me to love only the White sector of mankind.

Nicole: *"Canadians tend to be rather ethnocentric..."*

I know that if I were to enter a foreign country I would want to continue practising my usual traditions, such as Christmas, because this is important and something I would not like to live without. We Canadians tend to be rather ethnocentric and don't realize that immigrants have these same beliefs.

Andy: *"Awareness is of crucial importance..."*

It is my conviction that, although we are not born with racial and prejudicial concerns, through experience, observation, learning and interactions with society as a whole, we soon develop these characteristics and they become ingrained into our personalities whether we realize it or not. I was never told outright that one race was superior to another or that I should not like a certain individual because of their cultural and/or racial heritage. Nevertheless, I have been influenced by media stereotypes, by interactions with specific individuals whose behaviour I have subsequently generalized to their whole culture and by the thoughts and opinions of people I consider important. All these factors have contributed to the manner in which I view different races and cultures and I believe it would be unrealistic to pretend that even now they don't affect me, be it consciously or unconsciously. It is also my belief, however, that knowledge can lead to understanding and eventually, to compassion. Through an intelligent examination of our belief and value systems, we can perhaps begin to focus on where our biases have come from and help to change where they may be heading.

Questions:

1. What is the difference between ethnocentrism, bias, prejudice, racism and discrimination?
2. How would you describe the procedure by which ignorance leads to racism? How do lack of awareness, education and exposure combine to make a person "racist"?
3. What is the relationship between individual, institutional and structural racism? Identify some of the major examples of structural racism that are evident in Canadian history.

6

ON IMMIGRATION, MULTICULTURALISM AND EMPLOYMENT EQUITY

Three of the most significant issues that produced some of the most heated discussions and debates in classes were immigration, multiculturalism and employment equity. The significance of these issues to the participants at this particular stage of their lives not only had to do with their hopes of eventually realizing their career goals after graduation, but their understanding of how difficult the job market had become. For most of the students, particularly young white males, immigration, multiculturalism and employment equity were seen as impediments to their achievements. Immigrants were perceived as "a drain on our social services," who "were taking jobs away from Canadians," "causing an increase in crimes" (particularly Blacks and Asians), and were "coming into our country bringing their culture and changing our culture" (particularly Sikhs). Connections were often made between the increase in immigration and "what is wrong with multiculturalism." The latter was seen as facilitating changes in the "Canadian way of life." Employment equity was also perceived, like multiculturalism as making it difficult for "Canadians" to eventually achieve the jobs to which they aspire. Participants spoke about these factors causing "unneeded tension and frustrations among 'Canadians' (read white and British), 'immigrants,' the target groups and the government."

The following essays illustrate how participants, particularly young, white males and females related these three issues. The discussion that follows attempts to put into context and clarify the ideas and some of the misinformation and myths that underlie several of the prevailing attitudes and positions that are so often displayed in the general society. It is worth repeating that the ideas that are written here do not only reflect those of these participants, but are also ideas which represent many of the perspectives which can be found in our society generally and in major socializing institutions such as the media, schools, governments and others.

Immigrants and Immigration

Todd: *"It is expected that many traditional habits and practices have to be simmered down..."*

People coming to Canada should be informed or enlightened as to what to expect when they arrive here. It is for this reason the transition period is so difficult for so many people. I respect peoples' culture, traditions and beliefs and I expect people to respect mine. In many Middle Eastern cultures, westerners are often subjected to harsh reprimands if they dress in what we call western clothing, especially women. Many westerners often complain of the treatment they are given if they dress "disrespectfully" i.e., in the western clothing, especially women. Many times they are not allowed to commute or live in certain areas of the society, because it is felt they would corrupt the natives with their culture. Yet these very people come here to Canada and expect us Canadians to accept them in their traditional garments, and to work side by side with them. That is not fair. Canada is a sovereign nation with an identity.

I wonder what a foreigner would say when they arrive in Canada to find people with various modes of dress, some with turbans as police officers, some with daggers attending schools, while others wear kimonos (Japanese dress), saris, and a wide variety of dress. They would obviously be confused. I don't believe that Canadians should wear a national uniform or dress, but I disagree with immigrants coming to Canada and insisting on being employed with their traditional dress. The world must be able to recognize Canadians for who they are; Canadians should have an identity. This I believe is one of the many reasons that white people are viewed as Canadians and most non-whites are seen as immigrants. I am not saying that we (non-whites) should try to conform to the ideals and mouldings of the white, but the integration process is a blending-in process, where it is expected that

many traditional habits and practices have to be simmered down, because for the immigrant Canada is a new country, a different culture, and a new way of life.

How do we identify immigrants?

Nancy: *"I think that heritage is something that should be shared with others and not kept to yourself..."*

The issue that I wish to discuss deals with the immigrants that come to Canada and settle with their own ethnic group. I realize that when someone comes to a new country they feel safe in a community that is similar to the one they left behind, but I feel that this only brings people of different cultures further apart rather than closer together. I am not saying that it is wrong for people to be actively involved in their cultural community, I feel that it is important to keep up with your heritage and pass it down to future generations, but I think that heritage is something that should be shared with others and not kept to yourself.

I am an active participant in a Ukrainian dance group and have been for eight years, within this time I have seen how these people interact with other non-Ukrainians. It seems as though they want nothing to do with people that are not of their ethnic background. They all belong to Ukrainian churches, schools, sports teams, camps, country clubs, they have relatives in Ukrainian rest homes and on their vacation they drive up to their Ukrainian community cottages.

When I first joined this group it seemed as though the co-ordinators wanted me to forget my Scottish and Irish background and to just concentrate on being a Ukrainian. There came a time when I was almost embarrassed to admit that I also had another heritage.

When people of the same ethnicity cling together they become so involved in their own culture that they are not willing to open their eyes and experience what other cultures have to offer. This becomes impossible for them to do when they have spent so much time in their own community that they cannot communicate with anyone outside of it. For example, I knew someone who had been in this country for sixty years and could hardly speak a word of English, therefore how was he suppose to communicate with anyone outside his ethnic community, he had trapped himself in it.

I don't feel that to be a Canadian you have to change your name or behaviour but I do feel that a true Canadian is one that can admit that they are. I myself almost found that I was considering myself to be Ukrainian and I hardly ever called myself Canadian which my family has been for three generations.

Bill: *"I resented that a Canadian didn't come first...."*

I used to resent immigrants and refugees. I always looked at them as taking away from the Canadian social service system that I thought was unfair. This negative attitude was formed when I was out of work and looked into upgrading my education through the unemployment office. The waiting list was so long, and what infuriated me was the list of names waiting to enrol were names that I couldn't pronounce. All these people were ahead of me and I resented that a Canadian didn't come first. It has taken a bit of attitude adjusting to come to terms that—this is what Canada is all about. These people belong to Canada, just as I do.

Dave: *"I would like to see these people protesting only Canadian issues..."*

I cannot understand why immigrants coming to Canada, making the choice to leave their place of birth and adopting Canada as their new home, would protest in the streets of Canada about issues back in their country. Canada is filled with problems and the country needs people who would come here to contribute to the welfare, progress and development of the country. I would like to see these people protesting about Canadian issues such as the lack of jobs, the GST, no more taxes and other social issues that affect them and relate to Canada because here is where they are living.

Jane: *"Should protection from abuse be grounds for immigration?..."*

On the issue of immigrants (women) being allowed to stay in Canada because of persecution and harassment in their home country, I believe most of them should be allowed to stay. I say most of them because Canada cannot be seen as a dumping ground or a place where people can concoct a story and easily get in. Also Canada must respect the culture of laws of another sovereign country and we cannot be viewed as a judgemental country that decides what is right or wrong for other peoples or how they should live their lives. But I do believe once someone has embraced our shores and expressed a desire to remain here in Canada because of justified fears and a dissatisfaction with the oppressive, sexist and discriminatory policies of their government, then I believe they should be allowed to stay.

One of the issues I find irritating is immigrants coming to Canada, an English/French speaking country, and apparently making little or no effort to speak English or even to get involved in E.S.L. classes (English as a second language) and continuing to wear traditional clothes, and also wanting to be employed wearing their traditional clothes.

Claire: *"From immigrant to Canadian: How easy is the transition?..."*

Race and ethnicity are terms one rarely uses or prefers as a topic of discussion among friends, acquaintances or fellow workers. They seem to be taboo in Canadian society. And yet when people see each other, their first thought is "this person is yellow or brown or mulatto or black or white." It is known that visual images have a far greater impact than those produced by any of the other senses and hence the impact of skin colour or general features cannot be underestimated. As an individual, and being a first generation immigrant, I have been rather fortunate in not having had the nasty experience of a "culture shock" after having moved to Canada. My knowledge of English and previous experiences in dealing with people from different countries around the world during work and travel made my adaptation and integration into Canadian society easier than it might have been otherwise. Besides, having grown up in a large cosmopolitan city, awash in western influence, was also a major contributing factor in my familiarity with western culture.

Before arriving in Toronto I had never really given much thought to the importance of race, ethnicity and culture. In fact, I rarely thought about my own culture, probably because I lived it daily. However, after being here for a few days I realized that knowing the language and wearing Canadian-style clothing was not enough to make the transition to being a Canadian. Also, initially I wasn't sure if I wanted to be one. When asked who I was, my immediate reply was "Indian." I began to wonder if I was the target of discrimination and was going to be judged on the basis of my skin colour. I did my best to acquire the "Canadian" accent so as not to sound like a foreigner and even became rather good at blowing my own trumpet during job interviews (which is very much against my nature) but I could do nothing to change the way I looked. It was also very frustrating to know that my long years of education in India meant almost nothing here. I began to perceive discrimination in every rejection. Yet, I did manage to get a job and thought I'd won a great victory. One hurdle had been overcome and I felt nothing could stop me from becoming a successful Canadian. And yet, when at work, white-Canadian fellow workers would ask me "How come you speak such good English?" I could not take it as a compliment. In fact, I always felt insulted and angered that they thought only whites could master the English language. Unfortunately, I felt I was in no position to counter their perceptions except by making an exception of myself.

After being in Toronto for three years, watching people on the transit system, in malls and other public places, experiencing first hand what it's like to be a first-generation immigrant and becoming partly "Canadianized" I ask myself: "Is Canada a racist country?" The answer, of course, is "Yes." Not only do I see and hear and read about racist and discriminatory acts being perpetuated in this country, but also experience it first-hand—among neighbours, fellow workers, in the malls, on the transit system, etc. However, this does not drive me away from the country because, in spite of this, I have been able to achieve a certain amount of success and I'm sure I'll do even better in the future.

Anthony: *"Growing up as a child of immigrants..."*

I was born here in Canada. I am white, and have no trace of any accent. The language that is spoken in my home is English, and my family does not practice any religious customs other than status quo Christianity. Yet I think I can still empathize with the way in which many new, non-Anglo Canadians must certainly feel during this latest craze of immigrant-bashing.

My Mother emigrated from Poland at a young age, my Father, while being born here, is Italian and was socialized in Toronto's large Italian community, thus preserving many cultural traits. My name is obviously Italian and my physical features make it seem quite easy for everyone I meet to assume that I am Italian, a fact that brought me much grief growing up.

I was very aware of the stigma that was carried with the word "immigrant" while growing up in Toronto. Although it simply means a person who was born beyond the borders of one country and moved to another one, it carried other connotations as well. I didn't want to be called an immigrant, I perceived it as an insult. Although I was somewhat aware that the stereotypes of immigrants who were racial minorities were much more harmful and negative, the stereotypes of Eastern and Southern Europeans were still very much there. While playing down my Italian background as much as possible, I flat out denied being Polish.

There was no one single incident that brought these feelings on, I was never singled out in front of a large group to have my ethnicity ridiculed, I was not taught to hate myself the way Natives or Africans were, I have never known first hand the dehumanizing racism that people of colour must go through everyday. Most Italian and Polish people I have known have been very proud of their heritage. Yet, as a youngster I did not feel this way.

I can not in honesty remember the first specific incidents that I can justify my feelings with. But as far back as I can remember I thought that the word "immigrant" meant stupid, unclean, strange, outsider. I also remember the first day of school nearly every year when the teacher called my name and asked if I was Italian. The word instantly conjured up images of the greasy, over-sexed uneducated "wop" that seemed so prevalent on T.V. I was young, and wanted to be like everyone else, not an unwanted immigrant. I often answered "no" to the teacher's question. However, I was even more embarrassed to be

Polish. After hearing years of Polish jokes, I actually began wondering if Polish people were really inherently unintelligent.

I can remember when my grandmother dealt with the neighbourhood people; they were also immigrants. She was friendly and warm, she felt quite comfortable in her dealings with them. They appeared to me as neighbourhood people that were just like us, nothing to be intimidated by. When she had dealings with authority figures—they were exclusively Anglo, native-born Canadians—she became immediately apprehensive, telling me to always watch what I say around these people, to make sure to never insult them. Many of these people were polite, but I remember the ones who were rude and insulting towards her. She was just another dumb immigrant who couldn't speak English. Besides being intimidated by authority figures, these situations reinforced the idea that immigrants were second class citizens and native-born Anglos were the ideal Canadians who were to be revered and respected.

There were many days I went hungry as I could not bear to be seen eating the ethnic foods my mother made me for lunch. I often avoided having friends over for fear that they might hear my mother speaking Polish. These were the marks of the lowly immigrant that I desperately wanted no part of. I wanted the blond hair, blue eyes, and a cool, "Canadian" name like Brett Smith or Jay Johnson which were the marks of the Canadian.

To me, being other than Anglo meant being an immigrant. It meant being a janitor or cleaning woman. It meant dressing in strange attire and speaking peculiar languages. It brought images of my grandmother being scolded and humiliated by a cop, as if she were a child, it brought images of the leering immigrant who both steals jobs and drains the welfare system.

Through high school I never dated girls who weren't Anglo. I joined in with my exclusively "Canadian" friends in ridiculing the "wops" and "Ginos" and other immigrant kids at school. After twenty years of this, I systematically self-destroyed a very important part of who I am, a part I can never get back.

Maria: *"Having been born in a different country... I feel that being a member of the white race enables me to blend into the Canadian society much easier..."*

Having been born in a different country has enabled me to develop a greater awareness of my own ethnicity. When I first came to Canada, I realized that I was different from the people around me. Mainly because the language I spoke was Polish, not English. At that time I felt inferior because of the language barrier, but as my English improved, I was readily accepted by those around me. Since I spoke English, I was seen as a Canadian and no longer as an immigrant. Then and only then, I was able to say that I was Polish. At the present time I feel very strongly about my ethnic background. Even though I now live in Canada, I still want my children to speak the Polish language and practise the Polish traditions and customs.

I feel that being a member of the white race enables me to blend into the Canadian society much easier. My major barrier was being unable to communicate with the language of the dominant culture. But once that barrier was removed, combined with the fact that I was white, I was no longer considered as an outsider.

Multiculturalism

Ed: *"Is multiculturalism destroying Canadian identity?..."*

I was never a fan of the Multicultural Act and if anything I find myself even more opposed to it now. Although many people would like to say that this makes me a racist, I believe that I am not. A racist is someone who hates or discriminates against a person or people because of a difference (or perceived difference) in colour or religion. While I have never been like that, it sure makes my blood boil to hear that Sikhs can wear their turbans in police forces, or that schools are required to remove all references to Christmas from the classroom. Just because I do not like to see these events happen, doesn't mean that I dislike the person for succeeding in his or her quest. I am developing a strong discriminatory attitude towards the government.

On the topic of a Canadian identity, I can remember a government official (I cannot remember who) stating that one of Canada's greatest problems is that we haven't been able to create a feeling of being truly Canadian. This same politician stated that many of the problems that we are experiencing with Québec could be amended if we could just inspire a feeling of Canadian-ness within the people. That statement blew my mind. This same politician supports the very Act which is, with the government's blessing and money, destroying what remaining Canadian identity there was. Not only does Canada open its arms and borders to accept immigrants from all over the world, something that doesn't bother me, it also willingly changes CANADIAN traditions and

Is multiculturalism destroying the Canadian identity?

customs to accommodate them. In essence, what the Canadian government is doing is saying, "Hi, welcome, culture, don't worry about learning one of the two official languages of the country. In fact, if there are any traditions that have been around in Canada for a long time that you do not like, let us know, we will either exclude you from them or change them all just for you."

What this Multicultural Act has really done is given everyone a chance to change Canada and make it more like the countries they left in the first place. If you want to inspire a feeling of Canadian pride, leave Canada's laws and customs as they were and encourage people to assimilate, and contribute to the country in a positive way. As John F. Kennedy so eloquently put it, "Ask not what your country can do for you, but what you can do for your country!" Although this was an American President, I believe this country needs to do some real flag waving to wake it up

Ron: *"Religious Symbols: Do they contravene Canadian laws and policies?..."*

The idea that Sikhs are being allowed to wear their turbans on a police force makes me very, very mad. I know that in Canada everyone has the freedom of religion and there is nothing wrong with that. However, the Charter of Rights and Freedoms is like rules and regulations. The police force has rules and regulations and under those there is a uniform rule that states that every police officer must wear a hat. I don't think that it is right that a Sikh may change that rule. It is not fair to the rest of the police force. In fact, I think that it is an insult to this country. If I went to their country there would be no way in hell that I or any other white man would be able to change any of their rules. I do not have any prejudices against the Sikhs or any other nationality or skin colour but people from other countries are treating Canada like garbage and they are taking advantage of Canada and its people. I think that in order to change this problem Canada has to take away some of its privileges. One of these would be changing the Charter of Rights and Freedoms.

Simon: *"Freedom of Religion: Essence of the multicultural policy..."*

Although the past few decades have seen numerous changes in Canada's constitution regarding racist attitudes, statutes and laws founded on bigotry, the recent confrontation between the minority Sikhs and the majority white Canadians over the issue of the Sikhs wearing their ceremonial daggers in my opinion proves that the system of social stratification and inequality among minority groups is far from being eradicated.

Being labelled as a minority within the Canadian culture tends to lead to certain stigmas and attacks that are being built up around the colour of people's skin, as well as what rites or rituals take place within the sub-culture of minority groupings. Recently Sikhs have become the target for attacks such as these regarding this traditional dagger, which a great many Sikhs see as an essential part of their heritage.

When Sikhs come to Canada and become citizens of this country, they, as well as all other minority groups, are granted full freedom of religion, language and all heritage rights. I believe that by depriving the Sikhs of their right to wear the kirpan, the very essence of the multicultural policy within Canada is being ignored. The Sikhs view their dagger as something to be honoured and deeply treasured, just as Christians view their cross—not as weapons.

I think it is sad that the prevalent attitude among so many Canadians is the thought that "we let them in to this country so they should do as we tell them to. You don't see us going to their country and making all these demands." I believe that this type of statement reflects as a whole, the way in which the Canadian population has been reared, with close-minded and bigoted attitudes which have been handed down from generation to generation.

Many more changes need to be made before Sikhs or any other minority group can appreciate the freedom that they deserve. Although Canada is proclaimed to be a multicultural country we really are not, and until multiculturalism is fully enforced and regulated, minority rights will continue to be undermined and stepped on. Changes need to be made now.

Avinder: *"All I would like is the same respect back..."*

I am seen to others as a minority. Some people tend to see me differently because I am of a different race. But what they do not know is that I am not so different from them. I speak the same language, eat the same food, and do the same activities. Just because I am a different race they think that I do different things. I try to fit in with other groups and appreciably try to learn what others can teach me. All I would like is the same respect back. Religion is important to me and also very important to my parents. But that does not mean that everywhere I go I take my religion with me, because this is not so. Since I was brought to this country, I try to do what others do, and I practise my religion in my own home. I believe that my family and I carry out our responsibilities as Canadians ought to. Everyone should have their religion in them somewhere, but practice it on your own time.

James: *"Misconceptions about the French..."*

During the last week, Québec's sovereignty issue has been competing with the Gulf War for news headlines. The issue sparked after the failure of the Meech Lake Accord. The collapse of the Accord created an even stronger feeling of patriotism in Québec. This event sealed the fate of Canada's future. French Canadians are often thought to be extremists, separatists and selfish. I believe that English Canadians don't know enough about the history of French Canada to be able to be make a fair and unbiased assessment of the situation. During the next few paragraphs, I will express my opinion and try to clarify the situation as a "Québécois."

I don't believe anyone can get a full understanding of the situation unless they've lived it. I was born in Montréal and I went to a French school until I came to college in Ontario. I believe that this enabled me to see through many of the lies that the media was reporting. The greatest concern for the French is the preservation of their language. They live in a continent dominated by English. They feel this influence through the music that they listen to, television, the media and of course the political system. Many tactics taken by the Québec government to ensure the safety of the language are questionable. The greatest example is Bill 101; this affected the province on many levels: economic, educational, social, etc. ... I believe that it violates human rights especially in the domain of freedom of speech. But is it justified? I believe it is, if the rest of Canada is almost solely English (road signs, store signs), why not! Although there is one aspect that I haven't made up my mind on: Immigrants or Canadians whose parents never went to an English school are obliged to go to a French school, although I believe going to a French school is the first step towards becoming a "true Canadian" (most immigrants already know a bit of English)!

If you had taken a good history course, you will know that Canada did not start with equality among the English and the French. I remember learning that the English had tried to assimilate the French by forcing them to go to English schools and by not allowing them to have any Catholic establishments. Eventually, they got some of their rights back, not because of the fairness of the English, but because of their strong will and their patriotism towards each other. That is one thing that will never change, their devoted patriotism towards the Québec flag and their language. Proof of that is in Québec's music, theatre and especially on Saint Jean Baptist day (National holiday). For the first time this summer I participated in it and I was blown away by the amount of people in the streets with flags and chanting "Vive le Québec." That day I was proud to be a "Québécois!"

The thing that annoys me the most is when other Canadians complain that when they went to Québec nobody spoke to them in English. What do you expect? The French know just as much English as the rest of Canada knows French. If a French person were to travel in the rest of Canada, they wouldn't expect everyone to speak French to them. Let's not have double standards!

I believe it's time Canada realizes that Québec is a completely different culture. The way things are going, Québec will separate and it will prove to be a great loss to all Canadians. It's time we open our eyes and accept Québec for what it is and not for what we want it to be!

Without "La Belle Province," there will be no Canada. It's about time all Canadians discard their differences and try to live together as one!

Troy: *"Police and the Black Community..."*

We argued and argued over the matter of the Black community and the police. My argument, and I think I can speak for at least one quarter of the class, was that Black people tend to be more involved in crime. From statistics or police documents I can draw this conclusion. But one cannot make this type of conclusion because statistics mean nothing. All that they are saying is that so many crimes are being committed by these types of people. There are bad apples on every tree. I believe that all people are good, and just because there are some bad ones does not mean that the entire race should be discriminated against. I also hold the belief that a criminal has no colour. A criminal is a wrongdoer, and all criminals shall be dealt with by the law.

Employment Equity

Randy: *"Employment Equity: Discrimination against White Males?..."*

Almost every time someone begins to talk about employment opportunities, you can bet the topic of employment equity will come up. This seems to be on a lot of people's minds, especially those who are interested in police or fire fighting employment.

It doesn't really matter how these agencies wish to carry out their hiring procedures, because in the end they are all under close supervision. By who? By the N.D.P. government, that's who. Bob Rae, the party leader, has implemented an employment equity legislation. The rules were sent down to the agencies and it was explained that they were to hire a certain percentage of women and minorities within a given time. This is good because it forces police and fire agencies to open the doors to these prescribed groups that have been discriminated against in the past. On the other hand it's also kind of bad.

Being a member of the "white male" group, I have now come up against an annoying obstacle. Because of this new employment equity legislation the police forces are trying to increase their enrolment numbers of women, minority and disabled groups in order to meet Mr. Rae's requirements.

I think the phrase "employment equity" should be changed to "employment inequity." According to Webster's New World dictionary equity means "fairness and impartiality." From the same dictionary I found the word equal to mean "of the same value, having the same rights, to be equal to." Perhaps Mr. Rae has a different dictionary in which his translations come from.

The majority of the population should realize that women, minorities and the disabled have been discriminated against and in many cases still are. They may not admit it, but they know it's true. If this is the case ... why turn everything upside down by trying to make amends with these prescribed groups over such a short time? Why turn the white male into the minority, because this is what's happening, the white male is being discriminated against for something that happened beyond his/her control; it's a form of reverse discrimination. The police forces actually tell us (the white applicants), that our chances are slim of getting hired until the employment equity numbers balance out. This is where I start to get my back up. Equality should mean that everyone gets the same chance of being hired. If the top 10 applicants are black, they are hired, if they are white males, they are hired and the same if they are female. Forget about balancing the numbers, give the job to the person who best deserves it. That's equal!

Employment equity has played a minor role in my personal life. A couple of years back when this legislation came into effect I was applying to the Toronto Police with a East Indian friend of mine. I received a higher mark than him on the physical testing, and we were close on the written. After these tests the Toronto Police put out a hiring freeze and I was asked to re-apply at a later date. Two weeks after this, my friend received a phone call from Toronto Police asking him to come in for an interview. Toronto pushed him through the hiring process in less than two months and had him signed up to go to police college the following month. On average, the normal hiring procedure takes roughly six to twelve months, start to finish. The main difference between our two applications was that mine said "white male" and his said "visible minority," I'm sure there was more but this stuck out and bothered me. From that point I know I had to make myself a more attractive applicant to recruiters because the competition had just became tougher.

I'm a firm believer in the saying "two wrongs don't make a right," but this is what's happening now with employment equity. I truly wish I had a solution to offer that may rectify the situation and make it fair for everyone.

Will employment equity benefit society as a whole?, I don't think so. If anything it has created greater tension between the white applicants and the prescribed groups. It has brought our society into a state of disrepute. Eventually when employment equity has succeeded society as a whole may be better off, but then again I'm not sure. Even the minorities when asked say they want to be hired because they were the best, not because they were the minority. But on the other hand, if some recruiter told me I was wanted because I was white, and they were short of whites I wouldn't think twice about the so called "equity."

Competition is very tough in the job market these days and spreads further than the police and fire fighting professions. It's very common for someone to make an excuse, or to blame someone else for their own problems. For example, the fisherman always has ten reasons why the "big one" got away. Well, for some, not being hired on a police or fire department brings about a similar set of excuses, such as "I didn't get hired because some minority took my spot," and various other reasons. Being in a Police Education class I hear too many of these excuses every day, and it's usually before people even go to write their exam. In my opinion these people are probably not qualified and their preparing themselves for defeat, in turn using the minorities as their scapegoats. In the long run all employment equity is doing is making the competition that much more stiff. Therefore, if you want the opportunity, you have to go and get it because it's not going to come to you, and that's the bottom line.

Roger: *"Employment Equity: Reverse Racism?..."*

I come from an Irish-English family (75%-25% mix), and was raised in a white middle-class household. My family has never been overly rich, nor have we ever starved. I was born in Toronto, but raised in the suburbs, so in essence I have lived a rather sheltered life.

Even though I grew up in a good, financially stable home, I don't consider this fact to be an advantage created by my race or ethnicity. Through school and social clubs, I've had many friends from different races and ethnic backgrounds who were in a home of equal to greater financial stability. Like many others, my parents are both fairly unedu-cated, by today's standards, yet through hard work and determination have managed to make a success of themselves.

All through talking with other people, I've been trying to think of an instance where my race, or my ethnicity has been of an advantage to me, and I haven't been able to think of one. Sure, there is the fact that

I came from a stable home, but this has nothing to do with my race, it has to do with loving parents who have shown a genuine concern with what I do. Maybe the fact that I am fairly well educated can be considered an advantage, but my race didn't put me through school. My parents' guidance, my own drive to better myself and a desire to reach a certain goal, are what completed my education. Maybe always having money in my pocket can be considered an advantage, but even this fact is not a result of my race; the fact that I have always had a part-time job and worked hard to earn the money is.

So even after listening to other people's stories and points of view, I have found no situation were my being white is an advantage. I have always been a believer in the human spirit, I believe that what a person is, not what a person looks like, determines his or her future.

Employment equity in the workplace is a policy which has generated considerable controversy.

Just as I have not been able to think of a past experience or incident were my race or ethnicity has been an advantage, I am not able to think of an incident were my race or ethnicity has been a disadvantage. That is up until recently.

As my graduation quickly approaches, I am becoming more and more frustrated by the tough uphill battle which I will have to undertake. As is obvious, my future goal is to become a police officer, a profession which has been drastically affected by special interest groups, pathetic government policies and government appointed "overseers" such as the infamous Susan Eng. Through the media and schools, we are constantly bombarded with messages and slogans denouncing racism and discrimination. We are told that these types of acts will no longer be tolerated by society, and will be slushed through Government policies and public awareness. In our tireless search for racism and discrimination, two very interesting and disturbing phenomena have appeared: Everything has become a "racial issue," and "reverse discrimination."

This government's "Employment Equity Program" and "Multicultural Act" have in essence turned my race and my ethnicity into a disadvantage. The fact that I am a high school and college graduate no longer carries any significant merit when applying to a police force or any other Government agency. The prime qualification has become skin colour.

Although many "experts" and government officials will deny the existence of reverse discrimination and hiring quotas, professionals within the affected fields will give you a completely different story. The agencies' personnel tell horror stories about the government-imposed "hiring of minorities at all cost" tactics. Stories like these do little to add optimism to my view of a future career.

Many people talk about instances were they have been denied jobs in the past because of their race; well, in the near future I too will be able to relate to these people very easily. The only difference is I will be affected by a Government-endorsed policy.

The next question is, how does this make me feel? Quite simply put, nauseated. Now the fact that I am qualified, and possess more than sufficient skills to perform my job, has little to no bearing. I may now be forced to sit back and watch less qualified and less educated persons pass me in line because they are members of a race which the government has targeted.

The Employment Equity program is a topic of which I have very mixed emotions. The concept behind the program is good; it prevents employers from denying people positions within companies or agencies according to their colour or religion. The problem is in how the government has implemented the program. In government agencies, and in the public service sector, this program has made it extremely difficult to almost impossible for a white person (especially a white male) to find employment. In the business world, competition is not restricted to just business transactions, the whole application process is also a competition. If a person is more qualified because of English skills, education and experience he/she should get the job. This is not necessarily true now with the implementation of this Employment Equity.

My example of how this government has gone overboard with this program is the same as my cousin Brent's. During the summer, I had to go to the OHIP building to straighten up a problem I had with my health card. As soon as I entered the office, I was taken aback, not only was I the only white in the office, I was the only one capable of speaking English at an understandable level. After approximately 10 minutes of trying to understand what the OHIP employee was saying to me, the supervisor finally showed up (just returning from her lunch break). I was relieved to find out that not only was the lady capable of speaking English, but was also very understandable (and yes she also was of a visible minority group). My point here is, if these jobs are posted publicly, there would have to be applicants who possess good English skills. Did these people just not show up during the interviews for these jobs? In these economic times, I find that very hard to believe. Also if the purpose of the Employment Equity is to show an equal representation of the community which it belongs, someone obviously made a mistake.

Eugene: *"Employment Equity is a course of events which is inevitable..."*

The things that I feel have affected me the most while in this class were the topics of reverse discrimination, and of whites of this generation "paying" for the mistakes and ignorance of our forefathers. This in particular because I have Chinese background and I also have white background. Is it necessary then, to split me in half so that my white half may be condemned, and my Chinese half may receive retribution? And finally, the ignorant and extremely racist attitudes that were displayed by certain classmates really appalled, shocked, dismayed, and insulted me. Having people like this in my class really made the issue of racism hit close to home.

The topic of reverse discrimination basically made me realize that even though I am willing to make this effort to understand, it does not mean that those I encounter will feel similarly. And I cannot allow these people to make me lose sight of what I feel is right, nor let them weaken my determination.

The topic of whites of this generation paying for the mistakes of their forefathers also affects me greatly. I realize that this is a course of events which must inevitably come about but it is hard to see past the fact that I am losing out. I guess where one stands on this topic depends on whether they feel their life is more important than the future or vice versa.

Radcliffe: *"Employment Equity—A necessary hiring practice..."*

I intend to discuss that employment equity is a necessary hiring practice that needs to stay in effect until an acceptable balance in employment is achieved.

When I first learned of employment equity I felt that it was reverse discrimination. I thought that minorities were getting an unfair advantage over those who had more experience in their field. Now I understand that equity means giving people a fair chance at getting hired. Equity means that other factors are taken into consideration when hiring. A man who has worked just as hard as a man who has been hindered by prejudice and unfair hiring practices should be credited for what he has endured to enter the job market.

As children we learn through example. When minorities are growing up in our society they are socialized with cultural bias and unequal representation in their curriculum. If at a young age they are taught that positions of power are open to all people and yet no minority has occupied such powerful positions, they will not perceive themselves "Good" enough for the job. For common sense would dictate that if there were a equitable hiring practice in effect there would be people of all races occupying such power positions. For example a young black female has never seen a black woman police officer. So she does not take the necessary steps in order to reach that position. With the employment equity in place the disadvantaged youth is given merit for enduring a culturally biased educational system. Now when a young black girl sees someone like her in such a power position she will take the necessary steps to become a police officer and she can get the job regardless of whether or not employment equity exists. When equal representation of cultures is met within the police force, or any other profession for that matter, employment equity should be discontinued. As the demographics of the surrounding area fluctuate employment equity should be able to go with those changes.

Discussion

A poll conducted in 1989 found that 49 per cent of the people polled agreed that immigrants take away jobs from Canadians. The same study also found that Canadians were concerned that newcomers, particularly racial minorities, do not make enough effort to integrate into the society (Angus Reid, 1989). These ideas remain and are reflected in the above essays. More generally, it is felt that the changes in the economy, the double-digit unemployment rate, the need to preserve "our" cultural identity, and the rising tensions among the various ethnic and racial groups are enough reasons for "the Canadian government to stop immigration altogether or drastically reduce the numbers coming in." Unfortunately, this position fails to take into consideration Canada's needs and the significant role of immigrants in the economic wellbeing of Canada.

Before proceeding, it is important to clarify the difference between an immigrant and a refugee, a confusion that was often reflected in the comments made by participants. An immigrant is a person who takes up permanent resident in Canada, while a refugee, or Convention refugee, according to the United Nations definition and adopted by all member countries like Canada, is:

Any person who, by reason of a well-founded fear of persecution for reason of race, religion, nationality, membership in a particular social group or political opinion, (a) is outside the country of his (her) nationality and is unable or, by reason of such fear, is unwilling to avail himself (herself) of the protection of that country, or, (b) not having a country of nationality, is outside the country of his (her) former habitual residence and is unable, or by reason of such fear, is unwilling to return to the country.[1]

It is estimated that we would experience a decline in population if we were to significantly reduce the number of immigrants and refu-

---

[1] It should be noted that people just do not enter Canada and claim refugee status, Canada must first recognize the country of which claimants are citizens as refugee-producing countries, of course with reference to the United Nations definition. Other factors that are taken into account to qualify as a refugee are: age, level of education, job skills, knowledge of English or French and security and health considerations.

gees entering Canada. This is so, since according to Statistics Canada, we have a birth rate of 1.8 and an aging population; there are more Canadians dying than are born; and well over 10,000 people emigrate from Canada (most going to the United States) each year. This is the situation that makes the Canadian government, despite many Canadians' opposition to immigration, continue to allow some 250,000 immigrants into the country each year. This supports the claim made by many demographers and statisticians that we need this number of immigrants entering Canada each year if we are to have a viable economy and social stability.[1] The aging of our population is of particular importance here. It is estimated that by 2036 one in every four Canadians will be 65 years or older (Gauthier, 1994). So as the post-war baby boom generation gets older and drops out of the labour force, there will be an increased need for immigrants to fill the labour force's needs, which in turn will provide a steady tax base to fund the high quality health and social service needs of that generation.

In order to sustain population levels and meet labour force demands, Canada's immigration policies have traditionally sought to attract the youngest, healthiest, best-educated and most resourceful people. Since the introduction of the immigration point system[2] in 1967, all immigrants except close family relatives of Canadian citizens and permanent residents, have been assessed according to age, education, training and experience, demand for their occupation in Canada, presence of pre-arranged employment and/or knowledge of one or more of Canada's official languages. Over three quarters (77 percent) of all immigrants admitted to Canada during the 1980s were under the age of 40; over half (57 percent) were under 30 (Logan, 1991: 11). Adjusted for age, the 1986 census shows that 28.2 percent

---

[1] In fact, according to the Law Union of Ontario (1981), Canada's population would begin to decline to by the year 2000 with an annual immigrant rate of 100,000.

[2] In addition to the refugee class of immigrants, there are also, as set out by the Immigration Act of 1976, family and independent classes. The family class refers to those who may be sponsored by relatives (e.g. parents, siblings, children), or nominated by husband, wife or fiancee who are Canadian residents or citizens, 18 years or older. Sponsors must agree to provide maintenance for up to 10 years. Independent immigrants include assisted relatives (not in the above category), entrepreneurs, investors and retirees. Those entering through this class must qualify by scoring a minimum of 70 points out of a possible 100 based on age, level of education, job skills, occupational demand, knowledge of English or French, "personal suitability" (i.e. capacity to adapt to Canada), and security and health considerations. Entrepreneurs must intend to operate a business and employ one or more Canadians. Investors must have a net worth of $500,000 and must invest a minimum of $150,000 in a project that create jobs and is economically beneficial.

of immigrants compared to 22.3 percent of native-born Canadians had some university education (Jansen and Richmond, 1990: 6). More current data indicate that this percentage has increased in recent years. Although educational attainment data includes pre-school and school age children, a full 33 percent of newcomers had some postsecondary education; among refugees, 28 percent had some postsecondary education (Employment and Immigration, 1989b: 22).

People are particularly sensitive to factors which might operate as barriers or hurdles to the realization of their aspirations and goals when they are at the point of entering the job market. It is understandable therefore that the class participants would think, given the degree to which this view is supported in the media, that immigrants are taking jobs to which Canadians citizens are entitled. Economists argue that by creating demands for goods and services, immigrants create jobs for Canadians. According to one government study, immigrants and refugees admitted to Canada between 1983 and 1985, created 9,000 jobs over and above those they filled, and that single immigrant entrepreneurs were expected to create or maintain an average of six jobs (Employment and Immigration, 1992a). Another study estimated that immigrant investigators created an estimated 10,000 jobs between January 1986 and December 1991 (Employment and Immigration, 1992b). While immigrants are to be found in significant numbers, and are in some cases over-represented, in some industries and businesses compared to native-born workers, this is certainly not the cases in the labour force as a whole. As has already been mentioned, because the majority of immigrants are selected on the basis of education, skills, experience, "national and regional population goals and labour market needs" (Employment and Immigration, 1978: 25), they tend to fill labour market gaps. So immigrants fill jobs which there are no Canadians to fill or jobs which Canadians do not want. The notion that immigrants are a drain on our social services is not supported by research data either. For instance, according to the Economic Council of Canada, between 1981 and 1986, 12.5 percent of the newcomers to Canada received some government social assistance cheques compared to 13.8 percent of Canadian-born adults; and only 3.5 percent of foreign-born received welfare in 1987 compared with 5.5 percent of those born in Canada (Jensen and Richmond, 1990). This indicates, as has so often been said, that newcomers tend to make less use of the social service system than native-born Canadians. In cases of social and financial needs they

Statistics illustrate that immigration is necessary for the maintenance of Canada's population and productive economy.

tend to turn for assistance from their sponsoring relative or community rather than to government. immigrants tend to aspire to be self sufficient and this can only be achieved through their own work efforts; they are inexperienced with such government assistance programs, particularly immigrants from "developing nations"; they would feel that accepting such assistance would be an admission of failure, something that is contrary to the reason for which they immigrated in the first place; and the immigration policies require that they are economically self-sufficiency and/or they are the responsibility of their sponsor for at least 10 years or until they become citizens.

Similarly, the myth that there is a correlation between an increase in crime and an increase in immigration is an example of media-fed xenophobia in Canada. This is fuelled by stereotypes based on race, ethnicity and the countries of origin of members of minority groups. The immigration act spells out that persons convicted of criminal offenses or believed to have committed a crime, and persons who would constitute a danger to national security are inadmissible. A study by Samuel (1989) showed that the criminality rate of immigrants from source areas like Africa, Asia and the Caribbean was less than one third of that of immigrants from the United States and Europe. Generally, the criminal behaviours of any population must be examined in relations to that group's access to opportunities. For immigrants, in particular, we need to examine how, as the host society, our accommodation practices provide immigrants access to the necessary employment and education opportunities. Before leaving this point, there is one question I think we should think about: When does a person cease to be regarded as an immigrant? What are the criteria that makes one a Canadian?

The above essays indicate that a distinction is not made between immigrants and racial and ethnic minorities. In fact, these minorities, especially racial minorities, are often constructed as immigrants. They are perceived as having "come to our country" settling within "their own ethnic groups" and protesting "in the streets of Canada about issues back in their country." Some suggest that Canada's multicultural policy is responsible for what is seen as immigrants (or racial and ethnic minority group members) "taking advantage of our liberalism" to the extent that they try to change "our identity," "our laws," and "our culture." But an honest examination of our demography will indicate that "ethnic" neighbourhoods abound throughout the country, and have for many, many generations. Neighbourhoods populated by people of similar background, whether by language, social class, ethnicity, race, nationality or sexual orientation, provide members of that community with an available support system. Associations, organization and businesses located in these neighbourhoods strengthen individual and group identity, nurture community spirit and foster economic self-sufficiency and productivity. As one minority member of metropolitan Toronto comments: "You have to understand that back home, we don't have social insurance or anything of that kind ... Everyone's social insurance policy is [their] relatives and friends. If you grow older, or you are somewhat poor, you always rely on the people you know and your relatives. We always depend on each other" (Watson, 1991: A11).

Insofar as immigrants must adjust to a new environment, and they are likely to experience barriers to full participation in the society, particularly as racial and ethnic minorities, then it is inevitable that they would seek alternative ways of participating. It is within these communities that they find the space and the voice to experience the life they would wish. Further, we maintain that in a democratic society, everyone has the right to live where and with whom they choose, as well as participate in the way they wish. Hence, where they live and the ways in which they participate are individual choices rather than prescribed options or privileges.

In one of the above essays, the writer points out that immigrants should not "protest in the streets of Canada about issues in their country, " they should protest "about Canadian issues." An interesting question that this raises is: Do not *all* Canadians have the freedom to exercise their rights as citizens—the right to express their political positions about—and hence influence—local, national and international issues? Similar objections about how people choose to participate and explain their opinions are not often articulated when members of the dominant group protest about international issues. In such cases, they are not perceived to be protesting out of self-interest but from a position of concern and empathy. This same behaviour, when exhibited by racial and ethnic minorities, is invariably interpreted as the actions of "others"—"outsiders" and "immigrants."

In Chapter One, we observed that all societies are multicultural and that racial, ethnic, religious, linguistic and regional groups have different subcultures. In Canada, with the exception of Aboriginals, all of our ethnic groups are immigrants, some more recent than others. Tensions and conflicts are often found within culturally diverse societies. They are sometimes a result of differences in political perspectives, lack of recognition of respective differences, lack of access to political and economic resources, and the society's inability to manage and accommodate these differences. Canada is not unique with the difficulties we experience between the various subcultural groups. The French-English issue is an example of historic tensions that exist in culturally diverse societies such as ours. Similar tensions and conflict can be observed in other nations. How we address these issues and tensions reflect how we come to understand and accept our cultural diversity, as well as how we accommodate our minority population.

One aspect of our cultural diversity with which many Canadians seem to struggle is that of "religious freedom"—individuals' right to engage in their particular religious practices. As some of the essays indicate, religious practices, for example those of Sikhs (the ones that are often cited) are perceived to contravene our laws, and to change "our Canadian identity." Particular references are made to "Sikhs being allowed to wear turbans on the police force, or the RCMP." Participants insist that religious practices such as those of Sikhs are contrary to our laws even when informed that the Constitution of Canada and the Multiculturalism Act support these practices. Specifically, the Constitution

provides that every individual is equal before and under the law and has the right to equal protection and benefit of the law without discrimination and that everyone has the freedom of conscience, religion, thought, belief, opinion, expression, peaceful assembly and association ...

And the Multiculturalism Act states in part:

And whereas Canada is a party to the International Convention on the Elimination of All Forms of Racial Discrimination, which Convention recognizes that all human beings are equal before the law and are entitled to equal protection of the law against any discrimination and against any incitement to discrimination, and to the International Covenant on Civil and Political Rights, which Covenant provides that persons belonging to ethnic, religious or linguistic minorities shall not be denied the right to enjoy their own culture, to profess and practise their own religion or to use their own language ...

Very often criticisms are made by dominant group Canadians whose religious practices and symbols are very well preserved by the laws and institutions of our society. Generally, Canadians do not know that the Sikh religion has been in Canada for generations, that the first Sikh temple or *gurdwara* was opened in Vancouver, British Columbia in 1908 (Burnet and Palmer, 1989). On the basis of longevity alone, this should be seen as an established Canadian religion.

The principle of equity and social justice underlie any practices that is established to ensure the rights and privileges of Canadians. The fact that the multiculturalism policy exists is because in a democratic society, measures must be taken to ensure that the rights and freedom of all members of society are protected; that there is full and equitable participation of all members of the society; and that barriers to participation do not exist. Similarly, the employment equity[1] policy seeks to remove barriers in accessing employment opportunities. Employment equity policies, as Fish argues in his essay: "Reverse Racism or How the Pot Got To Call The Kettle Black," are "not intended to disenfranchise white males. Rather the policy was driven by other considerations, and it was only as a by-product of those considerations—not as a goal—that white males have been rejected" (Fish, 1993: 136). These considerations include such things as minority representation and an acknowledgement that barriers to employment opportunities have existed historically and systemically, and continue to exist for racial and ethnic minorities. In making this point in class, I often get the response: "Two wrongs don't make a right; if it is unfair to discriminate against Blacks, it is just as unfair to discriminate against Whites." This position is posited on the notion that everyone is or should be the *same,* and ignores the historical fact that groups have been excluded historically or treated inequitably. It is a dismissal of individual and group differences, and a disregard for the existing power imbalance that provides advantages to some members of society and forces disadvantages upon others. Fairness is a notion that must be evaluated in relation to the histories of respective groups to which individuals belong. Equity programs are "attempts to undo the effects of arbitrary and racist policies and practices that have historically been barriers to access and opportunities" (James, 1995) for some.

The claim that employment equity is "reverse racism" or "reverse discrimination" has merit only if racism or discrimination are constructed in terms of individuals' attitudes and ignorance, rather than a product of historical and structural factors. But we know, as discussed in Chapter Five, that racism is not based merely on individuals' ignorance or negative attitudes, but more importantly on structural inequality. It is more than individuals' attitudes and acts of discrimination. It is a cultural and historical fact that structures the

---

[1] The term employment equity is seen as uniquely Canadian. It was coined by the 1984 Royal Commission on Equity in Employment (Judge Rosalie Abella). It is used to "describe programs designed to improve the situation of individuals who, because of they are or can be identified as being in a particular group, find themselves adversely affected by certainly systems or practices in the workplace" (Moreau, 1994: 147). The four groups that have been identified as disadvantaged because of their labour force participation, unemployment rates, levels of income, and persistent occupational segregation are: women, Aboriginal people, "visible" minorities, and people with disabilities (Moreau, 1994: 147).

norms and values of this society, consequently finding expressions in the laws, policies and practices of institutions. As I argued elsewhere:

Essentially, the phase "reverse racism" seems oxymoronic. It negates the inherent inequalities in resources and power among groups posited by racial categorization in our society. It is a phrase that has important carriage for young white males, for it gives political weight to their feelings of powerlessness and loss of privilege. The term allows them to wear the banner of oppression as victims of a system over which, like racial minorities, they have no control ... It fails to construct power in structural and historical terms which would account for the cultural capital that they possess because of their membership in their particular racial group. Inherent in their conceptualization of racism is their neglect to acknowledge their own power and privilege, and to recognize that their own power is rooted in the historical and cultural conditions upon which this society has been built. Not to recognize the structural roots of racism and their white privilege is a way of denying their own racism, the benefit they derive from its existence, and their responsibility for participating in changing it (James, 1994.)

We cannot minimize the importance of the fact that some who articulate this sense of victimization are students. As young people, they attend postsecondary institutions, with the hope that they will "have the edge" on other job applicants, eventually realizing their occupational goals. They are particularly sensitive to the job market and the employment opportunities that await them. Whatever is perceived as a barrier would contribute frustration and anger. Their anger and frustration stem also from what they see as meritocracy being compromised. As an article in *Business Week* magazine points out, "At the heart of the issue for many white males is the question of merit—that in the rush for a more diverse workplace, they will lose out to less qualified workers" (January, 1994: 52). This might in part explain why, in their bid to maintain some sense of self-confident and optimism, some individuals see employment equity as premised on a quota system in which "less qualified minorities are being hired."

But studies reveal that racial and ethnic minorities experience significant barriers to employment opportunities. For instance, in a survey of employers in Toronto, Billingsley and Muzynski (1985) found that most employers relied on informal employee and friendship networks to recruit and fill job positions. Moreover, a survey of 672 corporate recruiters, hiring mangers and agency recruiters conducted by Canadian Recruiters Guild in 1989 showed that 87 percent of corporate and 100 percent of agency recruiters surveyed received direct discriminatory requests. Nearly three-quarters of corporate and 94 percent of agency recruiters complied with these requests. The survey also showed that out of 6,720 available positions, only four target group members were placed by the recruiting agencies (Currents, April 1989: 19-20). In their 1985 study "Who Gets the Work: A Test of Racial Discrimination in Employment" in Toronto, Henry and Ginzberg concluded that:

> ... there is a very substantial racial discrimination affecting the ability of members of racial minorities to find employment even when they are well qualified and eager to find work ... Once an applicant is employed, discrimination can still affect opportunities for advancement, job retention, and level of earnings, to say nothing of the question of the quality of work and the relationship with co-workers (1990: 20).

And in a study of Black youth employment experiences, James (1993) quotes respondents as saying that racism and discrimination were "challenges" with which they had to contend, both in terms of obtaining a job and while they were on the job. They suggested that "who you know" is even more important than education, "particularly in competition against a white person for a job." As one respondent stated, "while education can help, I have seen that who you know gets you further" (p. 10).

Information that challenges the myth of meritocracy is difficult for anyone to accept, particularly middle-class, postsecondary students, when they have been socialized to believe that the principles of democracy and correspondingly, meritocracy, work well to provide all Canadians the same opportunities and chances to succeed once they have gained the ability, education, training and skill, and the opportunity to apply themselves. Such people subscribe to the notion that it is individuals' efforts and ability, and not systemic factors that determine achievement. It is inconceivable therefore, that governments and other institutions should support what these students perceive as "unfairness"—a situation in which race or gender or ability is seen as operating to advantage some (ie Aboriginals, women, racial minorities, and people with disabilities). When governments and institutions by these practice admit to inequalities, they appear to deny the young men's traditional beliefs in meritocracy. This raises doubts in their minds, shakes their confidence in the system, and has them asking questions such as "why me, why now?" Or, "why do I have to pay for things that I am not responsible for creating?" Nonetheless, it remains that at some point, remedies like these must be developed to address the situations of those citizens who are, and have been in the past, disadvantaged by structural inequalities. If not now, when?

SUMMARY

The essays on immigration, multiculturalism and employment equity tend to suggest that participants see these phenomena as impediments to economic growth and positive social relations in Canada. Immigration is perceived as largely unnecessary particularly at this time of high unemployment and social tensions due to crime and ethnic differences. But as Darren rightly mentions in his answer to the question: "Are immigrants a strain on our society?"

> One of the benefits from having immigrants come into the country is economic. The immigrants will obtain jobs and receive wages in return, they then will spend the money on necessities, such as food, shelter, and clothing. When more products like these have to be supplied, the companies that produce them have to accommodate the demands of the new immigrants. When this happens new jobs are created. This is also beneficial to economic growth, and will eventually benefit all the country. This is the aspect that a number of Canadians do not take into consideration when they oppose new arrivals to the country.

> Without immigrants, we would not be able to increase in population. The reason for this is that the number of children born is very low and will not compensate for the number of deaths and emigration that occur each year. The influx of new immigrants into the country will help to compensate and eventually even out and expand the population. This will enable Canada to become economically stable and prosperous.

And as Fleras and Elliot (1992) state: "the immigrants of today are likely to underwrite the costs of the delivery of social services in the future. For this reason alone, we are as dependent on immigrants as they are on us" (p. 46).

Many people see a link between immigration and multiculturalism—two unnecessary evils. It is believed that the large numbers of immigrants, their assertiveness and expectations that their ethnic and religious values and practices be recognized, contribute to disharmony and a loss of "Canadian identity." But as one participant argues, this perception of multiculturalism, immigration and immigrants is due to the fact that "we are resistant to change and anything foreign. What we don't understand, we destroy. The cold hard fact is that we need immigrants more than they need us." The subcultures expressed by minority group members is related to the social situ-

Legislation like employment equity has forced many Canadians to re-evaluate their views about equality and fair hiring practices.

ation or context in which they find themselves. "It is identification with select objective markers of that cultural lifestyle—not the degree of intensity of involvement or the number of distinguishing cultural traits—that is crucial" (Fleras and Elliott, 1992: 51). Furthermore, remind us, the ethnic culture is not necessarily based on the original immigrant culture but on a "reconstructed" ethnicity in which tradition is "invented" on the basis of ongoing adaptations to the environment and to the social situation in Canada (Fleras and Elliot, 1992: 51).

On the issue of employment equity many of the white class participants see it as "reverse racism," "reverse discrimination," and/or an unfair policy in which "less qualified racial minorities" are being hired. One participant argues that because of employment equity "white males are not being hired and this causes some sort of negative feelings towards the designated groups. I believe this created more tension and frustration among each other." However, with reference to the career to which he aspires, he admits that as "a corrective measure," employment equity "would definitely help" since having coworkers from "all racial minority backgrounds can and will benefit a multicultural society."

It can be said that myths, misinformation and half-truths characterize much of the discussion about immigration, immigrants, multiculturalism and employment equity. These myths are largely based on the lack of acknowledgement of the inherent economic and social inequities within our society, a fear of social change, and an anticipated loss of political, economic, and social power and privilege. They are also coloured by prejudices, stereotypes, and racism aimed toward the groups who are characterized as their benefactors. If we are to build a democratic and equitable society in Canada, then we must be prepared for social change and we all must play a part in initiating and fighting for that change.

Questions:

1. Discuss the historical significance of immigration and immigrants to the economic, social, political and technological development of Canada. How will immigration play a role in the future development of Canada?

2. What is meant by the term "hyphenated Canadian"? What role does the population in general play in maintaining the "hyphen" in some Canadians' lives?

3. Is there such a thing as "reverse racism"? Do multiculturalism and employment equity contribute to reverse racism and discrimination in Canada?

7

REFLECTIONS: ASSESSING THE LEARNING

Joanne: Although I realize I cannot change the attitudes, beliefs and values of society overnight, I can work to change them over time. In an earlier essay I said that I did not believe I had the ability to change society's attitudes, but if no one tries to change them we will never grow past the racial discrimination we experience today. If I can change the views of the people around me and try to get them to see past the racial discrimination, at least it will be a start. I feel that in order to understand something, you first have to educate yourself on the subject. If we educate ourselves about our own culture and come to an understanding of that, maybe it will be easier to look at another person's culture objectively. We all live on the same planet and it is time that we realized that no one ethnic group is better than another. We are all equal. We are all just human beings.

In the above quotation, Joanne captures the sentiments of many of the participants in this project. Their essays are a documentation of the crucial role that personal development plays in career development and education as a whole. Education goes beyond academic requirements. It includes building an awareness and knowledge of self and of others.

In their comments, some of which appear in this chapter, participants tell of their need to understand the significance of culture in people's lives, the process involved in overcoming ignorance about racism, prejudice and ethnocentrism, and the importance of accepting the diversity of our society.

For some, attitudes did not change, only their level of awareness.

For others, the process meant discovering the true meaning of racism, and finding that it applied to themselves. Some of the essays are presented in their entirety to provide insight into participants' process of learning and self-discovery. The chapter concludes with an essay by a racial minority participant who, reflecting on her experiences in the class and in society generally, contemplates what it would be like to be unaware of inequity.

Concluding Notes

On Culture

Jay:

In my opinion, all cultures have more similarities with each other than differences. They all have a religion of some sort, view family in a special way, and maintain themselves through viable economic means. The difference between cultures is the degree and method by which they practise religion, view the family, and support themselves economically.

William:

Cultural differences will always be present in Canada but the acceptance of these differences will become less of a barrier when people can handle the fact that within this country there is not just one way to live. They must accept that a "Canadian culture" is a mixture of many cultures combined together.

Everybody, including myself, seems to dwell on the "unique" aspects of cultures. Indeed, all cultures are unique in some ways, just as individuals are; but all these cultures reside in Canada and are therefore part of our Canadian culture … I think that comparing cultures … would shed a great deal more light on the similarities between people. We could learn more about ourselves in the process.

Tina:

In an earlier essay, I had the opportunity to think through some of the assumptions I hold about my culture. The familiarity and power it has so often disguises the fact that it is only one culture among many. I could see clearly how success, for example, can be defined culturally. I could see how the priorities of this society are reflections of White, English-Canadian culture. And I could see myself as a product of that culture—how it could trap me. I could see that so much can only be understood if you step outside and look back in.

From this course, I have learned about how culture is internalized. Although I often feel at odds with my culture, I can perhaps see more clearly now how my individual identity will always be rooted to some extent in my Whiteness and my Englishness. But to some degree, as a result of seeing myself in those terms, I can also more deeply question the culture which is part of me. In doing so, I hope I will be less afraid of my own inevitable ignorance and that I will be more open to other ways of life. I hope I will also be more determined to challenge my own view of the world and the assumptions that lie within it as well as those of the society in which I live.

On Immigrants and Refugees

Jeff:

How could I have been so ignorant? I have always prided myself on being "a man of the world." I have travelled to many places and thought I had a good understanding of other cultures. I was shocked to learn of the positive effects of immigrants on our society. It is because of immigrants that we are able to live in a buoyant labour market. I was also shocked to learn of how early immigrants were manipulated and suppressed. I had always thought of Canada as a warm, caring country. My investigation of Jews almost made me embarrassed to say I am Canadian. How could such a warm country refuse thousands of Jews who were fleeing for their lives during the Holocaust? As for education, I had to ask myself why many immigrants became successful while I remain financially stagnant. Could it be I am the uneducated one?

Maureen:

I was annoyed to hear comments such as, "Why should those boat people be allowed into Canada?" and, "They should have gone through the proper channels." I thought to myself, obviously these people do not know anything about political and religious persecution and about living in fear for their lives as many refugees have. In drastic

Through interaction, people of different backgrounds are often surprised to learn that their cultures have more similarities than differences.

situations, people do drastic things. We have been so fortunate to live in a good land, true and free and to have not experienced such realistic nightmares. I grew up aware of the political dissidents in the Soviet Union who were languishing in labour camps and psychiatric hospitals. I was aware partly because of my Ukrainian-Canadian background. I felt that in some small way this set me apart from the other students. They seemed so ignorant, although I now realize that I might also have been making assumptions about these students.

From hearing of the various racial and ethnic groups, I was saddened by reminders of the part played by my country in denying entry to certain groups of refugees—putting their very lives in jeopardy. That this was none of my doing personally does nothing to reduce the sense of guilt I feel as a Canadian.

On the expectation that immigrants should be expected to speak English?

Lisa:

I always held the firm belief that immigrants arriving in Canada should learn English and should adopt the customs held by the majority; to not do so was a snub to all Canadians and an implication that, "Although I am here now, I shall carry on as I did before." Nothing infuriated me more than seeing "immigrants," especially of college or university age, conversing in their mother tongue while ignoring the language that surrounded them—English. I figured that if you were willing to live in "Rome you should live as the Romans do." This belief included dress, attitude and especially language.

This very point was discussed numerous times in class and though at times I was in vehement agreement with the side that upheld what I have just stated, my view now, although not completely changed, has somewhat softened.

I realize that assimilation does take time and that there is security in conversing in one's mother tongue amongst friends. I also realize that culture is an integral part of one's sense of being and that without it, an essence of the self is lessened. Although I still feel my old sense of ire stir whenever I am on public transit and situated near to others who are using a foreign language, I can now at least comprehend some of their troubles functioning in perhaps a different society and why they continue to maintain their old behaviour.

Experiencing a minority situation

Kendra:

The research I did on Blacks was a real learning experience for me. As I had never been exposed to the Black community before I had perceived them as they are shown on T.V. Although I knew that everything on T.V. had to be taken "with a grain of salt," I was still not sure what to expect. The trip to the community was very scary for me. Since I am White and never been in a minority situation or experienced discrimination, going to a place where I was clearly in the minority was very uncomfortable. I had never given my colour much thought until I was in a situation where it slapped me in the face. It was a rude awakening for me. I never got over the feeling of being uncomfortable, but I realized how wrong my perception of Blacks was. They were friendly, helpful people, no different from the people I had grown up with. I know that our cultures make us different, but if we look past those differences we are all human beings. It was a very rewarding experience for me.

Janet:

When I think about the word Indian, I think of my Grade Eight history class. We were taking the War of 1812. I will always remember how the Indians helped Canada win the war at the battle of Queenston Heights. They seemed so proud and determined ... and now they look defeated. I have always wondered what they must be thinking and feeling about the way most of their people are living.

As I got older I heard about their living conditions—the cramped shacks they lived in, no plumbing, and so on. I was horrified. How could anybody be so cruel? I had also heard that many Indians used alcohol to escape from the realities of their lives. I did not want to believe these stories, and thought that if they were true, the number of Indians was exaggerated.

I could not bear to think that these once proud and strong-willed people would be alcoholics, nor did I want to face the facts about some of the reasons why they might be drinking. I wanted to believe that most people care about each other.

I was glad to have the opportunity to investigate the Indians. Now I could learn about the truth and face some of the reality that the Indians live in. The day I went to an Indian Centre I had mixed feelings. The Centre was located in a slum area, and we had to walk about eight blocks to get there. I had dressed up for the occasion, believing that the Centre was a place where Indians come together to practise their culture, spiritual beliefs, and feast.

Once I got to The Centre I learned that it was like a shelter for the Indians to come and talk and have a meal with friends. Unfortunately, my worst thoughts of how these people live were true. I did not know what to think. I could not imagine how our society could treat them like they have. On the other hand, what happened to their will to be strong, and to control their own destiny?

My feelings for the Indians have not changed greatly, but the research has definitely opened my eyes to how some of the people in my own country live. I still believe the Indians have the power to change their lives, to stay together as they once were. This will all happen with time. I do not think any less of them because of their alcoholism, or poverty, but I am ashamed that as Canadians we let it happen and subject them to it.

On Prejudice, Racism and Ethnocentrism

Doreen:

The research on ethnic and racial groups brought me to the conclusion that prejudice is based upon ignorance. I also believe that knowledge forces a person to confront his or her beliefs with the facts. I believe that if more people were exposed to knowledge about other cultures in our society, much of the prejudice that exists would surely diminish.

A person must just become aware that his or her race, as well as cultural and ethnic background, affect our attitudes and behaviours toward others who are both similar and different based on these factors. When a person becomes aware of this, he or she is well on their way to understanding their prejudices. Anything that is unknown or strange to us is susceptible to discrimination on the basis of our fear …

I cannot say that my prejudices have diminished, as they have not. But I now have an understanding that these factors do exist. I find that to a certain degree, I am now able to stop myself when I am about to discriminate against others by reminding myself that my prejudices are based on ignorance and fear of the unknown …

I feel that in order for my prejudices to diminish, I must confront them directly, and also understand why I have these feelings toward people who are ethnically, racially and culturally different from me.

Lorna:

I am now more aware of how much my Ukrainian background has affected my view of the world and of other ethnic groups. I learned that I am indeed ethnocentric with respect to immigrants not learning English. All my life I have heard, [that] "When my grandparents and parents came to Canada, they didn't know a word of English, but they learned it. Therefore, all should learn English." I do not think I am as rigid on this point now, as I realize that there are some who just can't learn another language despite making the effort.

I think about the people I consider ignorant. How can I blame someone for being ignorant if she/he has not had the chance to experience or to have empathy for another's suffering?

Pat:

Every one of us sees other cultures through our own set of "rose-coloured glasses." We see what we want to see and no more. This is sad but true. If people say that all their biases and prejudices were laid to rest after learning about another culture, I think they are being untruthful to themselves. We have all grown up being influenced by our parents, siblings, peers and significant others and these influences have shaped our behaviours into what we are today. We are taught to be prejudiced. We don't teach ourselves but others teach us. We are influenced by what is said in ethnic jokes, by what our family has encountered, and even by what we encounter in day-to-day life. We may have learned about different cultures in general but unless we know people intimately we can never get over our prejudices about people who are different from ourselves ...

Kathy:

I am ashamed to admit what a prejudiced and ethnocentric person I am. I had thought I viewed and treated all ethnic groups with equality in relation to my ethnicity, but I do not. Now certainly there are individual people of ethnic backgrounds different from my own whom I respect and admire for whatever their accomplishments. However, I do not regard ethnic groups in general on an equal basis. I have also come to realize that minority groups of a different colour stand a lesser chance for equality than those who are White. For some reason I possess the deep-rooted notion that White English people are superior. Their colour is a ticket to success. If I were asked to categorize all minorities, the bottom of the file would consist of the coloureds leading up to those who are White with a foreign accent.

My only consolation is that I am now more aware of my biases and with luck the impact will create a positive change. I can realistically admit that a 14-week course cannot change 28 years of prejudice.

However, I do feel I have acquired a new appreciation for all ethnic groups and feel confident that my outlook has been altered enough to approach them with more understanding and tolerance. I have once again been reminded that Canada is a multicultural country and I should not allow the difference of skin colour to set the standards of superiority.

We all have different backgrounds which will assuredly lead to differences in many areas, but I feel confident that I will now approach these differences as such and avoid the urge to criticize and view others through ethnocentric eyes.

During our first class we were asked about our prejudices. The general response was that we had none. Some suggested they see everyone equally, be they black, white or purple, and if I recall correctly, one student ventured to say there were absolutely no prejudices in his/her family. I venture to guess that this response reflected our naivete. One's physical features such as skin colour and shape of eyes cannot be hidden and I find it difficult to believe that someone could look at, for example, a White person and a Black person at the same time and view them in the same way. I feel quite sure that I would have viewed the instructor differently had he not been Black. In fact, the moment he walked into the classroom on the first day I thought to myself, "Oh, he's Black. This course will be right up his alley."

The Consequence of Trying Not to Show Prejudice

Jane:

Although one part of me still possesses the steadfast belief that I do not patronize people or treat people of different races with exaggerated kindness, another part of me acknowledges many preconceived stereotypes I have towards people of racial, ethnic and cultural backgrounds that are different from my own. I have also realized that I feel an astounding sense of intimidation by these people. What I mean by this is that sometimes I actually feel that it is necessary to be nice (not in an exaggerated fashion, however) to a person of a minority group even if he or she is not a friendly person. Why?? Perhaps because I would prefer to be accepted on a first-impression-basis, so that the person would recognize me as an individual who is unlike prejudiced people.

On Interracial Marriage

Rita:

I get the impression that people are very naive about interracial marriages. Their first reaction to the question of interracial marriages is a quick, "Yes, it's okay." They defend that quick answer by professing that love will take care of all of the troubles such marriages may bring. They never even take time to consider any factors realistically, such as parents, churches, social groups, children and unknown prejudices.

I have experienced such a marriage, but before I got married I went through dozens of scenarios making sure that I could back my thought with real convictions. I had to know the answers before the questions were asked. I have a five-year-old daughter, and when she came home from school upset, wanting to know if she was White like mommy or Native Indian like her daddy, I had the right answer for her. I would not walk into an interracial marriage with only love to use as an answer, for too many lives are at stake.

On Employment Equity

Dana:

... Also, this new equity system, they are going to put into place is unbelievable, I don't agree with it at all. I don't feel that all of the people are qualified for the job. You can't tell me that we, the white people, are getting treated fairly in this system. But there are some plus and minus points about this system of hiring.

For whatever reasons, it is obvious that a person's race and cultural and ethnic background does play a large part in establishing a set of values or in explaining an individual's behaviour pattern ...

When a person recognizes that these factors do indeed exist, he (or she) is well on the way to better understanding and appreciating not only themselves, but other people as well—people who may previously have been represented as strange and unknown, who appeared threatening and were to be avoided at all costs.

In an ever-changing world, the word "understanding" is often not only misused, but abused. For if a person cannot understand himself, how can he understand others?

Does the Canadian educational system adequately present the contributions of all ethnic and racial groups in the nation's development?

It is very obvious to me that many ethnic or cultural groups react with surprise, anger and frustration when their values are being threatened. They make assumptions and take things at face value, as if in fear of examining them further, for it may mean changing. Human beings are funny creatures, many have a hard time admitting they were wrong. No one likes to admit they might have jumped to conclusions. It makes people feel insecure and unsure of their judgement—or at least that's what it does to me.

Similarly, when cultural groups feel like they are not being listened to, or that people are trying to change their ways, there is an initial shock. They ask themselves, "Why us? What did we do?" Once they have established where they stand and how they feel about it they usually establish some sort of goal to work towards, so that they can begin to change what they are unhappy with. This is unavoidable; it is a natural problem-solving process that one uses in most situations that arise. However, this is often a slow, painful process, especially when attempting to change or adapt one's personal values and belief system. As I did with my fellow students, many groups meet with more discrimination and stronger feelings directed at them as they begin to implement this process. The education of both parties as to their differences and their similarities is a difficult process for both sides; however, if we could do this, the rewards would be immeasurable.

When examining my cultural group and when watching other presentations, I realized, as a relatively intelligent, educated Canadian citizen, how little I know. As was stated many times, you cannot really understand a culture unless you spend some time with the people and begin to see how they view the world. So much of how they have been treated historically influences where they stand and/or what they experience currently. Again, gathering all the information which is accessible to you is so important.

Learning about racial and ethnic groups may or may not directly reflect the nature of a specific program of study; however, it deals with developing an important skill that is essential in my field: interacting with others, especially those who are different.

I have come to realize the importance of learning about racial and ethnic groups as it pertains not only to my career as a social worker but also as a Black Canadian. I used to think that it didn't matter what ethnicity, colour, or culture a person is, they should all be treated equally. That is true to an extent, but it is also questionable. I now realize that I must not only treat every individual with respect and as an equal, but I should also be aware of the individual's differences in terms of their ethnicity, culture, and colour; and I should not be ignorant to these differences, but I should be able to understand them in order to better cater to the needs of individuals.

On Awareness of Differences

Robin:

Interaction from our group assignments and personal interaction with people of other racial and ethnic origins have always had positive effects on myself. It is a lack of knowledge which breeds discrimination and stereotypes. Without personal contact with other racial/ethnic groups it is understandable that a person can fall prey to stereotypes of people they know very little about. It is the interaction which gives you a foundation to base relations with other groups, enabling the people involved to see the similarities and differences in culture and background. From here a relationship of understanding and compromise can evolve.

The most important part of understanding other people is first under-standing yourself. This includes your background, culture, and per-sonal biases. If you can objectively assess these traits, then a more understanding relationship can be built with [people of] different ethnic or racial origins. This seems to be a problem for some Canadians such as myself. My ethnic origin has somewhat become lost as generations have gone by. It wasn't until this course that I became interested in my ethnic origin, for [before the course] I was told that I was Canadian, and that whites such as myself are real Canadians. When in fact many other races have been here since the formation of Canada. This is a fact very few are aware of, which increases the belief that Canada is a "white country." This makes me better understand just how institution-alized racism is in Canada.

The lack of history taught about Canadians of non-white origin is harm-ful to these people by making it seem as though they don't belong. Taking away their roots in Canada takes the foundation from which these people can base their pride in their country. Among the people this creates a feeling of alienation from their own country. From this I became aware of the need for multicultural programs. Programs at the federal level as well as at the community level. Programs like Employ-ment Equity are needed to try to balance the scales of power which can open the door of opportunities for minority groups. The importance of ethnic associations are especially prevalent at the present time. These associations give a person a forum to share their culture with others of the same background. Plus their history which is lacking in the public school system. The lack of history or information may make the minority student lose interest in school, thus dropping out and continuing the cycle racism creates. Then the student who does turn to crime is exploited by the media. The media's portrayal of the minority groups further reinforces the stereotypes in the minds of both minority and majority groups.

The awareness of the differences among people of various ethnic/ra-cial origins is valuable to the person who considers a career in human services. A person in this field is going to encounter various people on the job and how you handle the situation is key. If the person is equipped to deal with people of various ethnic racial origins the out-come of the situation can be quite different. This idea is based on an individual level of relating, but if more individuals are better equipped to deal with people then the relations between the various communi-ties can be improved.

Hugh:

I found that my open-mindedness was not all that was required in order to gain a better understanding of people of different racial and ethnic backgrounds. Although I realized that I should not always accept other people's opinions and stereotypes as true, nor should I accept media "statistics" as 100% factual, when this is all you have to base your opinions on, you feelings are affected by them. This is why being open-minded must be combined with being educated. When people are educated about something, they are less likely to assume things and less likely to be swayed by the "opinions" of others. I don't profess to be totally void of prejudice and possibly racist thoughts, but I do make an effort to dissolve stereotypes and feelings that have been built up within me for 22 years now. I constantly make an effort to give all people the opportunity to impress me, based on the merit of who they are as a person; not what they are. This at times is difficult because our present social system unknowingly/knowingly promotes segregation, prejudice, racism, and ostracism. We are "brain washed" by what is around us throughout our lives and I/we cannot be held responsible for what society taught us as we grew up. But we can and should be held responsible for educating ourselves and learning the difference between what is wrong and what is right. Because whether we like it or not, we are all human and we all possess one very important part of being human, the ability to feel compassion. No matter what differences we have, we will always be bonded by a far greater amount of similarities. Whatever good we have, we can find in others; whatever bad we see in others, we will find within ourselves.

Reflections

PAUL'S DIARY

March 27

In earlier essays, I used such words as bigot, racist, prejudiced and White supremacist to describe myself, my ideals and my upbringing. Certainly strong words to describe oneself but all not entirely untrue. To a certain degree, I know that I will put on one of those masks in order to deal with or to explain away any given situation. Am I a racist because I think that White people as a whole drive better than Oriental people? I can back up my theory with statistics such as the number of accidents caused by Chinese people compared with White people or with the number of times I've been cut off and who has committed the offense or even the fact that you would be hard pressed to find even one Oriental involved in the Pro Driving circuit. These facts wouldn't sway me either. The simple fact is that I grew up with the "knowledge" that they cannot drive, and now I believe that to be a truth. I admit to my prejudice. Does that make me a racist though? I do not believe so. I think that one has to cross a hidden boundary that separates racism from being a normal human who will hold prejudices that don't affect how one looks at the person behind their ethnicity. As soon as one takes malicious action against someone based strictly on their ethnic origin, or holds prejudices against them in such a manner as to cause them emotional or physical harm, they have crossed the line. True, I have given my own definition for racism, but I think it is a fair one that takes into consideration the fact that we are all human, and therefore susceptible to beliefs bestowed upon us. I can honestly say that I have never crossed this line as my best friend is an Oriental and I rented the upper two-thirds of my townhouse to a Black family. In both cases, I looked beyond the origin of the person and saw them for what they were; human, just like me. Well, I've done it. I've absolved myself from any guilt for possibly being a racist by giving my own definition to it.

April 10

So, you again ask if I am a racist? I want to believe that deep down in my heart I am not. I'm a nice guy who gives to charity and helps old ladies cross the street. I'm the first person to give up my seat on the bus for a blind person and have more than once helped a distraught mother carry her groceries. I have never gone gay-bashing nor have I burned any crosses on lawns, nor do I want to. That makes me not a racist, right? Wrong. My best friend for more than six years, with whom I have shared all of life's ups and downs is Oriental. This must mean I am not a racist, right? No. I rented the top half of my house to a Black family. Is that the mark of a racist? Doesn't that prove that I'm not a racist? No, no, no. I do sound like a helluva nice guy though, don't I? So, am I a racist? Yes.

How did I come to that conclusion? Well, first I looked up the meaning of the word racism in Oxford's dictionary. The definition reads "belief in the superiority of a particular race". That is what the classified defini-tion is. I defined it in a different way. I thought it meant when one person takes malicious action against another person based strictly on the colour of skin or their religious beliefs. One racial slur here and there doesn't a racist make, does it? I mean, okay, as a rule I think that

Oriental people can't drive. And, if the truth be known, I do sort of feel superior to Black people. Deep down I don't believe I'm any better than they are, but because Black people are highly discriminated against in today's society, I feel I have an advantage over them because I enjoy a relatively discrimination-free lifestyle. This course has caused me to find something out about myself that I didn't necessarily want to find out. It has made me realize that I am a racist. Yes, my best friend is Oriental, but I take the ethnicity out of him. I don't take him for the Oriental that he is, I take him for the White person I have made him. I enjoy knowing that Black people are discriminated against because it gives me a decisive edge over them. As said before, maybe I am not a demonstrative racist but a rose by any other name ...

I guess the saddest part of all is knowing that I will not change. I am probably worse than those who run about actively showing their racism. If nothing else, they are up-front about it. I lobby for equal rights for minority groups knowing full well they will never get them. I give them my charity because it makes me feel good; makes me feel like not a racist.

Corey: *Smart, Sly and Naive: Barriers to Confronting Racism*

During the course of this semester I have come to realize my racism and must now make a conscious effort to change my way of thinking. I honestly believe that it is people like me that are the most dangerous in our society, smart enough to know better, sly enough to keep it hidden and naive enough to convince myself that I am not a racist. Whether or not we choose to admit it, we are all racist in one way or another. Some like myself are able to hide it much better than others. When we walk down the street, interview someone for a job or look at our neighbours. It is perfectly acceptable to criticize, compare and look out for one's self in our society at the expense of others. Children are conditioned ever since they first start school to follow these rules. The problem begins here and is considered as an innocent lesson on the facts of life but the underlying reality is that it teaches racism and discrimination.

It amazes me how some people—myself included—can be so blind to our own actions. I always find ways of justifying what I say and how I say it. I have perfected this down to a fine performing art. I can cover up anything I want if I have to. The thing that amazes me the most is that once you lie to yourself for long enough you actually start to believe it.

I have a responsibility as a Canadian and as a person to be fair and honest but yet I want desperately to fit into society and get ahead myself that I ignore those around me whom I abuse in the process. I have been taught that this is what life is all about and it is o.k. because I am white and middle class. Anything less than the best for me I am told is unacceptable and that I am entitled to so much more.

Eric: *Reflecting on Myself is a Reflection of You*

Any course that requires you to rethink your values and beliefs is bound to be interesting and of some merit. Sometimes it can even turn into a heated debate. Anything that questions our validity and goodness is bound to raise our emotional level a little, some more than others. Having to think about what you think about others, never having had to think about it before is also difficult. We may even question the sanity of the teacher that stands before us. We may even dislike the course because we are not able to see where it is leading us.

I hated seeing the discrimination that actually does happen from day to day in front of our very eyes. Is it that we really do not see what is happening or is it that we just believe our way to be right? I watched a program on a White Supremacist Group a few weeks ago, my curiosity now peaked by this course, and I was disgusted to discover that these are average people, the kind of person that you might meet in the grocery store or at church. What was even worse was that these people actually believe deep in their hearts that they are supreme. They do not think they are doing anything wrong.

So then I had to sit down and think about my brother and my father. Here we are, immigrants in Canada and they think they have the same right to every opportunity as every other Canadian, yet they do not think that other immigrants have that right.

I had to stop and really wonder what the difference was between them and the White Supremacists. All it is, is degrees. My brother and father would never kill anyone for taking a job that they were applying for if another immigrant happened to get it, yet I believe a White Supremacist might. Then I had to stop and think again about which was better, letting them know you hate them or spreading vicious remarks about them as a group. In one of the class presentations the presenters said that the group they studied wanted to know up front where they stood, at least then they could deal with it.

Then I was made to think about me. Oh no, I could never be a bigot, or could I? Having to sit down and reassess who I was and what I

Confronting one's racial views is the first step. But learning about living in a multicultural society is a life-long process.

believed was very hard for me because I have always considered myself an open minded person. But then, who ever admits that they are closed minded? So I thought. That was when I discovered that I did not know anyone from another race. I thought immediately that this meant that I was a bigot. I condemned myself then and there. So what if I did not know anyone of another race? It is not because I am a bigot, it is because I come from a town where there are only White people. I had not been exposed to other groups until now. Besides, what is better, admitting that you do not have any culturally different friends or going out in search of that "token Black" or "token Jew"? I feel strongly that I do have an open mind and that if the opportunity arises where I do come in contact with another person of a different race that I happen to get along with, things will be fine.

So, by now I was feeling pretty okay about myself, I was not that bad and then came the question, "Why am I still tied to Scotland if I am happy here?" Does this mean that I think of myself as not fully Canadian, as different from you out there who drink beer, eat potato chips and say, "Eh"? It was only after my research projects, the question of the conversion law in Israel, and my meeting with Mehul (the subject of my second essay), that I discovered what it was that made me so anxious to keep my Scottish roots and the path to Scotland open. There is a certain security in knowing who you are and where you come from. After you know that, there is an even bigger sense of belonging in knowing that you can return at any time.

Being told that I would never be able to return to Scotland because I had come to Canada or that I was no longer able to consider myself Scottish would be devastating. But I have only just recently discovered why that is. My history is there, it is part of me, no matter what. Yes, I am Canadian and I love Canada, but I was not born here. I was born in Scotland. It holds my heart even though I cannot remember what it looks like. It is me and if you try to take it away, you destroy part of me.

Through this course, we have been tested to see if we could analyze ourselves, if we could look deep into ourselves to see if there were faults and if there were, what to do about them. We have been made to see the discrimination around us and become aware of other cultures, and what they might have to offer us. The best part for me was testing myself and believing that I passed. The worst part was finding our that there are others who will fail because it is easier to hide and not change than it is to challenge and come into the light. A faith never tested does not constitute a complete faith. A person who does not test himself is also not a complete person.

Todd: *Challenge ideas and opinions on an ongoing basis*

When I started this course in September I thought "Oh good, this should be interesting. I'll get to learn about different cultural groups and how to deal with them when I eventually come across them as clients. I am not a prejudiced person and I have been to many different and diverse countries in the world and so this course should be easy for me. I'll probably be able to contribute to the class discussions more than the other students because of my knowledge of different cultures."

What a shock I received when I realized that this self-assured and narrow-minded attitude was torn apart by my own discoveries during the course. There is no handbook for social service workers that can effectively teach you how to deal with East Indians, Blacks, Italians or any other race, colour or culture. This was just my own stereotypical view of people that I hoped would make my job easier. To say that we can treat all people of one culture in a certain way would be a disastrous mistake.

I was also sure that I had no prejudices. Many of us in the course said that we had none. We backed this up by saying that we couldn't be prejudiced because we had friends who were Black, Vietnamese, Italian or East Indian (these were my examples of friends that proved that I was not prejudiced). When I look at my relationship with these friends objectively I realize that I had mentally put their differences from me out of my mind. My Vietnamese friend was so like me that I unconsciously considered him to be Canadian. When I think of the Vietnamese people as a whole group my immediate thoughts are of people with large families that are poor and who used to spend most of their time in the learning centre at high school because of their difficulties with the language. I hate to admit it but this stereotype still comes to mind when I think of them as a group. Why then did I not categorize my friend in this stereotypical way? Because I had seen him as the person he was, a wonderful, extremely intelligent man who would do anything for anybody, but in my eyes I had taken away his culture. Had I not known him personally would I have grouped him with the impressions that I have of the group as a whole? I hate to admit it but I think I would have and, more frighteningly with my awareness, maybe I still would. My East Indian friend was a wonderful girl who was sadly killed on the Air India jet that exploded and took so many lives. I was saddened by her death (she was only twenty-one and so pretty that she was in the preliminary stages of being a model). Had I taken away her ethnicity too?

To say that we are not prejudiced is a lie and it's one that I am guilty of too. I loathe the idea of the Ku Klux Klan and other groups that display their prejudice so openly and with such hatred but at least they are being honest. To say that you are not prejudiced but to hold ideas that are stereotypical is just as dangerous but in a more subtle way.

An aspect of the course that I found most interesting was the difficulties that we all had in examining Canadian culture. What was strange was that during class discussions I found myself saying things like, "when immigrants come to our country they ..." and yet I am an immigrant too. Would an East Indian find himself saying that or have I mentally grouped myself with Canadians because I am white and speak English? I fit in so easily, but an East-Indian that is born in Canada and is a Canadian would have people questioning him if he were to say the same thing. No one questioned me, despite the fact that I had openly admitted that I was an immigrant. As a class we may have been showing our racism without even realizing it.

I can at least recognize the mistakes that I have made and am still making. To be critical of myself I must answer the question, "have I come to these conclusions because I want to pass the course and because I want to think that I am objective, or do I truly believe this?" The real test for me will come when the course is over. Will I continue to apply this knowledge and question my thoughts and feelings when I am no longer forced to do so just because I am writing an essay? I don't know the answers. I hope that it is yes, this course has made me challenge my own ideas and opinions, I hope this is a new habit that has just begun. I feel that this course is just the beginning, my concepts must be analyzed and challenged on an ongoing basis but at least I have made a start.

Dorne: *What would it be like to be unaware?*

A young boy of 9 or 10 walking down the street encounters a car full of people of a different cultural group. Something causes him to do something out of the ordinary. He sticks up his middle finger at the three female passengers, scowls and resumes strutting as if nothing else is required. Shock and fear registered on his face as the car swerved into the driveway not three feet from where he stood. As it dawned on his mind that his actions brought consequences, he is spurned to run. Arrogance gone he flees the situation, yet is unable to escape the pursuit of his victims. He is brought up short, face to face with the youngest of the three. He has no response, no reason, no conclusions when faced with the meanness of his racism. The young girl returned to the car, turning her back on yet another dirty incident.

As the driver of the vehicle, a black female aged 26 at the time, I was yet again disappointed with the white youth of today.

Racism exists, and it is ugly. It has damaged countless individuals through the ages, and it has damaged me. Through the duration of this class, I have been given the opportunity to consider reasons not to succumb to bitterness.

People are generally motivated to act due to various forces both external and internal. One such factor is fear. Fear causes many individuals to react contrary to the principles and morals driven into them by their civilization. Fear of the unknown, fear of change, fear of the loss of status, fear of losing control, all can lead a person to regrettable action. Police officers shoot black youths before they have an opportunity to vindicate themselves. Government officials falsely put countless Sikh men and women behind bars to satisfy the public's need for a scapegoat in the destruction of the Air India flight in June 1985. Hong Kong policies deter the immigration of non-Asian groups into their country. Such action has no credible long term benefits without the need for apologies or under the table pay-offs.

We are forced to act not only due to a primitive response to fear but to the cobweb-like tug of insecurity. I am shocked when my sister's

The lessons we learn at school about positive interactions are an important beginning to the larger changes we must consider as we enter the world of work.

teacher actively prevents non-white students from studying autobiographies of their own cultural heroes in an assignment where they are given supposedly free reign in reviewing figures of historical portent. Teachers who inadvertently colour history to suit their own agenda influence the minds of our children. I grew up in basic ignorance of the major contribution my race has made to not only Canada, but the world. I am ashamed that only recently have I even had the slightest interest in peering out from under my perpetual shell of belief that racially I am inferior, unsuitable, not worthy to seek equality. I had grown as accustomed to the thought "I am black, I cannot rate what the white race rates" as to the thought "I am female, I cannot rate what the male rates."

With the recognition of being duped came rage. I deliberately recalled what my mother had told me growing up. "Don't trust the white man," she said, "they will friend you up, then use you." I looked at everything they did and said for a double meaning. So absorbed had I become with what they had done to my race in the past, I lost sight of my personal goals for the future. No cultural group can afford to spend all their time looking back at the ravages of time.

With the fading of rage came resolve. As a *female* member of a *minority* race I have much to offer this world. My impact will be left on the friends I have chosen and acquaintances both casual and fleeting. My past both racially and individually is mine. No group or individual can diminish my experiences. I am determined that my skills and abilities will receive the nurturing they need to develop. That means relating with my society fully. The POWER group might not be of my ethnicity, but they cannot exist without mine and every other minority group in this country. As we discover the power we each hold in the unity of our individual groups we will create our own history for future generations to look back on. I am as proud of my heritage as the Jews are of theirs, the Greeks theirs, the Asians theirs. It is our very hardships that have made us as resilient as we are. We are more alike than we are willing to admit.

I am still disappointed at the imbalance of Global POWER, even a little envious. What would it be like, I ask myself, to not be aware of inequality because it is to my benefit? What would it be like if my only concern for a job interview were really my credentials? What would it be like to raise teenage sons and not worry if the police will mistake them for troublemakers or drug addicts? What would it be like to apply for a bank loan and not have the additional worries of racial distinction applied? What, I ask myself, would it be like?

Because I have no answers for these questions I cannot relinquish the nagging tendrils of mistrust. It would be foolish for me to do so, for would I not protect these "benefits" if they were truly mine. Maybe the only place they exist is in my homeland, but even there the POWER group's hand can be felt. Maybe with all the intermarriages taking place we will escape white dominance, or any distinct group dominance for that matter. Then again, maybe not. As mentioned earlier, people have done and will do unnatural deeds to maintain their "natural balance".

As it stands, we can learn to live with the present balance or we can develop a new balance. Either way we will have to do away with ignorant non-educated assumptions of other people groups. We are truly different, as different as the seasons, the flowers that bloom and the animals that roam this planet. And yet, we are more alike than we care to admit. We are humans. Isn't that worth celebrating together? What potential such a concept would hold for this world's future!

Questions:

1. Can multiculturalism really compromise "Canadian identity"?
2. To what extent is it possible for you to interpret another person's ideas and actions completely independent of your own worldview?
3. What does "seeing ourselves" mean? What can be gained in terms of human relationships and interactions through being self-reflective?

POSTSCRIPT

[T]he most important learning experience that could happen in our class-room was that students would learn to think critically and analytically, not just about the required books, but about the world they live in. Education for critical consciousness that encourages all students—privileged or non-privileged—who are seeking an entry into class privilege rather than pro-viding a sense of freedom and release, invites critique of conventional expectations and desires. They may find such an experience terribly threatening. And even though they may approach the situation with great openness, it may still be difficult, and even painful (hooks 1988: 102).

This book is a further attempt to build an understanding of culture, race, ethnicity, prejudice and racism, and expand the issues in, and range of perspectives on, the dialogue that currently exists in this field. The comments and essays which appear in this book provide insights into how students locate their experiences in the critical discussions and reflections about these issues, and how the issues in turn affect them. This educational process is premised on, as articulated by bell hooks in the above quotation, "education for critical consciousness." hooks (1988) argues that such an approach to pedagogy should be taken if we are to prepare students to live and act more fully in the world—if they are to develop awareness of themselves and the existing social structures so that they may be active participants in the social change movement.

I do not believe that these essays reflect only the ideas and opinions of the writers. Surely, these views, interpretations and analyses have support and consensus from ourselves and/or others we know. What might be different here is that these writers have expressed on paper what many of us say privately, or think but dare not articulate publicly. While the essays reflect an awareness and a sensitivity that we would wish Canadians to hold, there are many unsettling comments from which we would like to disassociate our-

Author:
Carl James

selves. We should not dismiss these negative comments and disturbing perspectives as merely those of a minority of Canadians, for these too have an impact on defining our social relations.

The book begins with a discussion of culture as a structure which is socially constructed and which impacts on everyone's life, and is also something upon which everyone has an impact. To understand ourselves requires us to understand Canadian culture in its entirety. Racism, stereotyping, prejudice, sexism and other factors play a significant role in defining, maintaining and perpetuating the culture. It is by understanding how the existence and expressions of sub-cultures are dependent on the extent to which they are not in conflict with the values and norms of society's culture that we also come to understand the meaning of race and ethnicity in the Canadian context. Our identities are a product of the social construction of race and ethnicity in Canada. For example, while I may have cultural practices that are sometimes attributed to my racial group (Black), they are not independent of Canadian culture—they are part of it. My identities and behaviours are just as much Canadian as any other Canadian person, for I am a product of, and I am responsive to, the Canadian social structure. My behaviours are a result of my understanding of, and interaction with, the institutions of Canada, and the values and norms that have been communicated to me. My behaviours will also be a product of how I perceive my situation in the society and will be influenced by my capacity to participate and influence social, political and economic structures and events.

Any educational process is political (Friere, 1968; hooks, 1988). It provides insights into the structures that determine the relationships between racial and ethnic groups, between the dominant and subordinate, and between individuals. As a result, we can expect participants to have both positive and negative reactions. It is understandable that many of the class participants would express that they have been affected in some way by this learning experience. And from Chapter 7, we might conclude that discussing issues of race, ethnicity and culture have made individuals begin to develop the understanding and sensitivity necessary to confront the issues. This would include engaging in self-criticism and admitting negative things about themselves. However, this is only the beginning of what will be, in many cases, long and painful lessons in race and ethnic relations. And without nurturing, coaching and encouragement, these initial insights, the commitments and determination to take up the challenge might be lost.

Despite awareness, sensitivity and understanding, there are some things which individuals still find difficult to discuss. Racism is one issue from which some shy away. If we are to meaningfully discuss prejudices based on race, and the power factor that accompanies racial prejudices, then we must talk of racism and all the related painful and negative conditions. Insofar as we choose to see differences and tensions between Canadians as a product of "multiculturalism" and "cultural differences," then we are avoiding the issues of race and power. It is an insufficient analysis to attribute the problems and tensions individuals experience to cultural differences. Differences and tensions can in part be attributed to attitudes and ideologies such as racism, something which, as Adrienne Shadd explains, is inherent in the structure of our society (Chapter 5).

It is hoped that through these essays we have initiated a dialogue which will bring into focus many of the critical issues that must be discussed if we are to move to a more equitable society. It is time to implement an anti-racism perspective, particularly in our approach to education, for the multicultural and cross-cultural approaches have not helped to alleviate the social and educational problems that we are experiencing today. The issues which we identify currently as rooted in cultural differences, due to a large minority population which is comprised largely of immigrants, will still be here in the year 2000. By then, many more racial minority people will have been born, been socialized and reached adulthood in Canada. Today's immigrants would have been living here for decades. What will our explanation be then? Moreover, estimates indicate that by the 2000's Canada's racial minority population will have grown to over 15 per cent, with a greater concentration in the large urban centres. In metropolitan Toronto, the racial minority population will be more than 35% (Samuel, 1992).

We need to equip ourselves for working and living in the multiracial and multicultural society that has always existed.

1. We must begin with our education system. Curricula and materials must reflect our diverse population and represent all groups as Canadians—not as "immigrants." Education must be rid of its Eurocentric approach, and must strive to inculcate in students the critical thinking and analytical skills that are necessary for living in a diverse society. We must be educated about the contributions that all groups have made to the historical, political, economic, social and cultural development of Canada today.

2. We need to commit to understanding ourselves since it is an important part of the process of understanding others requires. We must recognize that we are all cultural, racial and ethnic beings; we contribute to culture and are affected by culture. As Canadians, the differences between us are a result of our various social locations in society and the social conditions under which we exist.

3. Racism and discrimination as social mechanisms, rooted in our Canadian history, must be acknowledged and addressed directly. We are all affected by them. Issues and situations that are racist and discriminatory must be identified explicitly as such. They must be named, and we all must engage in the use of the language that names the issues and events. For we need to use language that will allow us to act together while cherishing each other's individuality. And as Steinem (1983) writes, there can be no big social change "without words and phrases that first create a dream of change in our heads" (p. 2).

4. With the appropriate awareness, knowledge, skills and language, we must proceed to engage in action for social change. Engaging in social change activities means accepting that we all have varying degrees and sources of power, and combined they can be used to transform the system that provides advantages to some people and disadvantages others.

The individuals who have shared their works with us and have given us insights into their thinking, attitudes and the process of change in which they have been involved, admit that this is only the beginning of a long journey of self-discovery and social awareness. These two are necessary if we are to build understanding of, and between each other. Only then can we work toward building a society where all members have equality of opportunity and access.

A Final Note

Before ending I wish to share a conversation I had with a friend and colleague, about this book. C. Geddis had read and commented on the earlier edition of it some years ago. Upon completing a draft of this edition, I passed it onto her for her comments. The following is part of our conversation:

C.G. You talk about things like self-awareness and increased understanding of others (in fact, largely, "the Other") as being central and important to any kind of individual change as well as social change, over time, towards a more equitable society. Why do you believe that? Why do you think that if I understand myself better and increase my understanding of people who are racially and culturally different, that somehow that will all accrue to the good?

C.J.   I don't think that it *necessarily* follows that because I am more aware of myself that I will be much more active in social change. But I do think that personal awareness is a critical and crucial aspect towards the whole issue of social change. If you are going to be involved in social change, you have to understand yourself—and understanding yourself involves understanding how the structures have impacted on you; how they have affected your life; and consequently how you can influence the structures in order to bring about change. So personal awareness is an important starting point in the process of social change.

C.G.   It seems to me that something more than self-knowledge and understanding of others is going to be required for substantive change to come about. Or do you believe, in your heart of hearts, in the "perfectibility of human kind?" That you can take anyone from anywhere, teach them some things, and that this will turn them around?

C.J.   I believe, like you do, that more than self knowledge is required. It is a matter of how we get people toward collective action. We can move toward collective action if we have a common understanding of the forces that shape all our lives. These forces impact racial minorities differently from racial majority people. In knowing that, a person—either racial minority or racial majority—will understand the role she or he will have to play individually and collectively in bringing about change.

C.G.   Whether or not they accept that role is another thing, though, isn't it?

C.J.   Oh, yes. But some will accept the role and others will reject it.

C.G.   Yes, they do. You did not answer my question directly. I asked you if you believed in the perfectibility of human kind. I think that at some level you must, if you believe what you are saying to me now.

Let me react to you as a white person. If I accept the fact that racism as we know it in Canada is a white problem, given the historical forces like colonialism that have helped to shape this society, then, as a white person, I also need to clarify my responsibility—or the role that I could be playing to help make society more equitable than it is. When I interact with other white people around that issue, it seems to me that it comes down to the big question of power and privilege. I am too often left with the question, what is it going to take to have white people share, relinquish, or somehow modify our power and privilege? Or even to have us realize that we have such things as power and privilege? Even when there is a recognition of white power and privilege—then the issue often becomes—once I know that I have it, why should I give it up? It seems to me that it is not only a matter of white folks holding tight to our power and privilege because it is to our advantage to do so, sometimes it is also a matter of risk and fear. I have had white people say to me, for example, if they challenge racism, as an expression of white power, among family or friends, they are putting themselves in some jeopardy. By which they mean that they run the risk of damaging the relationship of setting themselves apart from their group. That is a powerful combination—self interest and wanting to maintain power and privilege, on the one hand, and not wanting to pull away from the group, on the other. I would like to know what is it going to take to get people beyond those major road blocks.

C.J. It is going to take lots of efforts and struggle. When you were talking, I was thinking about the students whose experiences are documented in this book. Most are white and are 21, 22 up to 24 years old. Their understanding of their own power and privilege, and of social structures and their impact on individuals and groups—is limited. They seem to think they don't have any power. For example, when employment equity was being discussed, the assumption was that racial minorities have all the power now, and they are taking over. So much work remains to be done in terms of bringing people to an understanding of their power and privilege. There is nothing wrong in recognizing one's personal power. One has it because of his or her skin colour and because of the meaning given to such things by our society. Understanding the structural aspect of power could hopefully lead to an understanding of how one can use her or his power towards social change.

C.G. I think the employment equity issue moves the discussion of power, and the recognition and acceptance of differential power as part of the problem, past the academic. It remains true that the notion of unearned power and the part it plays in advantaging the lives of those that have it, is a complex and difficult issue for some people to come to grips with. Not only 20-years-olds but also 40- and 50-year-old people find the notion of power difficult to understand. They have trouble perceiving themselves as having power, of understanding power as a function of how things are structured, as something that works in some people's favour and to the disadvan-

If social change is to occur through our education system, we must start early in discussing issues like racism and multiculturalism.

tage of other people. They have difficulty relating this understanding of power to their own experience. My concern is that as we try to lead people through this type of analysis of power, too often the discussion remains academic. Employment equity is going to take it away from the academic. People, for the first time, are going to experience what it feels like to have a system or structure that does not automatically work in their favour. Employment equity is going to be a "test case" for this society and for those of us who see ourselves as change agents.

C.J.   Yes I wonder about those people who participated in the classes, and who expressed a growth in their level of awareness. I wonder what changes I will see in them if I meet them 10 years from now. The changes they write about in their essays will only be evident then, through sustained efforts. There is only so much that can be done in the course of 12 or so weeks in terms of getting people to seriously understand that they have a role to play in social change.

C.G. I could not help but think, as I read the works of the students, that there were varying degrees of growth around the understanding of the issues. In the case of some people, it seemed superficial. In other cases it was quite profound—the degree of self-insight and so on that the writers were gaining. I must also admit that the insights, understanding and emotions that I found most telling were in the writings of minority group people. I am reminded of the woman who put herself in the place of a majority group person and asked the sort of questions that a majority group person should ask about things like power. She asked, what must it feel like to be able to do A,B,C, without reservation or restrictions? She also asked, what must it feel like to be expected to give up some things? She admitted, did she not, that she was not sure if she could, if she found herself in such a situation? This woman demonstrated a level of insight and empathy I found in no other piece of student writing.

C.J. Sometimes that kind of awareness produces empathy. Sometimes it produces anger and frustration. It is also possible that people just go through the exercise to fulfil course requirement—and then just leave it behind them when the course is over. One of the challenges of this type of course is to have people see it as more than an academic exercise—that it can be a combination of intellectual insight and insights into the structural operation of society.

C.G. It also shows the danger of the path we tread when we open these issues in a classroom setting. Some people can approach it academically and just walk away. For others, it is keeping a wound bleeding. As the person facilitating such discussions, how does one manage all that so that there are not deeper scars left from what is supposed to be an enlightening experience?

C.J. We also get a sense of guilt emerging as a result of such discussions.

C.G. I am less patient with guilt than I used to be. I find it is self-defeating; and too often it can become a ploy to prevent people from getting beyond a certain point to a deeper analysis, and ultimately, action.

C.J. Guilt is not a productive consequence of these exercises. It is important to present this kind of material and manage these kinds of discussions in order not to produce the kind of feelings that are counter-productive in terms of moving towards action.

C.G. You mentioned that many of the students you worked with were in their early 20's. Presumably, many of them have gone through the school system here, up to the college and university levels. The fact that they were approaching the course material as if it were the first time they were exposed to the issues, for me, is an indictment of the school system in general. One should not have to wait until the post-secondary level before one is given the opportunity to contend with the major issues that are central to the health of this society.

C.J. Yes. And as our society becomes even more multiracial and multi-faith and multicultural, we are going to have to do a better job in the schools to prepare students to live and work in our diverse society. You are correct. Since we are not exposing students early to the issues, then we are failing in our education of students. If social change is going to take place, if education is to liberate and be meaningful to the students, then we must start early to educate our students about issues of classism, sexism, racism and other forms of oppressive mechanisms.

C.G. You realize that you are talking big change?

C.J. Certainly. And a re-education of teachers who are responsible for educating the students.

C.G. Yes, re-education of existing teachers and re-conceiving of teacher training programs.

As hard as it may be to believe,
In Canadian society, issues of race and ethnicity are often ignored.
With so little acknowledgement of our diversity,
We will remain blind to our reality.

- Kai James

BIBLIOGRAPHY

Abella, Rosalie (1984). *Equality in Employment: A Royal Commission Report.* Ottawa: Ministry of Supply and Services.

Adams, Howard (1989). *Prison of Grass: Canada from a Native Point of View.* Saskatchewan: Fifth House.

Adhopia, Ajit. (1988). "Prejudice and Pride." *Mississauga Magazine, Premier Issue,* July.

Adler, Peter S. (1977). "Beyond Cultural Identity: Reflections upon Cultural and Multicultural Man." In R.W. Brislin (ed.) *Cultural Learning.* Honolulu: East-West Center.

Agocs, Carol (1987). "Ethnic Group Relations." In J.J. Teevan (ed.) *Basic Sociology.* Scarborough: Prentice-Hall.

Ahlquist, Roberta (1992). "Manifestations of Inequality: Overcoming Resistance in a Multicultural Foundations Course." In C.A. Grant (ed.) *Research and Multicultural Education: From the Margins to the Mainstream.* New York: Falmer.

Allport, Gordon (1958). *The Nature of Prejudice.* New York: Doubleday Anchor.

Anderson, Alan B. and Frideres, James S. (1981). *Ethnicity in Canada: Theoretical Perspectives.* Toronto: Butterworth.

Angus Reid Group Inc. (1989). *Immigration to Canada: Aspects of Public Opinion.* Ottawa: Employment and Immigration Canada. October.

Apple, Michael (1993). "Introduction." In C. McCarthy and W. Crichlow (eds.) *Race, Identity and Representation in Education.* New York: Routledge.

Arnold, Rick; Burke, Bev; James, Carl; Martin, D'Arcy; Thomas, Barb, (1991). *Educating for a change.* Toronto: Between the Lines.

Avison, William R. and Kunkel, John (1987). "Socialization." In J.J. Teevan (ed.) *Basic Sociology.* Scarborough: Prentice-Hall.

Barlund, Dean C. (1988). "Communication in a Global Village." In L.A. Samovar & R.E. Porter (eds.) *Intercultural Communication: A Reader.* New York: Wadsworth.

Benedict, Ruth (1983). *Race and Racism.* London: Routledge & Kegan Paul.

Berry, Brewton (1958). *Race and Ethnic Relations.* Boston: Houghton Mifflin.

Billingsley, Brenda and Musznski, Leon (1985). *No Discrimination Here! Toronto Employers and the Multi-Racial Workforce.* Toronto: Social Planning Council of Metropolitan Toronto. May.

Brislin, Richard (1993). *Understanding Culture's Influence on Behavior.* Orlando: Harcourt Brace Jovanovich.

Britzman, Deborah P. (1991). "Decentering Discourses in Teacher Education; Or, the Unleashing of Unpopular Things." *Journal of Education.* 173, No. 3.

Burnet, Jean (1981). "The Social and Historical Context of Ethnic Relations." In R.C. Gardener & R. Kalin (eds.) *A Canadian Social Psychology of Ethnic Relations.* Toronto: Methuen.

Burnet, Jean R. and Palmer, Howard (1988). *"Coming Canadians": An Introduction to a History of Canada's Peoples.* Ottawa: Ministry of Supply and Services.

BusinessWeek (1994). "White, Male and Worried." January 31. pp. 50-55.

Calliste, Agnes (1994). "Race, Gender and Canadian Immigration Policy: Blacks from the Caribbean, 1900-1932." *Journal of Canadian Studies.* Vol. 28, No. 4. (Winter) pp. 131-147.

Carroll, Michael P. (1987). "Culture." In J.J. Teevan (ed.) *Basic Sociology.* Scarborough: Prentice-Hall.

Carter, Robert T. (1991). "Cultural Values: A Review of Empirical Research and Implications for Counselling." *Journal of Counselling and Development*. 70 (1): 164-73.

Christensen, Carole Pigler (1992). "Enhancing Cross-Cultural Understanding in Multicultural and Multiracial Educational Settings: A Perceptual Framework." In K. A. Moodley (ed.) *Beyond Multicultural Education: International Perspective*. Calgary: Detselig.

Cryderman, Brian K., O'Toole, Chris N. and Fleras, Augie (1992). *Police, Race and Ethnicity: A Guide for Police Services*. Toronto: Butterworth.

Currents: Readings in Race Relations (1989). "Canada's Employment Discriminators." Vol.5, No. 4, March.

Curtis James, and Lambert, Ronald D. (1986). "Culture." In R. Hagedorn. *Sociology*. Toronto: Holt, Rinehart and Winston.

Dei, George J. Sefa (1994). "Reflections of an Anti-Racist Pedagogue." In L. Erwin and D. MacLennan (eds.) *Sociology of Education in Canada: Critical Perspectives on Theory, Research & Practice*. Toronto: Copp Clark Longman.

Dobbins, James E. and Skillings, Judith H. (1991). "The Utility of Race Labelling in Understanding Cultural Identity: A Conceptual Tool for the Social Science Practitioner." *Journal of Counselling and Development*. 70 (1): pp. 37-44.

Driedger, Leo (1986). *The Ethnic Factor: Identity in Diversity*. Toronto: McGraw-Hill Ryerson Ltd.

Elliott, Jean L. and Fleras, Augie (1992). *Unequal Relations: An Introduction to Race and Ethnic Dynamics In Canada*. Scarborough: Prentice-Hall Canada.

Employment and Immigration (1992). *Background: The Immigration Management System*. Ottawa: Public Affairs Branch, Ministry of Supply and Services.

————— (1992). *Managing Immigration: A Framework for the 1990s*. Ottawa: Public Affairs Branch, Ministry of Supply and Services.

————— (1978). "New Directions: A Look at Canada's Immigration Act and Regulations." Ottawa: Ministry of Supply and Services.

Fanon, Frantz (1967). *Black Skin, White Masks*. New York: Grove Press.

Fish, Stanley (1993). "Reverse Racism or How the Pot Got To Call The Kettle Black." *The Atlantic Monthly*. November. pp. 132-136.

Fleras, Augie and Elliott, L. (1992). *The Challenge of Diversity: Multiculturalism in Canada*. Scarborough: Nelson.

Freire, Paulo (1968). *Pedagogy of the Oppressed*. New York: Seabury.

Frideres, James S. (1993). *Native People in Canada: Contemporary Conflicts*. Scarborough: Prentice-Hall.

Gill, Dawn and Levidow, Les (eds.) (1987). *Anti-Racist Science Teaching*. London: Free Association.

Haas, Jack and Shaffir, William (1978). *Shaping Identity in Canadian Society*. Scarborough: Prentice-Hall.

Hagan, John (1987). "Finding and Defining Discrimination." In L. Driedger (ed.) *Ethnic Canada: Identities and Inequalities*. Toronto: Copp Clark Pitman.

Head, Wilson (1975). *The Black Presence in the Canadian Mosaic*. Toronto: Ontario Human Rights Commission.

Henry, Frances (1978). *The Dynamics of Racism in Toronto*. Research Report. Toronto: York University.

————— (1994). *The Caribbean Diaspora in Toronto: Learning to Live with Race*. Toronto: University of Toronto Press.

Henry, Frances and Ginzberg, Effie (1985). *Who Gets The Work: A Test of Racial Discrimination in Employment*. Toronto: Social Planning Council.

————— (1990). "Racial Discrimination in Employment." In J.Curtis et al. (eds.) *Social Inequalities in Canada: Patterns, Problems, Policies*. Scarborough: Prentice-Hall.

hooks, bell (1988). *Talking Back: Thinking Feminist, Thinking Black*. Toronto: Between the Lines.

Hoopes, David S. (1981). "Intercultural Communication Concepts and the Psychology of Intercultural Experience." In M. Pusch (ed.) *Multicultural Education*. Yarmount: Intercultural Press.

Hoopes, David and Pusch, Margaret D. (1981). "Definition of Terms." In M. Pusch (ed.) *Multicultural Education*. Pittsburgh: Intercultural Network.

Hughes, David R. and Kallen, Evelyn (1974). *The Anatomy of Racism: Canadian Dimension*. Montréal: Harvest House.

Hutcheon, Linda and Richmond, Marion (eds.) (1990). *Other Solitudes: Canadian Multicultural Fictions*. Toronto: Oxford University Press.

Isajiw, Wsevolod W. (1977). "Olga in Wonderland: Ethnicity in a Technological Society." *Canadian Ethnic Studies.* 9 (1): 77-85.

Jackson, Anita P. and Meadows, Ferguson B. (1991). "Getting to the Bottom to Understand the Top." *Journal of Counselling and Development.* 70 (1): 72-76.

—————— (1994). "Reverse Racism: Is there such a thing?" Paper presented at Canadian Studies Class CAH 1300, Trent University, Peterborough ON, March.

————— (1993). "Getting There and Staying There: Blacks' Employment Experience." In P. Anisef and P. Axelrod (eds.) *Transitions: Schooling and Employment in Canada.* Toronto: Thompson Educational.

————— (1990). *Making It: Black Youth, Racism and Career Aspirations in a Big City.* Oakville: Mosaic Press.

Jansen, Clifford J. and Richmond, Anthony (1990). "Immigrant Settlement and Integration." Paper presented at the Symposium for Immigrant Settlement and Integration. Toronto, May 28-29.

Jones, James M. (1991). "Psychological Models of Race: What Have They Been and What Should They Be." In J.D. Goodchilds et al. (eds.) *Psychological Perspectives on Human Diversity in America.* Washington: American Psychological Association.

Kalbach, Warren E., Verma, Ravi, George, M.V., and Dai, S.Y. (1993). *Population Projections of Visible Minority Groups, Canada, Provinces and Regions, 1991-2016.* Ottawa: Statistics Canada, Interdepartmental Working Group on Employment Equity Data, December.

Kalin, Rudolf (1981). "Ethnic Attitudes." In R.C. Gardner & R. Kalin (eds.) *A Canadian Social Psychology of Ethnic Relations.* Toronto: Methuen.

Karapinski, Eva C. and Lea, Ian (eds.) (1993). *Pens of Colour: A Canadian Reader.* Toronto: Harcourt Brace Jovanovich.

Kinloch, Graham C. (1974). *The Dynamics of Race Relations: A Sociological Analysis.* Toronto: McGraw-Hill.

Lee, Enid (1985). *Letters to Marcia: A Teacher's Guide to Anti-Racist Education.* Toronto: Cross Cultural Communication Centre.

Li, Peter S. (ed.) (1990). *Race and Ethnic Relations in Canada.* Toronto: Oxford University Press.

Logan, Ronald (1991). "Immigration During the 80s." *Canadian Social Trends.* Ottawa: Statistics Canada, Spring pp. 9-13.

Mackie, Marlene (1986). "Socialization." in R. Hagedorn (ed.) *Sociology.* Toronto: Holt, Rinehart and Winston of Canada, Ltd.

McAndrew, Marie (1991). "Ethnicity, Multiculturalism, and Multicultural Education in Canada." In R. Ghosh and D. Ray (eds.) *Social Change and Education in Canada.* Toronto: Harcourt Brace Jovanovich.

McIntosh, Peggy (1988). "White Privilege and Male Privilege: A Personal Account of Coming to See Correspondences Through Work in Women's Studies." In M.L. Andersen and P. Hill Collins, *Race, Class and Gender: An Anthology.* Belmont (Cal.): Wadsworth, pp. 70-81.

Mills, C. Wright (1956). *The Power Elite.* New York: Oxford University Press.

Miner, Horace (1956). "Body Ritual Among the Nacirema." *American Anthropologist.* Vol. 58.

"The Multiculturalism Policy of Canada" (1988). Excerpts from the Canadian Multiculturalism Act, July.

Mukherjee, Arun (1993). *Sharing our Experience.* Ottawa: Canadian Advisory Council for the Status of Women.

Neufeld, Mark (1992). "Can an entire society be racist, or just individuals?" *The Toronto Star.*

Ng, Roxana (1993). "Racism, Sexism, and Nation Building in Canada." In C. McCarthy and W. Crichlow (eds.) *Race, Identity and Representation in Education.* New York: Routledge.

Office of the Prime Minister (1971). "Statement by the Prime Minister in the House of Commons, October 8." Ottawa: (Press Release).

Omi, Michael and Winant, Howard (1993). "On the Theoretical Status of the Concept of Race." In C. McCarthy and W. Crichlow (eds.) *Race, Identity and Representation in Education.* New York: Routledge.

Palmer, Howard (1975). *Immigration and the rise of multiculturalism.* Vancouver: Copp Clark.

Pettigrew, Thomas, F. et al. (1980). *Prejudice: Dimensions of Ethnicity.* Cambridge: Harvard University Press.

Philip, M. Nourbese (1993). *Showing Grit: Showboating North of the 44th Parallel* (Second Edition). Toronto: Poui.

——————. (1992). *Frontiers: Essays and writings on racism and culture.* Stratford (Ontario): Mercury.

Porter, John (1965). *The Vertical Mosaic: An Analysis of Social Class and Power in Canada.* Toronto: University of Toronto Press.

Quamina, Odida T. (1991). "Convenient Use of Race, Colour." *Share.* Thursday, October 10.

Ramcharan, Subhas (1982). *Racism: Non-whites in Canada.* Toronto: Butterworth.

Roman, Leslie G. (1993). "White is a Color! White Defensiveness, Postmodernism, and Anti-Racism Pedagogy." In C. McCarthy and W. Crichlow (eds.) *Race, Identity and Representation in Education.* New York: Routlege, pp. 71-88.

Samuel, John T. (1992). "Visible Minorities in Canada: A Projection." Ottawa: Carleton University (June).

Satzewich, Vic (1991). Social Stratification: Class and Racial Inequality. In B.S. Bolaria(ed.) *Social Issues and Contradictions In Canadian Society.* Toronto: Harcourt Brace Jovanovich.

Steinem, Gloria (1983). *Outrageous Acts and Everyday Rebellions.* Scarborough: New American Library.

Schoem, David (ed.) (1991). *Inside Separate Worlds: Life Stories of Young Blacks, Jews, and Latinos.* Ann Arbor: University of Michigan Press.

Schuster, Charles I. and Van Pelt, William V. (eds.) (1992). *Speculations: Readings in Culture, Identity, and Values.* Englewood Cliffs, New Jersey: Blair.

Seward, Shirley B. and Tremblay, Marc (1989). Immigrants in the Canadian Labour Force: Their Role in Structural Change. Ottawa: Institute for Research on Public Policy, September.

Shepard, R. Bruce (1991). "Plain Racism: The Reaction Against Oklahoma Black Immigration to the Canadian Plains." In O. McKague (ed.) *Racism in Canada.* Saskatoon: Fifth House.

Simon, Roger (1987). "Being Ethnic/Doing Ethnicity: A Response to Corrigan." In J. Young (ed.) *Breaking Identities in Canadian Schooling.* Toronto: Garamond.

Sleeter, Christine (1994). "White Racism." *Multicultural Education.* Spring.

Smith, Elsie J. (1991). "Ethnic Identity Development: Toward the Development of a Theory Within the Context of Minority/Majority Status." *Journal of Counselling and Development.* 70 (1): 181-188.

Sodowsky, Gargi R., Lai, Edward W.M. and Plake, Barbara S. "Moderating Effects of SociocultuRal Variables on Acculturation Attitudes of Hispanic and Asian Americans." (1991). *Journal of Counselling and Development.* 70 (1): 194-203.

Solomon, R. Patrick (1992). *Black Resistance in High School: Forging a Separatist Culture.* Albany: State University of New York Press.

Special Committee on Visible Minorities (1984). *Equality Now: Participation of Visible Minorities in Canadian Society.* Ottawa: Supply and Services.

Statistics Canada (1994). Housing, Family and Social Statistics Division.

Stebbins, Robert A. (1989). *Sociology: The Study of Society.* New York: Harper & Row, Publishers.

Stephen Leacock Collegiate Institute (History Department) (1994). *Our Roots 2: Personal and Family Histories from the OAC Stephen Leacock Black History Class, 1994.* Scarborough: Scarborough Board of Education.

Tatum, Beverly Daniel (1992). "Talking about Race, Learning about Racism: The Application of Racial Identity Development Theory in the Classroom." *Harvard Educational Review.* 62 (1): 1-24.

Taylor, Donald M. (1981). "Stereotypes and Intergroup Relations." In R. Gardner and R. Kalin (eds.) *A Canadian Social Psychology of Ethnic Relations.* Toronto: Methuen.

Tedesco, Theresa (1989). "The Moneyed Class: Rich Immigrants Jump the Queue." *Maclean's.* 102 (28): July 10.

Toronto Star (1986). *A Minority Report.* Toronto: The Toronto Star.

Vallee, Frank G. (1983). "Inequality and Identity in Multi-Ethnic Societies." In D. Forcese & S. Richer (eds.) *Social Issues: Sociological Views of Canada.* Scarborough: Prentice-Hall.

van den Berghe, Pierre L. (1967). *Race and Racism: A Comparative Perspective.* New York: John Wiley & Sons.

Watson, Paul (1991). "Somalis find home in Etobicoke." *The Toronto Star.* A11, September.

Wotherspoon, Terry and Satzewich, Vic (1993). *First Nations: Race, Class, and Gender Relations.* Scarborough: Nelson.

Yeboah, Samuel Kennedy (1988). *The Ideology of Racism.* London: Hansils.

Yi, Sun-Kyung (1992). "An Immigrant's Split Personality." *The Globe and Mail.* April 1, 1992: A20.